Notable American Indians
Indiana & Adjacent States

Alan J. McPherson and James Carr

Graphics by Lowell Hildebrandt

Bloomington, IN Milton Keynes, UK

authorHOUSE®

AuthorHouse™
1663 Liberty Drive, Suite 200
Bloomington, IN 47403
www.authorhouse.com
Phone: 1-800-839-8640

AuthorHouse™ UK Ltd.
500 Avebury Boulevard
Central Milton Keynes, MK9 2BE
www.authorhouse.co.uk
Phone: 08001974150

First published by AuthorHouse 6/6/2007

ISBN: 978-1-4259-9889-9 (sc)

Printed in the United States of America
Bloomington, Indiana

This book is printed on acid-free paper.

Front Cover: "Composite of Notable American Indians"
Back Cover: Meshekinnoquah's (Little Turtle) Signature

"The Father is the Sun,

the Earth is my Mother,

and upon her mighty bosom

I shall rest."

Tecumseh or Tecumthe
[*Panther Passing Across*]
(1768? – 1813)

Table of Contents

Preface

What truly is known of the indigenous peoples – "The First Nations" – who inhabited the wilderness between the Ohio and Mississippi rivers of the North American continent during the late eighteenth and early nineteenth centuries?

This geographic area of the southern Great Lakes was home to a number of clans and tribes who practiced what has become known as the "Eastern Woodland Culture." Located between two of America's most important fluvial arteries, this so-named "Middle Border" had for many years created economic and political buffers for enterprising European powers of Spain, France, and England. All were dependent on the indigenous culture for economic and political success.

With Spain's territorial claims laying primarily to the south and west, England and France wrestled for control of the Middle Border's lucrative fur trade. Their key to success was the cultivation of Indian alliances. Often tribes and even clans were divided and set against each other to curry European favor.

The so-named French and Indian War (1756-1763) resulted in British victory and domination, but tension and turmoil continued between tribal factions and Euro-American interests. Barely two decades later, following the American Revolution (1776-1784), a victorious United States--the newly formed "Thirteen Fires"--claimed this area and its inhabitants as the spoils of the war. In 1787, the "Middle Border" was re-designated as "The Northwest Territory," surveyed, divided, and opened to American expansionism.

The indigenous inhabitants, who had mutually husbanded this land for tens of centuries, resisted this invasion. A fledgling United States flexed its military muscle. The cultures clashed; resulting in a devastating series of events which dramatically dissipated this once thriving, intra-dependent indigenous culture. The repercussions of this conflict can still be felt today.

A primary goal of this work is to impart accurate historical information regarding Native American culture during these times. The chosen method presents thirty-one brief biographies of noted American Indians who first lived in what is now the State of Indiana or one of its adjacent states. Those men and women selected, primarily span the tumultuous times (1700-1850) of European and American exploration, exploitation, expansion, conquest and settlement of the area that has become known as 'The Old Northwest Territory." Selection of the lives presented was random; reaching the goal of historical accuracy presented heavier challenges.

During study and research of the thirty-one selected men and women, many questions were raised--many left unanswered—regarding the accuracy of some literary, periodical, and personal sources referenced. Upon locating and reading numerous primary and secondary sources, the authors have concluded that a considerable amount of documentation regarding Native Americans living in the Old Northwest is limited, fragmented and often conflicting.

Since the Eastern Woodland Indians of the southern Great Lakes had no written alphabet or language, factual accuracy of several events can be called into question; rarely was American history recorded from the Indian perspective. Oftentimes "historical" writings reflect a negative bias against the American Indian. In many cases, legend, personal opinion, and prejudiced observations have mutated into historical "fact;" in-depth, scholarly research has been frequently sidestepped. The ultimate fact is that non-Indian historians have dictated most of the final written accounts of Indian persons and events.

The authors, in their quest for historic "truth," have included some of these conflicting historic accounts for the purpose of comparison and contrast. Like history detectives, the authors have "tracked down" leads, drawn inferences from elusive clues and have pieced together fragments of documented fact into uncommon biographical stories of American Indians, many leaders and patriots of the Indian cause. [Some of the subjects lived at the time of European contact; some lived during the time of American military conflict; others were forced to confront choices of resettlement and acculturation in an alien society.]

These thirty-one biographical sketches are arranged alphabetically by their most recognizable and accepted Indian personal names. Variations in spelling and pronunciation and in some cases, sobriquets or nicknames also are included. The authors have attempted to present the most significant events from birth to death that occurred in the lives of these individuals, events that are often interrelated with other individuals in the collection. The authors also have included a number of native Algonquin words, phrases and terms within the biographical sketches.

For greater detail and accuracy, ongoing research by rigorous scholars is warranted. However, complete information about these Native American subjects will never be known; much is forever lost to the ages. Regardless, the authors contend that this book is an inspiring reference to readers interested in American Indian history of the Old Northwest Territory.

Several inspiring individuals have encouraged the development of this book. The authors are indebted to those who have contributed freely of their energy and time to the compilation of *Notable American Indians of Indiana and Adjacent States*. Especial thanks is due to reference librarians and county historians of Indiana and adjacent states, tribal members and other numerous interested individuals who provided clues and helped locate elusive documents. A special debt of gratitude goes to Lowell Hildebrandt, whose illustrations greatly add to the following pages. Also, the authors are deeply indebted to their parents, family, and friends who gave encouragement and support.

This book is dedicated to those "First on the Land."

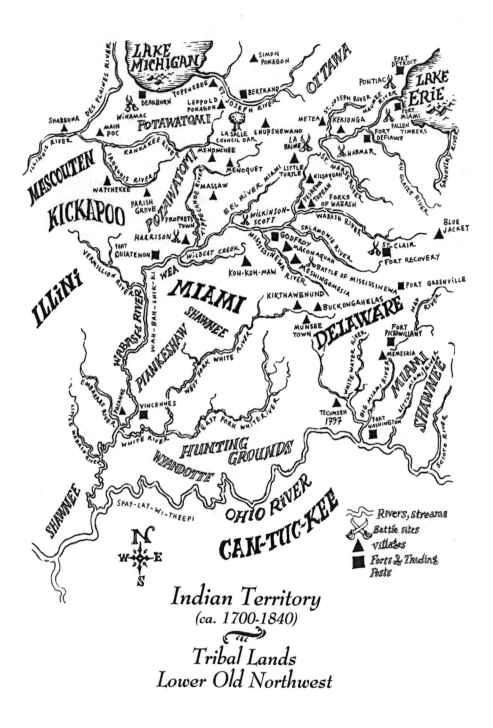

Indian Territory
(ca. 1700-1840)

Tribal Lands
Lower Old Northwest

Overview

"Indiana" is a place name derived from European roots. It combines the term "Indian" mistakenly conferred on the indigenous inhabitants, or "First Nations" of North America with the Greek suffix, "-iana," meaning "land of." The place name "Indiana" carries the definition "Land of the Indians."

Present-day Indiana historically experienced its largest and most varied American Indian population during the century prior to the adoption of statehood in 1816. This growth in the Indian population stems from the displacement of clans and tribes swept west before the tidal surge of Euro-American expansion and settlement. Others were displaced from traditional homelands by disease, warfare, and depletion of hunting and farming lands. Some had been pushed south and west by the more powerful traditional enemies; others emigrated from the south and east for similar reasons. Eventually, a large and varied population of Native Americans settled into the area designated on early United States maps as "Indian Territory" – The Land of the Indians – Indiana.

Following the American Colonial victory over Great Britain in the Revolutionary War [1776-1784] a vast wilderness north and west of the Ohio River was absorbed by a fledgling United States government. In 1787 the United States Congress passed the Northwest Ordinance, designating this vast new acquisition as the Northwest Territory. It was quickly surveyed, mapped, divided into squared sections and declared open for distribution.

This area, known historically now as The Old Northwest Territory, contained all or parts of six states: Ohio, Michigan, Minnesota, Wisconsin, Illinois and, of course, Indiana. The indigeneous populations were the people of the Eastern Woodland Culture of American Indians. They had lived on the land for centuries prior to and during the invasive arrival of European usurpers. Their sphere of influence would continue to shrink as America expanded.

More than a hundred years before the formation of the Old Northwest Territory, early explorers, mostly French, found the area inhabited by numerous tribes of native peoples, especially the Miami. Since the 1600s, the Miami had claimed the entire region drained by the watersheds of the Wabash and Scioto rivers, which empty into the Ohio River to the south; the St. Joseph River, which flows into Lake Michigan to the north and west; and the Maumee River, which empties into Lake Erie to the east. This Miami homeland included all of present-day Indiana, western Ohio and southern Michigan. The main Miami "capitol" of *Cecaahkonki* or Kekionga [Blackberry Patch] was located at the site of modern-day Fort Wayne, Indiana. From here the Miami guarded the most strategic fluvial routes of transportation and communication, making them the most influential tribe of the region.

During the final years of Indian occupation prior to removal west of the Mississippi, the Miami "permitted" several uprooted Algonquin-speaking tribes from other locations to occupy their lands, not always willingly or peacefully. Tribes and clans of people who were living or would live within the borders of what would become the State of Indiana and its immediate adjacent regions were Chippewa or Ojibwa, Delaware, Eel River Miami, Fox, Illiniwek, Kickapoo, Mahican, Mingo, Mohegan, Munsee, Nanticoke, Ottawa, Piankashaw, Potawatomi, Sauk, Seneca, Shawnee, Wea, Winnebago, and Wyandot.

Many of these tribes living in the area north of the Ohio River, east of the Mississippi River and along the southern borders of the Great Lakes had been displaced from earlier, distant homelands. Some had been forced westward from the Atlantic seaboard by encroaching European powers and American expansionism. Some had emigrated from the eastern Great Lakes and Atlantic Seaboard, driven west by the powerful, warring Iroquois; likewise, others came from the northern Great Lakes, also displaced by more powerful tribes, such as the Woodland Sioux and Chippewa. Yet, it was not these disturbing interrelationships alone that had the most dramatic impact on the Indian way of life.

Centuries before the European infiltration during the 1600s, the Eastern Woodland peoples had developed a culture of tribal interdependence, subsistence farming, hunting and gathering. The traditional Indian way of life was forever impacted by European intrusion deep into the North American heartland via the Atlantic Ocean, Great Lakes and connecting river arteries. Contact with French explorers, followed by the commercial fur trading ventures of French traders and businessmen and the "Black Robes," Catholic missionaries committed to conversion of the "noble sauvage," forever changed Indian destiny.

European fashion demanded furs, and fur-bearing animals were plentiful in Indian Territory of the New World. In return for these plentiful furs, French traders traded material goods made of metal. Metal knives, hatchets and cookware, once unknown, quickly became practically indispensable within the Woodland Culture. Guns, ammunition and powder replaced bows, arrows and spears.

While these new European tools made it easier for the Indian to procure the furs the French desired, traditional cycles of hunting, trapping, gathering and farming were altered forever as desire for trade goods increased. Indians exchanged their former "mixed economy" of subsistence for the "specialized economy" of hunting and trapping for trade. Social patterns of life changed. Life-altering religions, unknown diseases and spirituous liquor were introduced to the indigenous population. As valuable natural resources were becoming exhausted, competition and conflict among tribes--and between two encroaching European powers--increased.

While the French were more inclined toward intermarriage and adoption of Indian customs and language, the British, who came later, were more interested in occupation and colonization. The British regarded the Indian as savage and heathen, a culture that needed to be controlled, removed, or annihilated. A Franco-Anglo conflict, known as The Seven Years War, was fought on the European continent between 1755 and 1763. This military conflict spread to North America, where, as a series of smaller wars fought over commercial and territorial interests, it became known as the French and Indian War. On both sides, this conflict of European cultures enlisted Indian tribes as allies. This war ended in victory for the British. Unfortunately, most Central Algonquin-speaking tribes of the Great Lakes area had allied themselves with the defeated French, leaving them under control of the British policy of subjugation, removal or possible annihilation.

Considered by many historians as a continuation of the French and Indian War, the militant Ottawa leader, Pontiac, launched a unified Indian uprising against the occupying British in 1763. Deeply influenced by the Delaware prophet Neolin, a spiritual leader who advocated a return to traditional Indian ways, Pontiac, as a military leader, planned a series of attacks on British forts. Pontiac hoped victory over the British would bring back French influence. As a political figure, he was able to unite several Great Lakes tribes into a coalition that would carry out his plan of British expulsion.

In a brief period of time, Pontiac's followers had recaptured several British forts and carried out many successful raids on white settlements. When the French did not return as expected, Pontiac's Rebellion failed; his coalition dissipated by 1764 and the British remained in power. Although the uprising failed, the British had gained a deeper respect for the Indians as a political and military force.

In the Royal Proclamation of 1763, the British declared Indian lands west of the Appalachian Mountains and north and west of the Ohio River to be off limits to colonization. In 1768 the Treaty of Fort Stanwix officially set the western boundary of the American colonies at the Ohio River. However, neither document was honored; land-hungry colonists eagerly encroached onto Indian lands claimed by the Colony of Virginia, which included what are now the states of Ohio and Kentucky.

Indian reaction and retaliation to increasing colonial encroachment led to bloody warfare. Colonists attacked several Indian villages in Ohio territory. These events led to Lord Dunmore's War of 1774. Even Indian leaders seeking peaceful solutions, such as the revered Chalakatha Mekoche Shawnee chief, Hokolesqua [*Cornstalk*], were drawn into this conflict in an effort to protect their homeland. Hokolesqua, like many Indian patriots, paid with their lives.

Because of continuing encroachment onto Indian lands, most Indians sided with the British against the American colonists during the American Revolutionary War. Again, the Indians' allies were defeated, but not the Indians.

After the Revolution, a newly independent America disregarded the Proclamation of 1763 and Indian rights to the land. Without any consultation with the inhabitants, Americans sent surveyors into Indian Territory and renamed it the Northwest Territory by legislating the 1787 Northwest Ordinance. Maps were drawn and on paper, traditional Indian homelands were divided into squared sections of land by meridians, latitudes and longitudes without regard for natural geographic boundaries and traditional native homelands. When

Congress ratified the Northwest Ordinance in 1787, treatment of the native Indian inhabitants was specifically spelled out:

"The utmost good faith shall always be observed towards the Indians," the document reads, *"their lands and property shall never be taken from them without their consent; and in their property, rights and liberty, they shall never be invaded or disturbed unless in just and lawful wars."*

These noble words would ring hollow to the many Indians who held mutual title to the land on which they and their ancestors had lived for centuries.

A newly-formed American republic--one which espoused, in writing, that "all men ... are endowed with ... inalienable rights ..." - advocated a policy that brought about a few peaceful, but mostly violent, confrontations with Indian nations that stood in the way of America's "Manifest Destiny." America's socio-political philosophy advocated occupation, settlement and exploitation of the New World's natural resources from "sea to shining sea." A few "savages" would not stand in the way of a destiny that was perceived as "divine."

Dating from the formation of the Northwest Territory in 1787 to the Indian Removal Act of 1830, the timeline measures only forty-three years; but within those four decades, most tribes gradually would be displaced by white advancement or be relegated to tiny tracts within the vast areas they once occupied and called theirs. The "final solution," with few exceptions, was forced removal of all indigenous people from Indiana and the Northwest Territory to undesirable western reservations.

Following the American Revolutionary War formation of The Northwest Territory provided an opportunity for the debt-ridden republic to reward veterans of the war of liberation from Great Britain with land grants. Legally owned or not, land was sold to veterans and settlers for as little as one dollar an acre. Publicly, the United States demanded licensing of trade, and "forbid" the infiltration of unscrupulous traders and squatters, a policy rarely enforced.

As a justifiable military reaction to invasion by a foreign foe, Indian leaders, including patriot war chiefs, Meshekinnoquah [*Little Turtle*] of the Miami, Buckongahelas [*Breaker to Pieces*] of the Delaware and Weyapiersenwah [*Whirlpool*, or Blue Jacket] of the Shawnee, formed a military coalition of southern Great Lakes tribes. The coalition was known to the Americans by several names, including the Wabash

Confederacy and the Miami Alliance. Its main purpose was to stop the increasing western advance of American settlers from east of the Appalachian Mountains as they attempted to displace the Indians from the area north and west of the Ohio River. A series of military conflicts resulted.

To President Washington and the American military, the conflicts in the years between 1790 and 1794 were known by several names, including the Northwest Indian Wars, the Wabash Confederacy War and Little Turtle War. To the Indian, it was a nameless struggle of survival, preservation of culture and continued control of the land they had occupied since pre-European contact.

Regardless of what these conflicts were called, an alliance of Indian tribes united and fought to protect their homeland from aggression, deceitful treaties and subsequent forced removal. However valiant and moral the resistance may have been, eventually superior numbers and weaponry of the advancing enemy won out; the inevitable end was defeat for the Indian alliance and the erosion of an entire culture by an incessant stream of land cession treaties. After a few military successes, defeat at the Battle of Fallen Timbers in 1794 temporarily suspended the Indian coalition of resistance to American aggression.

Leaders of many tribes signed the Treaty of Greenville in 1795, the first in a long series of land cession treaties. The Greenville Treaty designated sixteen separate cessions of land and pushed the western boundary of the United States from the Ohio River into northwestern Ohio Territory, driving the Shawnee and other tribes from their homelands in eastern and southern Ohio. Lands west of the "Greenville Line," which divided Ohio Territory north and south, were to be Indian Territory:

*"In consideration of the peace now established, and of the cessions and relinquishments of lands made... by the said tribes of Indians, and to manifest the liberality of the United States, as the great means of rendering this peace strong and perpetual, **the United States relinquish their claims to all other Indian lands northward of the river Ohio, eastward of the Mississippi, and westward and southward of the Great Lakes and the waters, uniting them ...**"*

Once again, traders were to be licensed and American settlement of the area curtailed; and again, this policy was rarely enforced.

Continued American encroachment into Indian Territory set the stage for a renewed pan-Indian movement, which was initiated and headed by Shawnee leaders, Tecumseh and his brother, Tenskawtawa, The Shawnee Prophet.

By 1808, the Shawnee brothers had attracted a large following to their spiritual and politically motivated pan-tribal movement. While The Shawnee Prophet renewed the Delaware Neolin's spiritual message of a return to traditional ways, Tecumseh found a platform for his proposed pan-tribal "Indian Nation," similar to the earlier Ottawa Pontiac.

Tecumseh's message advocated that all Indian land was owned in common and all treaties signed by individual tribes or leaders were invalid. The Shawnee brothers' pan-tribal movement culminated at an Indiana village known to the Americans as Prophetstown. The village was located at the confluence of the Tippecanoe and Wabash rivers, just north of treaty boundaries in the area still designated as Indian Territory. Prophetstown's population may possibly have been several thousand and was perceived by Americans as a threat to their expansionistic policy. Once more the Americans found a military solution to the "Indian Problem."

In a show of force, Indiana's Territorial Governor William Henry Harrison and some twelve hundred troops advanced on Prophetstown. Following the ensuing Battle of Tippecanoe in November of 1811, the pan-tribal movement was crippled temporarily, but Tecumseh's allies and followers still numbered in the thousands. But the last major coalition of Indian resistance died with its Shawnee leader. Tecumseh had allied himself with the British and was killed fighting against the American forces, during the War of 1812, Battle of Moraviantown, October 5, 1813, also known as the Battle of Thames, Ontario, Canada.

Following his death, Tecumseh's coalition of tribes fragmented and was crushed. Although some individual Indian resistance continued after the War of 1812, eventually greed on both American and Indian sides led to a long series of questionable land cessions. Many Indians felt they had little choice but restricted acculturation into an American society that would not allow them citizenship or the right of suffrage. Many, disillusioned and homeless in a land they once called their own, fell victim to liquor, disease, and deprivation.

By 1830, the year President Andrew Jackson had signed the Indian Removal Act and most Indian lands in Indiana, with the exception of a few reservations, had already been ceded to the United States government.

Some Indians, such as Potawatomi chiefs Leopold Pokagon and Menominee, the "Potawatomi Preacher," converted to Christianity. They believed acceptance and practice of "white" Christian religion would allow them to remain on their lands. Pokagon signed the Treaty of Chicago in 1828, and was allowed to remain in Michigan; Menominee refused to sign the Treaty of the Yellow River in 1836, leading to his arrest by Indiana militia and forced eviction from his reservation. Menominee, along with his band, endured a six hundred sixty mile forced march to Kansas in 1838, now known as the Trail of Death.

Even the Miami, who managed to maintain ownership of sizable sections of land through the efforts of wealthy and influential leaders such as Peshewa [*Wildcat*], or Jean Baptiste Richardville, were eventually forced from Indiana onto reservations west of the Mississippi River. Today, three tribes remain in Indiana: the Miami of Indiana, headquartered in Peru; the Weas, centered in Terre Haute; and the Shawnees of Indiana, centered in Kokomo. Although formally organized with internal tribal government, the United States government does not officially recognize any of these forementioned tribal organizations.

Few Indian leaders stand out from the pages of Indiana history, individuals who caught the attention of historians of their day. Thirty-one noted Indian biographies, along with illustrations, are featured on the following pages. Some names will be immediately recognizable, while some will seem obscure. Most are men, and some are women; all have a place in Indiana's history.

The authors' intent is to bring together under one cover basic reference information regarding thirty-one historically notable Indians from the area which is now Indiana and the eastern north-central United States. Our selection of outstanding Indian historical figures was restricted by the amount of biographical information and images available. Convinced in the truth of the adage "History is written by the victors," locating accurate data about personal lives of the notable Indians herein has proved difficult; with numerous dead ends encountered Indian personal names were often transcribed phonetically and were written in many forms. Some personal names, as well as nicknames, changed over a lifetime. Often the true meaning of Indian personal names has been lost in translation into English. Furthermore, adding to the historical confusion, many Indians also adopted English Christian names, while some individuals shared the same name. Conflicting historic accounts regarding certain individuals have been questioned in many cases, and several equally influential Indian leaders were omitted for lack of information.

Historians for the most part have ignored the role of women in Indian culture. The term "unknown Indian woman" can be found often. Names are often omitted in favor of their husbands and tribal traditions. However, some tribes are matralineal, meaning the family name was passed through the mother. Among these tribes the influence of women is "observable," as in the case of the Potawatomi principal woman or chieftess, Mas-saw.

A few of the notable American Indians herein are not racially Indian, but are white captives "raised Indian." These include *Apekonit*, William Wells, and *Maconaquah*, Frances Slocum. Some adoptees chose to remain "Indian," while others returned to their Euro-American roots.

Indian leaders who resisted American takeover of their land appeared as patriots among their own people, but to an invasive alien race, these champions of Indian rights and lands were often vilified. Over time, resistance leaders such as Pontiac, Little Turtle, Buckongahelas, Blue Jacket and Tecumseh, have come to be recognized by the modern-day American public as iconic figures; while in their own time, these protectors, in an attempt to secure their homeland from foreign invaders, were feared, hated and subjected to violence from a vengeful United States government.

Some of the notable subjects were not admired among their own people. Some rejected their "Indian-ness" and acculturated into American society following many walks of life, becoming soldiers, businessmen and politicians.

Because of the time period, lack of technology or the personal decision of the subject, no official likenesses or image of some notable subjects exist. The artist has conceptualized some illustrations based on literary description and artistic imagination for unavailable images.

The literature listed in the Recommended Reading section is available at public libraries and universities.

Many of the notable American Indians described herein held significant roles in a time when two cultures, each with strong values, beliefs and determination, clashed as they wrestled for control of a changing landscape. Several struggled to retain dwindling lands and protect decreasing populations, to recall a fading culture or to gain recognition from America's government.

Even though most Indians are now gone from Indiana, their spirit is remembered and their spiritual values remain pertinent and significant today. The Indian spiritual philosophy of reverence for all life and the belief that the earth belongs to all humanity should remain alive and relevant as America faces increasing social, cultural and environmental challenges.

Although "the forest has gone silent with their voices," the Indian prophets believe the Indian spirit continues to live on in the land, and though dormant now, the Indian ways will once again flourish.

Apekonit

["Carrot; or Indian Potato"
Ma-kah-ta-ka-pa-quah, "Black Snake";
William Wells]

Anglo-American-Miami Adoptee
b. 1770 – d. 1812

*Adapted from an original, non-dated (circa 1794-1812) portrait
by an unknown artist.*

"He said to his men, 'that that family [Gaviahatte's] had fed him when he was hungry, clothed him when he was naked, and kindly nursed him when sick; and in every respect were as kind and affectionate to him as they were to their own children'."
    – From Biographical Sketches of ... Captain William Wells [et. al.] ... by John McDonald.

"Taking with him the War Chief, Little Turtle, to a favorite spot on the banks of the Maumee, Wells, said, 'I now leave your nation for my own people; we have long been friends, we are friends yet; until the sun reaches a certain height [which he indicated], from that time we are enemies. Then if you wish to kill me, you may'. If I want to kill you, I may.'"
    – From Little Turtle, the Great Chief of the Miami Indian Nation, By Calvin M. Young, 1917.

Apekonit [*Carrot*], or William Wells, was one of many individuals caught up in the clash between two cultures on the frontier of the Old Northwest. Some of these individuals were Indians, captured and adopted into the Euro-American culture, such as the Shawnee Spemica Lawba [*High Horn*], who became more widely known by his American name of Logan; some, like Wells, were on the opposing side - Americans captured and reared as Indians.

Wells grew to adulthood, married and began a family as a *Myaamiaki* [Miami], but eventually yielded to pressure from his biological family and changed allegiance. He joined General "Mad Anthony" Wayne's American Legion where he reached the rank of captain as a scout and spy. But when his death was imminent, he shed his American uniform and faced his final destiny wearing the regalia of a Miami warrior.

William Wells was born in 1770 near Jacob's Creek, Pennsylvania. In 1779, when he was nine, his family moved to the Beargrass area of Kentucky, near present-day Louisville. Wells' father, Captain Samuel Wells, a Revolutionary war veteran, was killed during an Indian ambush near Wells Station, Kentucky. With his mother already dead, the orphaned Wells was taken into the home of Colonel William Pope, a friend of Wells' father.

According to a traditional account, in March of 1784, young Wells and three friends were on a hunting expedition when a raiding party of

Miami warriors captured the youths. However, some accounts maintain that the teenaged Wells was found by the renowned Miami war chief Meshekinnoquah, or Little Turtle, following a Miami raid on Kentucky settlers and adopted into his family.

A more accepted account reveals that, after his capture, Wells was taken north into present-day Indiana, where he was held at a *Waayaahtanwa* [Wea] village along the *Kineepikomeekwa Siipiiwi*, [Snake Fish Stream, or Eel River] near present-day Logansport. The village, called Kenapocomaqua, was said to have stretched for three miles along the northern shore of the river. At Kenapocomaqua, the white youth was adopted into the household of the village chief, Gaviahatte [*The Porcupine*].

Wells was given the Miami name of Apekonit, meaning Carrot, in reference to his red hair. The fourteen-year-old Wells quickly adjusted to life among the Miami over the next few years. His close association with Little Turtle came after Wells had already gained warrior status. In adulthood, the Miami adoptee and the noted war chief became lifelong comrades, and Apekonit married Little Turtle's only daughter, Manwangopath [*Sweet Breeze*]. By some accounts, the marriage produced two daughters, Anne and Mary, and a son, Wayne, possibly named in honor of General Anthony Wayne, under whom Wells eventually served as a scout after returning to his biological family.

Members of Apekonit's biological family searched many years to find him. After some time, they finally came to Gaviahatte's village, discovered Wells and pleaded with him to return home to Kentucky. Apekonit did not accept their invitation. However, he did make one visit to his former home, although he insisted that an armed force of Miami warriors accompany him at least as far as the Ohio River.

Leaving his Indian companions at the Falls of the Ohio, Wells crossed into Kentucky by himself. Once there, his family members once again attempted to convince him that he should stay. His family showed him all the material wealth and comforts he had left behind, but Apekonit was not impressed. After just a few days with his birth family, he reunited with the party of Miami warriors and returned to his adopted Miami lifestyle. His biological family would not hear from him again for several years.

There is some evidence that, upon becoming a warrior, Apekonit may have changed his personal name to *Ma-kah-ta-ka-pa-quah*, meaning Black Snake. As a warrior he served with the Miami Alliance, or Wabash Confederacy, a coalition of several Algonquin-speaking tribes of the southern Great Lakes, formed to offer armed resistance against American encroachment into Indian lands. Accounts reveal that he fought savagely on the side of his Indian allies in victories over invading American armies led by generals Josiah Harmar in 1790 and Arthur St. Clair in 1791. However, after ten years of immersion in his adopted Miami lifestyle and becoming a warrior, he began to reflect. Now in his mid-twenties, several conflicting issues arose in his mind.

A few months prior to his ill-fated expedition against the main Miami village of *Cecaahkonki* [Kekionga or Blackberry Patch], located at modern-day Fort Wayne, Indiana, St. Clair, a former Revolutionary War general and now Governor of the Northwest Territory, sent a force of five hundred armed Kentucky militia to destroy other Miami settlements, including Kenapocomaqua, the home of Gavihatte, Apekonit's adopted father. This company of militia, under the command of Colonel James Wilkinson, destroyed several villages, including Kenapocomaqua on August 7-8, 1791. Apekonit's adopted mother and his wife, Sweet Breeze, were taken captive during Wilkinson's raid.

Gaviahatte and Apekonit traveled to the American military garrison at Vincennes [Indiana] in an attempt to secure the release of their wives. Once at Vincennes, they discovered the captured Miami women were being held at Fort Washington [Cincinnati, Ohio], not at Vincennes. Nevertheless, during the council for prisoner exchange at Vincennes, Apekonit happened to meet his biological brother, Samuel.

Samuel Wells told Apekonit, or William, that he had been commanding a company of Kentucky militia accompanying St. Clair during his recent defeat at the hands of the Indians and that many American soldiers were killed. Samuel's story affected his brother deeply. Considering that he could have killed his own brother, Apekonit had second thoughts about his life as a Miami. He also considered the uncertain future of the Miami as the forces of an emerging United States continued to press into their homelands. Wells decided to leave his adopted lifestyle and return to his roots in Kentucky.

In 1792, again using the name William Wells, he volunteered as an interpreter for American General Rufus Putnam, who was in the process of peace negotiations with local Indian tribes. Aware of Wells' language skills and his relationship with the influential Little Turtle, Putnam immediately accepted Wells' offer. Putnam had taken a personal liking to Wells and was able to secure the release of his new interpreter's Indian family members, along with several other Miami prisoners of war.

Before General Putnam returned to Ohio later that year, he sent Wells among the Miami, Shawnee and Delaware tribes to set a time and a place for peace negotiations. Wells had only limited success among the tribes. When Putnam did not hear from Wells for many months, he assumed that his interpreter had either deserted his mission or had been killed. Wells eventually returned, but had little good news for Putnam regarding peace negotiations with the tribes of the Confederacy.

In 1793, Wells joined the army General Anthony Wayne was forming at Fort Washington [Cincinnati, Ohio]. Wells escorted his wife and children to his brother's home in Kentucky, then took command of a group of some twenty scouts, comprised of other Americans, all of whom, like himself, had lived among the Indians. Over the next few years, Wells and his men rendered valuable service to the United States as spies, scouts and interpreters. Commissioned as a captain in the American army, Wells and his scouts, dressed as Indians, led the advance of Wayne's Legion through the forests of western Ohio on their way to strike Indian villages along the *Taawaawa Siipiiwi* [Maumee River].

In August of 1794, William Wells assisted General Wayne at the Battle of Fallen Timbers, which was fought near present-day Toledo, Ohio. But after the battle, Wells, who was recovering from a gunshot wound, rejoined his Miami family and friends at the recently-established American fort at the confluence of the St. Mary's and Maumee rivers. There at Fort Wayne, named for his commander, Wells resumed close ties with Little Turtle, who, following the defeat of the Indian Confederacy became a leading advocate of peaceful relations with the Americans.

Wells served as General Wayne's main interpreter during negotiations at the Treaty of Greenville [Ohio] in 1795. For his continuing services he was rewarded with a yearly government stipend of three hundred and fifty dollars. In 1800, Wells accompanied Little Turtle to Washington,

D.C. At the request of Little Turtle, Wells was appointed Indian Agent at Fort Wayne. Wells assumed those duties in 1802.

Over the next ten years, including a reappointment by President Thomas Jefferson, Wells maintained his position as Indian Agent at Fort Wayne at a salary of seven hundred fifty dollars a year. For his work in treaty negotiations among the Indians, Wells also was given three hundred twenty acres of land along the St. Joseph River. That area is now known as the neighborhood of Spy Run.

Although an employee in service to the United States, Wells also negotiated favorably for his former tribe, the Miami. Territorial Governor William Henry Harrison, who once regarded Wells as a close friend, became suspicious of Wells' friendship with the Indians and requested Wells be removed as Indian agent at Fort Wayne. But Harrison later recanted, citing Wells' intrinsic value to the American cause.

Wells resigned as Indian agent in 1812, following the death of his father-in-law, Little Turtle. He made plans to return to Kentucky, along with his wife and children. But due to a change in the political climate and with a war against England looming, Wells was recalled into military service by Harrison, who now held the rank of general and was in command of American forces in the Northwest Territory.

Wells and the Shawnee leader Tecumseh [Panther Passing Across] had been comrades during the days of the Wabash Confederacy. But now, during the early weeks of the War of 1812, Tecumseh had become a bitter enemy of the American captain and his "peace chief" father-in-law, Little Turtle. Tecumseh had stirred the regional tribes into an alliance the British. Word was received at Fort Wayne that Tecumseh's pro-British Indian allies were planning an attack on America's western-most garrison, Fort Dearborn, located at *Chi-cag-si-kag* [Place of the Wild Onion, now Chicago, Illinois] along the *Mischigonong* [Great Lake, or Lake Michigan].

Captain James Rhea, commandant at Fort Wayne, ordered Wells to proceed to Fort Dearborn. Wells was ordered to close the fort and escort the garrison's commander, Captain Nathan Heald, all soldiers and civilians to the relative safety of Fort Detroit. Since Heald's wife, Rebecca, was his niece, Wells readily agreed to the mission. About the third of August, 1812, Wells and an aide, along with a contingent of between thirty and fifty Miami warriors, traveled northwest to Fort Dearborn. Wells and his entourage arrived August 12.

At Fort Dearborn, Wells called a council with the hostile, British-allied Indian warriors, most of whom were Potawatomi. During the council, it was agreed that the fort's goods, excluding weapons, ammunition and liquor, were guaranteed to the Indians in return for safe passage. But Heald not only blew up all the powder, guns and liquor, but also all the supplies that could not be loaded onto the wagons. Just before departing, Heald set fire was set to the fort. Surrounded by more than five-hundred warriors, now infuriated by the loss of items they believed promised to them, the doomed evacuation party left the fort the morning of August 15 for Detroit.

Wells and his party of Miami brought up the rear of the column. He had traded his American captain's uniform for Indian attire; and, he had painted his face black, a Miami sign indicating impending death. A short distance west of the fort, along the dune-covered shore of Lake Michigan, the Indian ambush was sprung. The result is now known as the Fort Dearborn Massacre.

Captain William Wells, the Miami warrior Apekonit--who had lived in two culturally separate worlds--died from numerous wounds at the age of forty-two, August 15, 1812. After he had fallen, Potawatomi warriors beheaded Wells' and cut his heart from his chest. In the belief hat they may gain his courage, Wells' heart was divided among his enemies and eaten.

One of the leaders of the massacre, the Potawatomi chief Black Partridge, returned the next day and buried Wells' body in the sand where it lay.

Buckongahelas

[Packangahelis, "Breaker to (in) Pieces," "Giver of Presents," "One Whose Movements Are Certain."]

Lenni Lenape [Delaware]
b. 1725? – d. 1805

Adapted from a drawing by 20ᵗʰ century artist William Sauts Netamuxwe Bock.
No authentic image is known to exist.

"You see a great and powerful nation divided. You see the father [Britain] fighting against the son [American Colonies], the son against the father. The father has called on his Indian children to assist him in punishing his children, the Americans ... I took time to consider what I should do -- whether or not I should receive the hatchet of the father to assist him. At first, I looked upon it as a family quarrel in which I was not interested. At length, it appeared to me that the father was right ... I concluded from the many cruel acts his offspring [Americans] have committed ... against his Indian children, by encroaching on their lands, stealing their property, shooting at and even murdering without cause ... Did not they kill ... without the least provocation? Are they now, do you think, better men than they were?"
– *Buckongahelas, excerpted from a speech given during treaty negotiations at Fort Pitt (Pennsylvania), 1775.*

"I admit that there are good white men, but they bear no proportion to the bad; the bad must be the strongest for they rule. They do what they please. They enslave those who are not of their color, although created by the same Great Spirit who created us. They would make slaves of us if they could, but as they cannot do it, they kill us! There is no faith to be placed in their words. They are not like the Indians. They will say to an Indian, 'My friend! My Brother!' They will take him by the hand, and at the same moment destroy him. And as you will be treated by them before long. Remember that this day I have warned you to beware of such friends as these. I know the Long Knives; they are not to be trusted."
– *Buckongahelas, to the Moravian Christian Indian converts at Gnadenhutten (Ohio), overheard and recorded by Moravian missionary John Heckewelder, 1781.*

Buckongahelas [*Breaker to Pieces*] became one of the most prominent Indian leaders of his time, both in war and in peace. He was a major war chief among the Indian nation known as *Lenni Lenape* [Common People, or Original People]. The Lenape are more commonly recognized as the Delaware, a name given to them by the Europeans, stemming from the traditional geographic location in which they lived at the time of European arrival.

Buckongahelas was born on traditional tribal lands, somewhere in the vicinity of the Chesapeake Bay in the modern-day state of Delaware during the mid-1720s. A son of Chief Wandochale, Buckongahelas became a band chieftain among the pro-British faction of the Lenape during the American Revolution.

Between the ages of sixty and seventy, he became the most prominent war chief among the Delaware during the Wabash Confederacy War, or so-named Little Turtle's War of the 1790's. The Lenape was one of several Algonquin-speaking tribes living in the area of the Great Lakes that joined the confederacy, a combined effort to repel American expansionism into Indian Territory following the Revolutionary War [1776-1784].

For his considerable skill as a warrior and later as a diplomat, the admired and respected Buckongahelas became known among the *Shewanahkok*, his American foes, as the "George Washington" of his people - a reference to General Washington's having been referred to as "first in war, first in peace and first in the hearts of his countrymen."

During the French and Indian War [1756-1763], Buckongahelas cast his support to the British. After the war ended, pressure from encroaching Euro-American settlements and the warlike Iroquois Confederacy forced Buckongahelas and many of his pro-British followers from their homelands in Delaware and eastern Pennsylvania, westward over the Appalachian Mountains.

By May of 1773, Buckongahelas was living near what is now Buckhannon, West Virginia. It was there that an American militia captain, William White, killed his son, Mahonegon. (A statue, dedicated in 2000 by the State of West Virginia, stands in Buckhannon's Jawbone Park. It depicts the great Delaware leader holding his dying son.)

As a result of Mahonegon's death, Buckongahelas continued his support of the British in their fight against the American colonists during the Revolutionary War. His decision to remain staunchly pro-British divided the Delaware into two divergent factions. Buckongahelas split from the pro-American faction and its leader, Chief Koquethagechton [*White Eyes*], and continued moving *eheliwsikank* [west]. He eventually settled in present-day east central Indiana.

By 1781, Buckongahelas's band was living along the Mad River in what is now Ohio, near his close ally, the pro-British Shawnee chief, Weyapiersenwah [*Blue Jacket*]. While living there, Buckongahelas, although not a Christian convert, traveled to the Moravian mission at Gnadenhutten [Ohio] in the spring of 1781. His aim was to warn the Delaware Christian converts living there of the impending danger he felt would certainly befall them as a result of American aggression. He urged the Delaware Christian converts, for their safety, to leave the mission and move west.

Buckongahelas' eloquent speech to the converts at Gnadenhutten focused on the continuing demise of Indian culture at the hands of Euro-American settlers, dating from the first landing by European explorers on North American shores. In his address, Buckongahelas related how the Lenni Lenape first spied large sailing ships on the horizon of the Atlantic Ocean. Believing *Kishelemukong* [also *Kee-say-lum-moo-kawng*, He Who Created Us With His Thought], The Great Spirit, had come from the sea to visit his children in *Lenapehoking* [Land of the Lenape], the Lenape greeted these sea-borne arrivals warmly and prepared great feasts in their honor.

At first the Europeans called the Indians their friends and brothers in return, but, Buckongahelas continued, this contact with Europeans eventually brought only hardship and death for the native population. The Lenape called these first European settlers *Swanakens*, or *Shouwumnock* [Bitter, or Salty People].

Based on historical experience, Buckongahelas warned that even greater hardships were now in store for the Indian as America continued usurping Indian lands. Even peaceful Christian Indians, he said, would not be able to escape the wrath of the *Swanakens* and their unquenchable desire for Indian land. Unfortunately for the Delaware Moravian converts, Buckongahelas' warnings were ignored.

A year later, on March 8, 1782, at the height of the Revolutionary War, Pennsylvania militiamen marched on the peaceful Moravian mission. In what became known as the Gnadenhutten Massacre, the militia killed nearly one hundred Moravian Delaware converts, mostly women and children. This massacre created in Buckongahelas a deepening distrust of Americans – and of Christianity, which he viewed as weapon used by Europeans to alienate the Indian from his native culture.

In 1770, more than a decade before, the Miami and Piankashaw tribes extended an invitation to their "grandfathers," the Lenape, to settle in present-day Indiana. After the Revolution ended, Buckongahelas finally acted on the invitation. He established his village near present-day Muncie, Indiana, along the upper West Fork White River, *Opeksipu*, or *Wapahani*.

His town, the first of fourteen Delaware settlements along the stream, was known by several names: *Wapicomekoke, Wap-pe-kah-me-kunk, Outainink* and Old Town. Most commonly, the village was referred to as Buckongahelas' Town or Buck's Town.

Between 1790 and 1794, as American squatters and land speculators pushed farther west, resistance by individual tribes erupted into warfare. During this period, known to American historians as the War of the Wabash Confederacy, or Little Turtle's War, Buckongahelas was universally recognized among the tribes of the Indian Territory as the principal Delaware war chief.

Along with *Tuwehtuweyok* [Miami] war chief Meshekinnoquah [Little Turtle] and *Shaonu* [Shawnee] ally Weyapiersenwah, Buckongahelas was a primary architect of a pan-tribal coalition of armed resistance known as the Wabash Confederacy or Miami Alliance. At its peak, the coalition was more than thousand warriors strong.

As war chief, Buckongahelas was head of his Lenape warriors as the confederacy dealt two crushing defeats to invading American forces sent to annihilate Indian towns in what is now western Ohio and eastern Indiana. The first Indian victory came against General Josiah Harmar in 1790. The second, recorded as the worst defeat of American forces during the Indian Wars, was against General Arthur St. Clair in 1791. In light of these Indian victories, the United States continued to seek a "final solution" to the "Indian problem." President George Washington, who had an interest in land speculation in the Northwest Territory, directed General Anthony Wayne to form a more professional army to subdue the Indians and break the coalition of Indian resistance.

Wayne took two years to form and train his American Legion. In the face of Wayne's more professional approach to warfare, Little Turtle, often named as the coalition's overall leader, warned that the Americans could not be defeated a third time. He abdicated his leadership role in the confederacy. Buckongahelas, along with Blue Jacket, took his place as *Netupalit* [Brave Men in War].

Buckongahelas and Blue Jacket were principal commanders of Confederacy forces when they met Wayne's Legion at the Battle of Fallen Timbers near modern-day Toledo, Ohio, in the fall of 1794. Unlike earlier successes against American militia, and as Little Turtle had predicted, the Indian warriors were unable to surprise Wayne's well-armed, well-prepared, professionally trained troops. Despite limited support from British soldiers, the battle ended in defeat for the Wabash Confederacy. Indian survivors fled to a recently built British fort at the rapids of the Maumee River [Ohio], seeking protection from their "fathers."

Despite the pleas of the warriors, the British garrison, fearing retribution from Wayne's army and unwilling to risk war, refused to admit their Indian allies and would not open the doors of the fort. This rejection ended Buckongahelas' affiliation with the British. Now convinced of the futility of fighting American advancement, he became a *Welankuntuwakan* [Peacemaker]. Over the next ten years, he pursued the path of peace, trying to protect his people from being trapped between two conflicting cultures.

In 1795, Buckongahelas signed the Treaty of Greenville [Ohio], which ceded much of what was now known as Ohio Territory and a portion of southeast Indiana Territory to the United States.

Although he would not allow Christian missions built near his village, in 1801, he did allow brothers John and William Conner to establish the first trading post along the West Fork White River at Buckongahela's Town. He later signed two more land cession treaties with the Americans, one at Fort Wayne in 1803, the other at Grouseland [Vincennes] in 1804.

Recognized as a prominent peacemaker by Indiana Territorial Governor William Henry Harrison, Buckongahelas was selected as a member of an Indian delegation escorted to Washington, D.C., in 1803. While in Washington, he registered his protest of treaty violations and Indian treatment directly, in English, to President Thomas Jefferson. Through his words and actions, Buckongahelas acquired the reputation of being "fearless, frank and magnanimous." Among most of his former

Indian allies and foes alike, his reputation was that of a principled, independent thinker.

Within the next few years, a pan-tribal movement sparked by The Shawnee Prophet, Tenskwatawa [*The Open Door*] and his brother, Tecumseh [*Panther Passing Across*], would gain a large following among the tribes of the southern Great Lakes. Buckongahelas agreed in principal with Tecumseh's message of Indian unity. According to some undocumented sources, he invited the leaders of the pan-tribal movement to live at his Wapahani village for a time so his people could listen to their message. Possibly at Buckongahelas' invitation, the Shawnee brothers lived among the Delaware during 1804 and 1805.

After hearing the Tecumseh's pan-tribal message, Buckongahelas not only refused to join the movement, but he also attempted to dissuade his warriors from becoming active disciples of The Shawnee Prophet's spiritual renewal. In his view, the creation of another such coalition of resistance was futile and would only delay what he perceived as inevitable Indian subjugation and ultimate removal west of the Mississippi River. Despite these views, it was Buckongahelas' death in May of 1805 that inadvertently increased The Prophet's following and prompted the infamous *Nunchiheweokan* [witchcraft] trials among the Delaware and other tribes.

Buckongahelas most likely died of influenza; he was at or beyond the advanced age of eighty at the time. But his death allowed The Shawnee Prophet's fervent Delaware followers an opportunity to fan the flames of religious fervor. They told The Prophet, who was now living at a village near Greenville [Ohio], that the popular Buckongahelas had died at the hands of *Nihenuchiheweyewak* [They Practice Witchcraft].

To Tenskwatawa, all whites were devils, but any and all Indians, Christian or non-Christian, who did not faithfully follow his teachings, most likely were witches. Accusations that Buckongahelas' death was caused by witchcraft brought The Prophet back to the Delaware river town. His self-proclaimed ability to see into the souls of witches led to the tomahawking and burning deaths of several Delaware, including an elderly woman, her son and at least one Lenape leader, Tetapacksit [*The Grand Glaize King*]. Another Delaware leader, Hockingpomska [*Hard Walker*], was driven from his village.

For this reason, added to the warnings of the influential Buckongahelas, most Lenape eventually came to distrust The Shawnee Prophet's motives. Subsequently, the Delaware played a relatively minor role during the creation of The Prophet's centralized village of Prophetstown, located at the confluence of the Tippecanoe and Wabash rivers, near present-day Lafayette, Indiana, in 1809, and at the Battle of Tippecanoe, which brought about The Prophet's downfall in 1811.

Buckongahelas was most likely buried in eastern Indiana, near the site of his village, located along the north bank of the West Fork White River, about three miles southeast of today's Muncie.

Kiilhsoohkwa

[Kilsoquah, "Sun Woman," "The Setting Sun," "The Sun;" Angelique Revarre]

Miami
b. 1810? – d.1915

Illustration adapted from a photograph taken by Vern Huffman, dated 1910.

"Marvelous are the changes I have seen; great are the improvements of the years, I have noted. My people are gone; those I knew are dead, but the changes about me have been too great and too marvelous to be of the hand of man alone. I see in the progress of things about me, the hand of the Great Maker himself, for man alone could never accomplish so much, only the maker of the bronze man and the white man could give us the old canal, then the railroad, then the interurban and now the automobile. Yes, the Great Spirit of my forefathers has wrought and wrought well."

– *Kiilhsoohkwa, from her speech given during her 100th birthday celebration, Roanoke, Indiana, 1910; interpreted by her son Wahpimongwah [Little White Loon], or Anthony Revarre.*

"My father said our people had occupied this country for ages, and Eel River and the Maumee and its tributaries were the heart of our possessions. The Potawatomi and some other came among us, but the country was ours."

– *Kiilhsoohkwa, from an interview with the Columbia City Post, dated 1906.*

Kiilhsoohkwa, or "Sun Woman," was born during *Cecaahkwa Kiihswa,* or the Sandhill Crane Moon [May] of 1810, near *Paawikami Siipiwii* [the Forks of the Wabash River] at present-day Huntington, Indiana, two years before the death of her grandfather, Me-she-kin-no-quah, [*Little Turtle*].

Her Miami father was Mak-e-shen-e-quah [also Wakshingay, or Wakshingwah, meaning *Crescent Moon*], a son of Little Turtle. Her Miami mother was Wah-wa-ka-mo-quah [*Snow Woman*], a daughter of Chief Shimaakanehsia, or Shemockenish.

While still a young girl, her father, through treaty negotiations, was granted an entire section of land in Ohio. However, reluctant to move so far from his boyhood home, Mak-e-shen-e-quah traded his Ohio section to another man for a half-section, three hundred twenty acres of forestland, near present-day Roanoke, Indiana. He cleared an area large enough to build a log cabin and moved his family there. Kiilhsoohkwa lived on this reserve the most of her long life.

Around 1826, when she was sixteen years of age, Kiilhsoohkwa married John Owl, a mixed Miami. The couple moved to Seek's Village, along the *Kineepikomeekwa Siipiiwi*, or Eel River, east of modern-day Columbia City, Indiana. After only two years of marriage, John Owl died, and Kiilhsoohkwa moved back to her father's home.

In 1832 she married Shawpenomquah [*Thunderstorm*], also known as Antoine Revarre. Like her first husband, Revarre was a metis of French and Miami heritage.

Six children were born to Kiilhsoohkwa and Revarre; four of the six died in infancy. One daughter, Wan-nog-quan-quah, [*Snow Mist*, or *Fog*], also known as Mary Revarre, and a son, her youngest child, Wahpimongwah or Shap-pe-ne-maw, [*Little White Loon*, or Anthony Revarre, Junior], also known as Tony Loon, survived.

After attending Roanoke Academy, Wan-nog-quan-quah married and moved to Oklahoma, where she became a schoolteacher. Wahpimongwah also attended the academy, but stayed on in Indiana.

Kiilhsoohkwa's father died in 1846, and her mother died shortly thereafter. Both parents were buried on the family's forested Roanoke reserve. Her husband, Revarre, died in 1850 and was buried near her parents at the family farm. By special decree of the United States government, when most of the Miami were forced into selling their reserves and moving across the Mississippi River, Kiilhsoohkwa and her family were not required to remove from Indiana.

For many years, Kiilhsoohkwa cared for a flag, which had been given to her by her grandfather, Shimaakanehsia. According to one version of the flag's origin, General Anthony Wayne presented it to her grandfather during the signing of the Treaty of Greenville [Ohio] in 1795. Another Miami source says that the flag had been taken from General Wayne's troops during a skirmish in Ohio. Regardless, according to authorities, the flag appears to have been hand-sewn by Indian women, based on the method of construction and materials used.

Kiilhsoohkwa 's later years were spent living with her son near Roanoke on what was known locally as the Miami Loon Reserve. At the time of her passing, Kiilhsoohkwa was one of the last full-blood Miami remaining in Indiana. A devout Roman Catholic, she lived to be 105 years of age and died September 4, 1915, at her log cabin home. She was buried in Glenwood Cemetery in Roanoke.

She never learned to speak English.

Her obituary in the Indianapolis News, dated September 5, 1915, states: *"But until rheumatism kept her indoors, each spring her birthday was celebrated by great gathering* [sic], *and from the platform on which the Indian princess sat speeches were made, and she smilingly and calmly received the applause of hundreds."*

In 2005, an Indiana Historic Bureau marker was dedicated at Glenwood Cemetery in her honor.

Kik-tha-we-nund

["Making A Cracking Noise,"
"Causing To Crack, As A Tree About To Fall In The
Forest;" Captain William X. Anderson]

Lenni Lenape [Delaware]
b. 1750-1757? – d. 1831

Illustration adapted from a sculpture by Kenneth Ryden.
No authentic image is known to exist.

"I do not like the evil conduct of our young people, neither do I like to see whiskey brought here, for my grandfather told me that if anyone should die while drunk, he would go straight to the Devil. I often talk to my people about it, but they will not listen."
   – Kikthawenund to Moravian missionary, c. 1801.

"Father: We did not think that big men would tell us things that weren't true. We have found poor, hilly, stony country, and worst of all, no game to live on ... Father: You know it is hard to be hungry, if you don't know it, we poor Indians know it ... We are obliged to call on you once more for assistance in the name of God, you know that one God that made us all, and we know it."
   – Kikthawenund, letter to government agent Richard Graham, Kansas, dated 1824.

Kikthawenund [Making A Cracking Noise], or William X. Anderson, despite being only half Indian, was regarded as one of the most influential sachems and major chiefs of the Lenni Lenape [*First People, Original People, or Common People*], or Delaware Indians, living in eastern Indiana and western Ohio at the time of their removal to the west in 1820.

Anderson led his people first to Missouri, then later to Kansas, where he died in 1831. During those eleven years as sovereign chief of the Delaware, Kikthawenund fought tirelessly for tribal unity, better living conditions for his people, and for peaceful relations with other tribes and with the American government. His leadership policy was one of adaptation to American values for the purpose of maintaining a modified Anglo-Indian culture.

Kikthawenund was born in western Pennsylvania between 1750 and 1757. His father, John Anderson, was a Swedish-American trader; his mother was Lenape. His mother's Delaware grandfather was Netawatwees, head chief and "keeper of the wampum" of the *Unami* [Down River People, or Turkey Clan], one of three Delaware sub-tribes. Since ascendancy among the Delaware was through matrilineal lines, Kikthawenund eventually rose to be, first a clan chief, then, in 1806, principal chief of the Delaware. He was about fifty years of age at that time. During his years of leadership, 1806 to 1831, Kikthawenund was a *Welankuntuwakan* [peacemaker] and an unwavering supporter of American policies.

Depending on accounts, Kikthawenund was born either at his father's trading post along the Susquehanna River, near modern-day Harrisburg, Pennsylvania, or possibly at the confluence of Beaver Creek and the Ohio River, northeast of today's city of Pittsburg – then known as Fort Pitt.

In July of 1758, Kikthawenund's band moved near present-day Cayuga Falls, Ohio, along the Tuscarawas River to a place called Newcomer's Town, a village his great-grandfather, Netawatwees, had founded. Principal chief of the Unami, Netawatwees was evidently a man of substantial means. His house is described as having two stories, a stairway, wood flooring and a large fireplace.

Kikthawenund's father opened a trading post at Newcomer's Town, but he was often absent from home. John Anderson worked as a governmental interpreter and messenger to many of the tribes displaced through American expansion. With his father gone, Kikthawenund spent much of his youth visiting and speaking with his great-grandfather, most likely learning the traditions of the Lenape. Netawatwees died in October of 1776.

By the time Kikthawenund was twenty years old, he had married a Delaware woman, a relative of Hopocan [Konieschquanokee, or *Tobacco Pipe*]. Also known as Captain Pipe, Hopocan was leader of the Wolf Clan. Kikthawenund and his first wife had a daughter, Swan Nuck, and two sons, Pushies and Sacondi. His second Delaware wife was a member of the Turtle Clan and a sister to Mehshaquowha, also known as Captain Patterson. His second wife bore him three more children, a son, Saroxie, and two daughters, Sosecum, and Mekingees.

Known among the Algonquin-speaking Indians as "grandfathers," the Lenape were considered to be the oldest tribe living on the North American continent. By their own traditions, the Lenape claimed first contact with Europeans. They welcomed their foreign visitors with open arms, only to later be underhandedly exploited. The Lenape signed the first known peace treaty between Indians and settlers – the only one never broken – with Quaker leader William Penn, founder of the colony of Pennsylvania.

However, over the years, other treaties were signed and then broken. Rifts between the Delaware and the Iroquois Confederacy, along with westward American expansion, eroded their claims to their native lands in the eastern United States. The Delaware clans began to scatter.

Some Lenape moved north into Canada, others moved south into the Carolinas, and others, like Kikthawenund's family, first gaining permission of the Miami, moved west into western Ohio Territory, eventually settling in what would become eastern Indiana between 1770 to 1800. As peacemakers the Lenape often found themselves in the unenviable position as buffer between the advancing Euro-Americans and other Indian tribes.

About 1790, Kikthawenund's clan settled along the *Wapahani*, or West Fork White River, near the site of the present-day city of Anderson, Indiana, the current county seat of Madison County. A village of some twenty families, it was known as *Wapeminskink*, or "Chestnut Tree Place." Due to a continuing influx of Indian refugees during its latter years, Wapeminskink's population swelled to one thousand residents.

Kikthawenund became chief of the Turkey Clan in 1795, after the death of his uncle, Gelelemend [*Big Cat*], known among the Americans as Killbuck. When Netawatwees died in 1776, the position of principal chief of the entire Lenni Lenape had fallen to Koquethagechton [*White Eyes*]. White Eyes had served as a scout for American forces during the Revolutionary War, and attained the rank of lieutenant colonel. He died in 1778, while in the service of the American colonial army.

Since White Eyes had no immediate successor, a triumvirate of three Lenape clan chiefs--Tetapacksit [*Grand Glaize King*] of the Turtle Clan, Meshingwe Pooshies of the Wolf Clan and Gelelemend of the Turkey Clan--was formed to govern the Lenape. A quick-moving turn of events would make Kikthawenund the singular principal chief within the next few years.

Gelelemend resigned his position after converting to Christianity, and Kikthawenund, his nephew, became clan chief. By 1805, Meshingwe Pooshies and his successor, Captain Pipe, were both dead. Hockingpomska and Tetapacksit succeeded Meshingwe Pooshies and Captain Pipe, but that same year, both were accused by Tenskwatawa [*The Open Door*], The Shawnee Prophet, and his Delaware disciples of practicing *nunchiheweokan* [witchcraft] and sentenced to death.

Tetapacksit and Hockingpomska were charged with causing the death of the popular Delaware war chief, Buckongahelas [Breaker to Pieces] through witchcraft. Tetapacksit was executed, and Hochingpomska fled.

With these two leaders gone, the position of principal chief came to Kikthawenund, who by now was known among the Americans by his Christian name of William X. Anderson – sometimes called Captain Anderson. He was known as a friendly, peaceful man, but one who stood firmly for his beliefs.

Although there is no proof that Anderson practiced Moravianism or any other form of Christianity, in 1801, he allowed a mission to be built a few of miles from his village. He also offered his village as protection for Moravian missionaries and Delaware Christian converts during a series of "witch hunts" and "witchcraft trials." He sometimes called on missionaries to write and translate correspondence for him.

Anderson preached temperance and worked with missionaries to stop the use of alcohol among his people. He campaigned strongly against Tenskwatawa's anti-American message and Tecumseh's [*Panther Passing Across*] pan-tribal movement. He forbade his warriors to join the Shawnee brothers' cause.

During Tenskwatawa's witchhunts, Anderson openly defied The Shawnee Prophet, daring Tenskwatawa to accuse him of witchcraft. The Shawnees left his village soon after. After the Indian defeat at Prophetstown in 1811, Tecumseh sent a belt of war wampum to Anderson, trying to enlist the Delaware in his battle against the Americans. Anderson refused to accept the belt and again tried to keep his followers from joining the pro-British Indian alliance during the War of 1812. Despite his refusal to go to war, Anderson's Delaware Village of Wapeminskink was burned by American troops in 1813.

Anderson did not retaliate. As peace chief and sachem or spiritual leader of the Delaware, Anderson is not recorded as having joined any battles against the Americans. As one of two principal Delaware chiefs, along with other tribal chiefs, he signed the Treaty of Greenville in 1795 and other land cession treaties in 1803 [Fort Wayne] and 1805 [Vincennes]. In 1818 he signed the St. Mary's Treaty, along with the other principal Delaware chief, Lapanibi [*Big Bear*].

The St. Mary's Treaty relinquished remaining Delaware claims to Indiana lands and required them to move west within three years. This angered the Miami and Shawnee, who felt the Lenape had no right to sell any land in Indiana. Later, as an act of revenge, the Miami attacked Anderson's Delaware, who were then living in Missouri.

Some unfounded legends say that Anderson died before the Delaware removal from Indiana. One of these legends claims he fell from a horse along the White River, another says he died of disease, and still another that he moved to Ohio and was killed.

However, documentation proves that Anderson led his people out of Indiana in 1821. He was about sixty years old at the time. His daughter, Mekingees [Ma-cun-chis, *Dancing Feather*], chose to leave her husband, William Conner, take their six children, and follow her father and people west.

Using canoes and traveling along water routes, Anderson's Delaware started from their village on the Wapahani and traveled southwest through present-day Indianapolis, onto the Wabash River, then down the Ohio River to the Mississippi River.

Anderson and his people settled a few miles north of the confluence of the Ohio and Mississippi rivers at Cape Girardeau, Missouri. By 1824 the Delaware were challenged by a lack of game and poor farming conditions. There was also trouble with the resident and militant *Wakon* [Osage Indians], who killed one of Anderson's sons. These circumstances prompted Anderson to move his people to a reservation in Kansas.

In 1829, he signed his final treaty with the Americans at James Forks along the White River in Missouri. Anderson led his people to Kansas, ironically settling just a few miles from his former nemesis, Tenskwatawa, The Shawnee Prophet.

During his later years, Anderson spent much energy trying to unite all Delaware into a single nation. Some clans had stayed behind in Indiana, while others were living on a reservation in Ohio. Still others, mostly Moravian converts, moved to Canada. Some clans moved to Mexican-held territory in what was transforming into the Republic of Texas. For the rest of his life, Kikthawenund never ceased his efforts to unite the scattered Delaware into a single tribe.

He also worked tirelessly to improve conditions on his reservation, writing numerous letters to governmental officials on behalf of his people. One of his last letters was written in 1830, less than a year before his death in the fall of 1831. In the letter Kikthawenund asks that Major John B. Campbell direct a group of Lenape, which he calls "his relatives," to his Kansas cabin. He signed the letter designating his position as "The Sovereign Chief of the Delaware Tribe."

Always a peacemaker in the tradition of the Lenni Lenape, his very last letter tells of his peaceful offerings to a tribe of neighboring Pawnee. Following his death, his son-in-law, Captain Patterson, succeeded Kikthawenund as principal chief.

No one is certain where Anderson's body is buried, but most believe his remains to be interred near his Kansas home. Regardless of where he now rests, his life is depicted through his untiring efforts on behalf of his people.

Koh-koh-maw

[Mahkookima, Kokomoko, Kokomo, Kokokama,
Kokama, Co-co-mo; *"The Diver," "Black Walnut,"
"Bear Chief," "She Bear," "Old Woman"*]

**Miami
b. 1785? – d. 1840-42?**

*Illustration adapted from a painting by Ida Gordon, based on the artist's conception
dated 1962. No authentic image is known to exist.*

Koh-koh-maw [*The Diver*] is shrouded in historic mystery. Documented information about Koh-koh-maw's life is sketchy at best, although the alteration of his Miami personal name – Kokomo - has become one of Indiana's most recognized place names. Koh-koh-maw's homeland was within the area exempted from the New Purchase Treaty of 1818, an area called the Great Miami Reserve. The Miami called it "the bed we lie in" or "homeland."

At the time of negotiations with the United States for the Great Reserve, Jean Baptiste Richardville [*Peshewa*, or Wildcat] was principal civil chief of the Miami. The Great Reserve contained some 760,000 acres. The northern boundary of the reserve was the *Waapaahsiiki Siipiiwi* [Wabash River], from the mouth of the *Osahmonee*, or Salamonie River, west to the mouth of the *Kineepikomeekwa Siipiiwi*, or Eel River. The reserve stretched south from the Wabash to the present-day communities of Kirklin and Tipton, Indiana. The Miami "homeland" included parts of present-day Grant, Wabash, Miami, Cass, Clinton and Tipton counties as well as all of Howard County.

Koh-koh-maw's personal name, most often translated "The Diver," may possibly stem from the Miami word *akooka*, which means "frog." Several other meanings – and pronunciations – are also used, adding to his mystique. Regardless, he was a Miami who established his village in the unbroken wilds of the Great Reserve. His isolated village of some two hundred people has grown into Indiana's fifth largest city and the county seat of Howard County.

Although some accounts say Koh-koh-maw was Peshewa's son, and the grandnephew of the highly regarded Miami war chief Meshekinnoquah [*Little Turtle*], other accounts claim Koh-Moh-Maw was not a chief of any sort; nor did he hold any position of authority among the Miami. Still other local accounts claim that Koh-koh-maw "was the last of the fighting Miamis ... outspoken and fearless."

In 1841 transplanted Kentuckian David Foster bought a section of land in what is now Howard County from Miami head chief Topeah [*Frost on the Bushes*], or Francis LaFontaine. On this purchase, Foster founded what has become today's city of Kokomo, located at the rapids on the Middle Fork of Wildcat Creek. In newspaper accounts, Foster claims that he named "the orneriest town in Indiana after the orneriest Indian he ever met." And, indeed, a few early writers describe a "Co-co-mo" as mean, vicious and "nothing but a coon-hunting, root-digging, old redskin."

Since the town of Kokomo had no newspaper until a few years after Koh-koh-maw's death, there is little documentation of his life; his portrait was never painted, and since he died before cameras were commonplace, only an artist's imagined conception of his likeness exists.

Although few facts about his life are known, all accounts agree that Koh-koh-maw was a very tall person – perhaps seven feet - who "towered over everyone in town." Local Kokomo historian, Carl Leiter, cites an 1838 trading post ledger entry indicating that a twelve-dollar barrel of flour and some calico cloth was sold to "Koh-Koh-Maw and his squaw" by Palonswah, [*Big Bird*], the Miami chief Francis Godfroy. This is one of the few written records of Koh-koh-maw's existence.

Is it possible that contrasting descriptions of this noble, fearless "last of the fighting Miamis" and the "orneriest Indian" David Foster ever knew describe the same man?

If Koh-koh-maw was truly a warrior and war chief who was active in battles against the American army during the time of the Indian holocaust as well as an apostle of Miami sovereignty; if he desired freedom to wander the land; if his dislike of reservation life and his desire to maintain Indian customs are all accurate, all these hypotheses could certainly have put him at odds with early settlers – and perhaps even among his own people.

Modern Miami have said that Koh-koh-maw was driven from his former village near modern-day Peru at the confluence of the Wabash River and *Nimacihsinwi Siipiiwi* [It Slopes], or Mississinewa River. His ouster came because of "much disrepute" and his tendency to cause trouble among the tribe. If we consider Koh-koh-maw as an outspoken, fearless man of strong, unyielding pro-Indian views, then it is very possible that he offended those tribal members attempting to acculturate into modern American society. In this light, he easily could have been branded as a rabble-rousing troublemaker among both settlers and Indians struggling to leave the old ways behind and assume a new culture.

Regardless of the reason, Koh-koh-maw left his former village with several followers, "mostly squaws," and moved to a forty-acre site in the middle of the Great Reserve. Nearly two hundred Miami, the entire population of 1840 Howard County, lived in or near Koh-koh-maw's village. This village site was located at the heart of present-day Kokomo.

According to the public land surveyor's report of the summer of 1847, Koh-koh-maw's village occupied what is now the intersection of Main and Sycamore streets, near Washington Street, north of Wildcat Creek. There he remained until his death, which is assumed to have occurred sometime between 1840 and 1842.

Koh-koh-maw, this illusive figure of Indiana history first was buried in the old Indian cemetery on the north side of Wildcat Creek. But in 1848, excavation of a foundation for a new sawmill along that waterway unearthed several Indian graves, one possibly Koh-koh-maw's, in the middle of Buckeye Street, south of Superior Street.

One of the skeletons recovered was noted as "remarkably long," measuring nearly seven feet. Based on this measurement and early physical descriptions, the town's first doctor, Corydon Richmond, concluded that these bones must be those of Koh-koh-maw.

Koh-koh-maw's skeleton was disinterred from Pioneer Cemetery for reburial at the end of Purdum Street. A marker on the Purdum Street site reads:

"This stone marks/The burial place of/KOKOMO/War Chief of the Miami Indians/The former owner of the land along the river/and from whom this city derives its name."

Maconaquah

["Little Bear Woman"]
Frances Slocum
["White Rose of the Miami"]

Anglo-American – Miami adoptee
b. 1773 – d. 1847

Adapted from an original portrait painting by George Winter, dated 1839.

"No I cannot [leave]. I have always lived with the Indians ...
I am used to them. The Great Spirit allowed me to live with
them and I wish to live and die with them ... I should have
died sooner if I had left them. My husband and my boys
are buried here, and I cannot leave them. On his dying day
my husband charged me not to leave the Indians. I have a
house, and large lands, two daughters, a son-in-law, three
grandchildren, and everything to make me comfortable.
Why should I go, and be like a fish out of the water."
– Maconaquah's response to her brothers, Joseph and Issac
Slocum, and her sister, Mary Towne, asking her to return to
Pennsylvania; spoken through an interpreter, Peru, Indiana,
September, 1837.

"I am an old tree. I cannot move about."
– Maconaquah's response to her Pennsylvania Slocum relatives
when asked to return home with them, Peru, Indiana, 1837.

Frances Slocum was born March 4, 1773, in Rhode Island to
Jonathan and Ruth Tripp Slocum, a peaceful Quaker family. In 1777,
during the Revolutionary War, the Slocum family moved from Rhode
Island to Pennsylvania and settled along the Susquehanna River in the
Wyoming Valley, near the fort at Wilkes-Barre.

Due to the Slocum's peaceful religious beliefs and their friendship
with the Delaware Indians of the region, the family was spared any
violence during their first year in Pennsylvania. But on July 3, 1778, the
Revolutionary War came home to the Slocum family.

A British-led force of Indians attacked American settlers in what has
been termed the Wyoming Massacre. In retaliation for the Wyoming
Massacre, eighteen year-old Giles Slocum, Frances' older brother, joined
a military expedition to hunt down the perpetrators. After seeing
Jonathan Slocum's son bearing arms, the Delaware thought they had
been betrayed and sought revenge.

A force of Delaware warriors attacked the Slocum home on
November 2, 1778, and kidnapped Frances. The Slocum family would
not hear from her again for nearly six decades. In 1835 George W.
Ewing, an American trader living in Peru, Indiana, came to her home at
Kakipshah's [*Deaf Man's*] Miami village on the *Nimacihsinwi Siipiiwi*,

[It Slopes] or Missisinewa River, southeast of Peru. Ill and fearing her impending death, Maconaquah revealed to Ewing her true identity and the story of her life.

After her capture, five-year-old Frances had been adopted into a Delaware family, which had recently lost their own daughter named Weletawash. Young Frances was given the personal name Maconaquah [*Little Bear Woman*] in recognition of her physical strength. Maconaquah wandered with her foster parents from Delaware town to Delaware town, traveling through today's states of Pennsylvania, Ohio, Indiana, Michigan, on into Canada by way of the "Great [Niagara] Falls."

As a young woman, she had married a Delaware warrior, but in a short time the marriage failed. She would say later that he was abusive to her.

Traveling through the Ohio Territory, Maconaquah found a wounded Miami warrior named Shepoconah [*The Awl*] and nursed him back to health. They soon married. In later years as his hearing failed, Shepoconah became known as Kakipshah or "Deaf Man."

The couple first lived at *Cecaahkonki*, or Kekionga, at present-day Fort Wayne, Indiana. They later moved to Osage Village near the mouth of the *Nimacihsinwi Siipiiwi* [Mississinewa River] at its confluence with the *Waapaahsiiki Siipiiwi* [Wabash River], near Peru. They moved once more, this time a few miles farther upstream on the Mississinewa to the site of the present-day Mississinewa Reservoir. This was the place where Maconaquah finally revealed her white Anglo identity -fifty-seven years after she was abducted during the Delaware raid on her family's Pennsylvania home.

Over those years, Maconaquah had given birth to two sons, both of whom died young, and two daughters, Kickkesequah [*Cut Finger*], and Oshawsequah [*Yellow Leaf*]. Her husband, Kakipshah, a Miami chief, died in 1833, but left Maconaquah with enough land, livestock and money to provide for herself and her family. At the time she revealed her true identity to Ewing, both daughters and her son-in-law, Taquahkeah, [*Autumn*], were living with Maconaquah.

After discovering Maconaquah's identity--and against her wishes--Ewing sent a letter to the Slocum family in Wilkes-Barre. Ewing's letter was not immediately delivered. It languished in the local post office at Wilkes-Barre for two years. But the news of Frances Slocum, a white captive living among the Indiana Miami, finally reached her Pennsylvania family.

In the fall of 1837, Frances' two brothers and her sister traveled to Indiana. They visited Maconaquah at her home on the Mississinewa, and she met with them several times in a Peru hotel. On all occasions, she refused her family's continued offers to return east with them. Since she was no longer fluent in English, she spoke through an interpreter, telling them that she was an "old tree," which could not be replanted. Her Indian ways had become permanent, she said; she preferred to stay among the Miami. Finally, Maconaquah convinced her saddened biological family that she was entirely Miami, not only in appearance, but also in thought, word and action.

During the 1840s and 1850s, the Miami were forced to remove from Indiana and settle on reservations west of the Mississippi. By a special Congressional resolution passed in 1850, Maconaquah and her Miami family avoided the forced Indian removal. She remained along the Mississinewa River for the rest of her earthly days.

Maconaquah died on her birthday, March 4, 1847, at seventy-four years of age. She is buried near her beloved Mississinewa, northwest of present-day Somerset, Indiana. With the creation of the Mississinewa Reservoir, her grave was moved from the original burial site at Peoria and relocated to the present-day Somerset site.

A historical marker and gravestone monument, dedicated May 17, 1900, recalls fondly "The White Rose of the Miami." It is considered among the most significant American Indian memorials in the state.

Mas-saw
[Mis-sah, Massa, Mas-sau-kequa, Mes-quah, (*meaning unknown*); Marie Messah]

Potawatomi
b. 1800? – d. 1867?

Illustration adapted from the portrait painting by George Winter, dated 1837.

"[Mas-saw] had her cape covered with circular silver ornaments ... several strings of small blue beads hung around her neck. She wore a ke-chep-so-win *or belt pendant, from it were several steel chains with watch keys attached, falling as low as the knee over a* mich-a-ko-the, *or petticoat handsomely ornamented with silver rings ... her petticoat [skirt] was handsomely bordered by rows of ribbons of the primitive colors, an occasional row of secondary color. These ribbons were about two inches wide, cut into points and vandykes – very neatly sewed ... Her cloth blanket [shawl] too, was bordered by ribbons and silver rings ... Her blanket and petticoat were of good dark blue broad cloth ... her moccasins ... were neatly made and handsomely checkered on the laps with ribbons of primitive colors ... Red leggings ... completed the handsome costume..."*
– George Winter, from his Journal, describing Mas-saw's regalia worn for her portrait, Lake Kee-wau-nay Council, July 1837.

Mas-saw was a principal woman or chieftess among the Wabash Potawatomi, a hereditary position that held a great deal of influence among her people.

Mas-saw possibly was born around 1800, approximately the same time the Northwest Territory was divided into the territories of Ohio and Indiana. Ohio territory contained, basically what is now the State of Ohio. Indiana Territory included what would become the present day states of Illinois, Wisconsin and Indiana and large portions of Michigan and Minnesota. Mas-saw most likely was born in the area that would become northern Indiana or southern lower Michigan.. Little is known of her parentage or early life. Just prior to the Potawatomi removal from Indiana, she, like Menominee [*Rice Eater*], "The Potawatomi Preacher," converted to Catholicism.

Among the baptismal records of Father Benjamin Petit, the attending Catholic priest at Menominee's village chapel, Chi-chi-pi Outi-pe at *Ni-jo-de sa-ga-ig-an-og* [Twin Lakes], southwest of Plymouth, Indiana, she is listed as Marie Messah. Her baptism date is March 1, 1838. Father

Petit also baptized Mas-saw's sister, Archangel Messingagockoway, in May of 1838.

Father Petit, who accompanied Menominee's people on the Trail of Death to Kansas, records Mas-saw's father as Wassato, which could possibly be spelled Wasito. The name Wasito is listed among thirteen extended families of Chief Leopold Pokagon's [*Rib*] band of southwestern Michigan Potawatomi. Wasito is listed as a member of the Singowa Band of Lower Michigan between 1857 and 1866.

Similar spellings based on possible pronunciations of Mas-saw's personal name appear on several treaties signed with the United States government between 1832 and 1836. However, positive identification remains elusive due to several factors, one of the most significant being gender.

The Treaty of Tippecanoe, signed October 20, 1832, reserved "two section[s] of land at Wais-us-kuck's village for Mesawkequa, and her children. This could possibly be Mas-saw. Also, on October 26 of the same year, two more sections of land were reserved for "the band of Ma-che-saw." Confusion arises again in the signature, which is listed as Ma-che-saw, followed by "his mark." This could have been an error in record keeping, or Mas-saw — listed as Ma-che-saw - may have controlled a total of four sections of land [2,560 acres] in northern Indiana. To continue the mystery, two other signatures on the treaty are very similar to Mas-saw, and to each other, those being: "Mis-sah-kaw-qua, his mark," and "Mis-sah-qua, his mark."

In 1836 the Potawatomi "chiefs and headmen and their bands" signed three separate treaties along the Tippecanoe. In each of these documents, land reserves given to various *ogema* [leaders] by the 1832 treaties were ceded back to the United States. These treaties also exacted a promise that the Potawatomi would leave Indiana "within two years" and relocate to reservations in the west. Mas-saw may have been active in these negotiations as well.

On the first of these treaties at Tippecanoe, signed March 9, 1836, "Mes-quah, her mark" appears. This is most likely Massaw, who in this treaty, agrees to cede her land and move west within the allotted time. On the April 22, 1836, [Second] Treaty at Tippecanoe, the signature of "Ma-che-saw, his mark" is found again, with the personal name defined as "Bleating Fawn." This most likely indicates that Mas-saw and Ma-che-saw are two distinctly different individuals, although research turns up no definition of Mas-saw's personal name.

No variation of Mas-saw's name appears on a third treaty, also dated April 22, with the same stipulations and signed by several chiefs; but her signature seems, however, to appear on the Treaty of the Yellow River, signed August 5, 1836. Again, gender references become confusing.

In the Yellow River treaty, her signature appears among the "Proper Chiefs of the Wabash Patawattamies" as "Mas-saw, [and, again] *his* mark." In this treaty, Indian commissioner Abel C. Pepper was able to convince these "Proper Chiefs" to cede lands they did not own, including the reservation claimed by Menominee, the reserve on which Mas-saw later would be baptized. The forced removal of Menominee's band in September of 1838 led to the Trail of Death, a six hundred-sixty-mile march to Kansas, a trek in which Mas-saw participated.

Among several treaty signature lists, the various signatures that could be Massaw's often appear near that of Chief Ke-wau-nay [*Prairie Chicken*]. By 1837 Mas-saw was living at Kee-wau-nay's village, near modern-day Lake Bruce, Fulton County, Indiana, during the time of a treaty council between assembled Potawatomi chiefs, headmen and warriors and delegates of the United States government. The purpose of this meeting was to remind the Potawatomi of the terms of their 1836 treaty cessions, which required their removal from Indiana within the following year.

Among the American delegation to Lake Ke-wau-nay was George Winter, a self-trained painter and sketch artist, who was born in England in 1809. Although not considered a great technical painter, historians consider Winter the leading archivist of the rapidly disappearing traditional lifestyle of Indiana Indians during the 1830's and 1840's. His journal accounts, his sketches and his paintings are the main record of Mas-saw, along with several other Potawatomi, their dress and lifestyle, that Winter recorded during the council at Ke-wau-nay's village as well as other locations.

Winter came to America around 1830 and arrived in Logansport, Indiana, in 1837. That August, in hopes of gaining a governmental commission for his drawings, illustrations and writings, he joined Colonel Pepper's delegation to the lake and Indian village in western Fulton County.

Winter was quite impressed with Mas-saw. According to Winter, Mas-saw had inherited her title of chieftess, but her influence among her people was "very observable."

She was evidently also a woman of some financial means and a good businesswoman, "not indifferent ... to the silver dollar," Winter writes.

At the time of the council, Mas-saw was living in a double log cabin near the lake. Winter describes it "as good a home as the affluent farmer possessed, or aspired to, in the West generally." Her cabin became the headquarters for the American treaty delegation, and a "general rendezvous" for the Potawatomi who had assembled for the council and had not "[brought] their camps with them."

Winter describes Mas-saw's cabin as having two stories, and as being well made, but having few furnishings. Col. Pepper's bed, Winter notes, was the only piece of furniture in the upstairs, which like the downstairs, was divided into two rooms by "a wide passage or hallway nine feet in width." Like most of the delegates, Winter sat and slept on the floor, using his "saddlebags" for a pillow. He fashioned a makeshift desk, a place for him to write and keep his portfolio of drawings, paintings and sketches, from a wooden keg and a piece of board he had found.

Besides being the area's first innkeeper, Winter also notes that Mas-saw was something of a gambler. He writes that she was skilled at playing euchre and "adroit" at poker. She frequently held "receptions" in her upstairs, "often raking men of experience."

Mas-saw lived with a French-Canadian trader, Andrew or Andre Gosselin [also spelled Goslin and Gosland]. According to Winter, she was proud of her association with white people. Winter wrote that Mas-saw and Gosselin had a daughter, Maurie [also spelled Mauri and Marie], a girl of "about fourteen summers." Winter would paint finished portraits of both mother and daughter, but not without some convincing.

According to Winter, Mas-saw was good at cooking deer meat, but not very good at making bread. "She was much assisted" in preparing meals for her nearly two dozen guests by a woman named Doga. Doga was eager to sit for Winter and have her portrait painted. Pleased with the results, Doga finally convinced Mas-saw to sit and also have her likeness recorded by Winter. Winter's small watercolor portrait and writings describe Mas-saw's "full regimentals" as a "handsome costume."

Mas-saw's daughter, Maurie, also had her portrait painted by Winter. However, the young girl was much more reluctant than either Doga or her mother. Maurie had to be cajoled into sitting for Winter. Winter writes that Maurie was uncomfortable at first and would not smile. Eventually she became more comfortable and was pleased with her finished portrait.

After adopting the Catholic faith, and prior to her going west in 1838, Mas-saw was baptized and married Gosselin at Chichipe Outipe on May 8, 1838. Her daughter, Maurie, was also baptized in the chapel at Twin Lakes. A second daughter, Angelique, was about eight years old at the time, but there are no records of her baptism. By September, the Potatwatomi at Twin Lakes had been forced from their lands and were headed west.

On the rolls of the Trail of Death, Mas-saw may have been listed as "Missinoquah and with eight people;" however, sources also list a third daughter, Elizabeth Goeslin [sic], [also Lisette or Lazet Gosland], born in Indiana between 1839 and 1841. Her father is thought to be a Kickapoo named Keotuk or Keoduk, whose band many of the Potawatomi had joined. By 1846, the Potatwatomi who had been removed from Indiana were settled among the Kickapoo, near Fort Leavenworth, Kansas, north of modern day Kansas City. By the fall of 1847, Mas-saw's family, which now included a son, Autwain or Atwain, moved to a new reservation at St. Marys, now Pottawatomie County, Kansas.

Mas-saw's final documented signature appears on an 1861 Kansas treaty in which the emigrated Potawatomi separated into two groups: the Citizen Band and the Prairie Band.

The Citizen Band chose to divide their tribal lands into individual parcels of one hundred sixty acres, while the Prairie Band desired that title to their reservation lands be held in common. Mas-saw elected membership in the Citizen Band, so-named for the individual ownership of land and the desire for United States citizenship.

Perhaps Mas-saw's greatest contribution to American Indian history is through her daughter, Elizabeth.

After moving west, Elizabeth married Jacob Vieux [pronounced "vo"]. Jacob's father was Louis Vieux, Sr., a French trader who is credited with founding modern day Milwaukee, Wisconsin. His mother was Sha Note, or Charlotte, a Potawatomi also from Wisconsin. The Vieux family came west voluntarily about 1832. Sha Note's father, Chesaugan, was a member the St. Joseph Band of Potawatomi and had been with Menominee on the Trail of Death.

Jacob and Charlotte's daughter, also named Charlotte, became the second wife of Hiram P. Thorpe. One of the sons of Hiram P. and Charlotte Thorpe was the famed Indian athlete, Jim Thorpe.

Jim Thorpe, who was named Wa-tho-huck [*Bright Path*] by his mother, won both the pentathlon and decathlon during the 1912 Olympics, held in Sweden. Swedish King Gustav, when presenting Thorpe with his medals, proclaimed him the "greatest athlete in the World." In 2000, during a ceremony nearly a century later, Thorpe, who also played professional football and baseball, was named America's Greatest Athlete of the Twentieth Century.

Mas-saw, a notable Indiana American Indian, was Jim Thorpe's great-grandmother.

Memeskia

["Dragonfly," "The Lady," "La Demoiselle," "The Old Piankashaw King," "Old Briton (or Britain)"]

Piankashaw (Miami)
b. 1690? - 1700? – d. 1752

Illustration based on historic description and artist's conception.
No authentic image is known to exist.

"It is an ancient custom among us, when we speak of pleasant matters, first to present the calumets, we pray you have the goodness to listen to us. We come to reply to what you have said to us ... It is not with the tips of the lips that they speak to you, but from the bottom of the heart. You have bid us to reflect seriously on what you have said to us [about moving from this village]; we have done so ... and will continue to do so during the entire winter. We hope to have the pleasure of giving you a good word in the spring. If the hunting is abundant, we will repair our faults. We assure you, my father, we will listen no longer either to bad discourse or to evil rumors."

– Memeskia's reply to French military officer Celoron in the fall of 1749 at Pickawillany (Ohio), indicating his intention to continue trade with the British.

Memeskia was the most prominent civil chief of the *Peeyankisa*, or Piankashaw, one of six tribal divisions among the Miami nation, during the first half of the eighteenth century. He became a central figure in the struggle between England and France as the two European powers attempted to control the lucrative fur trade in the Indian Territory of the Old Northwest.

A French ally in his early years, Memeskia deserted the French and founded the first English trading post in what is now known as the Old Northwest in the days leading up to the French and Indian War [1754-1760].

No historical record is available regarding Memeskia's birth or his parentage, but based on Miami tradition, his mother was likely the sister of a chieftain. Memeskia is believed by historians to have been born in what is now northern Illinois, sometime before 1700. At some point, Memeskia became principal chief of the Piankashaw Miami. Known as La Demosielle [*Dragonfly*] by the French, he later was known by his British allies as "Old Briton" [also spelled Old Britain] and "The Old Piankashaw King."

During the early 1730s, Memeskia's village was located along the Illinois River, near modern-day Peoria [Illinois]. Like many tribes, including the neighboring *Kiwigapaw*, or Kickapoo [*Wanderer*], and

Muskuta, or Mascouten [*Little Prairie People*], the Piankashaw and the five other Miami-related tribes, including the Wea and Eel River Miami, were closely allied with the French.

In French the name La Demosielle also translates as "The Lady." This could, perhaps, refer to Memeskia's flamboyant, colorful wardrobe, his demeanor, or possibly the "heavy courtship" of his allegiance by both the French and British. Both European powers realized his considerable influence among other tribes living in the area, which would later be designated by the United States as Indian Territory under the Northwest Ordinance of 1787.

Despite British attempts to infiltrate the lucrative fur trade in Indian Territory, France continued to hold its trading monopoly among the Indians in the area. Sometime around 1696, the French established a trading post at the Miami village of *Cecaahkonki*, or *Kekionga,* [Blackberry Patch]. A few years later, between 1697 and 1715, a fort was established and garrisoned by some twenty soldiers. First called Fort St. Phillippe, and later called Fort des Miamis, it was located at the site of modern-day Fort Wayne, Indiana, and at the confluence of three strategic rivers. From this location, the fort, under the command of French officer Jean Baptiste Bissot, Suier du Vincennes, controlled the important fluvial trade traffic between French Canada and western Indian Territory.

Over time, the fur trade experienced a market glut. Simultaneously, as European demand for furs declined, France was experiencing financial problems stemming from the costs of ongoing hostilities with England, both in Europe and in North America. French goods gradually increased in price, while also declining in quality and availability. This decline allowed British traders to finally gain favor among the Indian nations of North America. Former French allies found British goods to be more plentiful, of better quality and at lower cost. British traders were warmly received among Indian tribes living the East, and these factors combined into a golden opportunity for the British to gain a foothold among the Indians living in the French-claimed valley of the *Oyo* [Ohio River].

Former Fort Miami commander Jean Baptiste Bissot was living among his longtime friends, the Miami, at the time of his death in 1719.[His son, Francois-Marie Bissot, Suier du Vincennes, who had served as a cadet under his father at the age of eighteen and was a commissioned French officer by the age of twenty-two.] He had spent most of his early life among the Miami. By 1730, the younger Suier du Vincennes had already held several commands, including the French trading center at Ouiatenon near modern-day Lafayette, Indiana. That year, he was directed by the French government to establish a new post on the lower *Waapaahsiiki Siipiiwi* [Wabash River]. This outpost was named Fort Vincennes for its founder and eventually became the first city in what is now Indiana. The location, some eighty miles north of the Ohio River, was considered a key to maintaining French trade dominance among the Indians of the region.

While the French-Canadian government in Quebec controlled Vincennes' earlier location at Ouiatenon, Fort Vincennes, located in what would become southern Indiana, was controlled through the French government centered in New Orleans. Many southern tribes, such as the Chickasaw and Choctaw, were allies of the British. It was hoped the French presence at Vincennes could keep British expansionism east of the Mississippi River and south of the Ohio River.

To that end, Vincennes urged the influential "Piankashaw King," Memeskia, to relocate his village on the Illinois River near present-day Peoria, Illinois, to be in closer proximity to with the newly established French trading center and fort. "La Demoiselle" agreed and established his new village along what is known today as the Embarras River, at its confluence with the Wabash, across the river from Vincennes, in what is now Illinois. The move backfired for the French.

While on a mission to New Orleans, Suier du Vincennes was attacked and captured by Choctaw warriors near present-day Memphis, Tennessee. He and his surviving party were later burned at the stake. After Vincennes' death, Memeskia left his village along the Embarras River and traveled northeast, into the area that would become northwest Ohio. There, he came in contact with a prominent chief of the Wyandot, known among the Europeans as Nicholas.

Nicholas' village was located along the southern shore of what is now called Lake Erie, at modern-day Sandusky, Ohio. Nicholas had allowed the British to build a fort at what is now Port Clinton, Ohio. At the time, he was urging the Indians of the Great Lakes to desert the

French and affiliate with the British. Nicholas introduced Memeskia to British goods, and the two chiefs created an alliance.

In 1747 Nicholas was able to convince Memeskia and his followers to relocate from the area near Vincennes and settle near Kekionga and the French-held Fort des Miamis. Nicholas also encouraged Memeskia to join in what ended as a failed *coup d'etat* against the French.

Memeskia, at Nicholas' urging and as part of an overall Indian uprising against the French, attacked Fort des Miamis. His warriors captured the fort, burned the buildings and stockade and took eight French prisoners. But when Nicholas' attempted coup failed, Memeskia released the prisoners unharmed. The following year, 1748, to avoid retaliation from the French and at the urging of the British, Memeskia moved southeast and settled along the Great Miami River its confluence with Loramie's Creek, near modern-day Piqua, Ohio. Over the next four years most Miami at Kekionga, the most populous of Miami villages, lost nearly all its population. Most Indians from the area followed Memeskia to his new village which he named Pickawillany.

Pickawillany's location allowed Memeskia's followers easier access to British goods, which were transported from Fort Pitt [now Pittsburg, Pennsylvania], down the Ohio River, then upstream on the Great Miami River, north to the new village which he named Pickawillany. As British goods arrived, Memeskia sent out messengers to western tribes, urging them to move to Pickawillany and share in the affluence.

One of those who responded was A-que-nack-que [*The Turtle*], war chief of the Atchatchakangouen Clan of the Miami. The Turtle, along with his wife and infant son, who would later become the noted Miami war chief, Meshekinnoquah, or Little Turtle, moved from their Eel River village in present-day Indiana in 1748 and joined Memeskia. The Turtle soon became Memeskia's second-in-command.

When the British invited Memeskia to attend trade treaty negotiations, the Old Piankashaw King sent The Turtle and two companions as his agents. Near what is now the city of Lancaster, Pennsylvania, the Miami and several other tribes pledged loyalty to the British "fathers." In turn the British vowed to increase access to trade goods and protect the Miami from French hostilities and invasion by warring Iroquois [*Real Adders*] raiders from the Northeast. [For his influence in convincing contemporary tribal chiefs to join in this agreement, Memeskia became known as "Old Briton." His new British allies showered him with gifts and adulation.]

British traders flocked to Pickawillany with a seemingly unending supply of less expensive, better quality knives, hatchets, firearms, powder and ball. As Pickawillany's population boomed to nearly two thousand, French officials feared that many years of influence among the Indians – and a major source of much-needed income from trade with the Indians of the Ohio and Wabash valleys – was nearing an end. Loss of Memeskia's influence among the tribes that controlled the main portages along the Wabash, Ohio, and Mississippi rivers also presented logistical and communication problems. A Miami alliance with the British could sever the main river routes and portages between the government in French Canada and the French port of New Orleans at the mouth of the Mississippi River in southern Louisiana Territory.

French officials hatched plans to bring La Demoiselle and his followers back into the fold. French "indignation" over La Demoiselle's defection prompted a dual mission to Pickawillany in 1749.

A contingent of some two hundred sixty five troops under the command of Suier Celoron de Blainville, historically known simply as Celoron, headed toward Pickawillany on a two-pronged mission. Celoron's highest priority was to convince Memeskia to return to Kekionga at the headwaters of the Maumee River, closer to French influence; and, secondly, along the way, he was to reinforce French claim to all lands in the Ohio River Valley.

In the fall, Celoron and his troops left Canada. He met with tribes in what is now eastern Ohio and western Pennsylvania; then he traveled down the Ohio to the Great Miami River, and finally upriver to Pickawillany. All along the way, he had buried lead tablets at the confluence of the Ohio and each of its tributaries. The embossed inscriptions on each tablet underlined France's ownership of all lands in the Mississippi watershed. However, Celoron had better success reclaiming the land for France than he had in reclaiming the Franco-Miami alliance with La Demoiselle.

Memeskia listened agreeably to Celoron's "kind words" and thanked him for his gifts, which the old chief considered scanty. Despite Celoron's cajoling, Memeskia made no firm commitment to leave his new, rapidly growing village. Also, Celoron and his small force found

Memeskia's Miami warriors armed with British muskets and possessing plenty of ball and powder. Not wanting to risk armed confrontation, the disappointed Celoron returned to Detroit after four days of failed negotiations.

Following Celoron's failure to convince Memeskia, even more British traders rapidly replaced the humiliated French. These traders made sure the Indians had ample supplies to prosper through a long winter. This generosity cemented British relationships with the Piankashaw leader. British soldiers, at the urging of The Turtle, also constructed a small stockade and surrounded it with several cabins, which doubled as homes and trading posts.

French-Canadian officials, their original offers thwarted, again tried to entice Memeskia back into their fold with more gifts, money and promises. When Old Briton refused their gifts and overtures a second time, French officials were convinced that only La Demoiselle's demise could quell British influence among the Indians.

French military forces attempted their first attack on Pickawillany in 1751. But upon arrival, the French found that Pickawillany was not only still heavily armed and manned, but also protected by British soldiers and fortifications. The French turned back, but were far from finished with Memeskia.

Canadian officials encouraged a French-Indian metis [mixed blood] named Charles Langlade to raise a military force and finish off La Demoiselle once and for all. Over the winter, Langlade assembled more than two hundred Ottawa and Chippewa warriors at Fort Michilimackinac, a French-controlled fort at present-day Mackinac, Michigan. The following spring [1752], as soon as weather permitted, Langlade's Indian-French force began the long march south to Pickawillany.

According to accounts, Memeskia had ample early warning of Langlade's advance, but evidently felt secure under the protection of his British allies and their stockade. He paid little heed to the warnings of Langlade's arrival. In fact, he even encouraged the majority of his warriors to leave Pickawillany for a spring hunt along the Ohio River. This decision left only a few warriors behind to protect the women and children who were engaged in tending the freshly planted fields of corn and squash – and proved to be Memeskia's undoing.

After his arrival at Pickawillany, Langlade most likely used deception to carry out his mission. Most accounts tell of his coming into Memeskia's fortified village with only a small force. He gained the chief's trust with flowery words and many presents. After putting Memeskia at ease, Langlade left. But the following morning, his full contingent of Indian warriors attacked suddenly with brutal force. At the time, no British military were present, and the village, protected only by a few warriors and traders, was easily overrun.

Caught off guard as they tended their crops, some of the women and children of Pickawillany were killed and many were captured, including Memeskia's wife and children. Meanwhile the aging chief, along with about twenty warriors and a handful of British traders, fled into the fort. Under siege and outnumbered ten-to-one, without food or water, Pickawillany's few defenders realized the inevitable.

The siege lasted just a few hours before Langlade proposed a peaceful solution. The French officer promised to spare women and children, the chief's family and all the stockade's defenders - if Memeskia surrendered peacefully. With several of his warriors already wounded, short on powder and ball, and with no provisions, Old Briton capitulated.

But once the defenders were outside the stockade, Langlade's Indians set upon the British traders immediately. One trader was killed outright, as were several of Memeskia's wounded warriors. All remaining traders, except for two who escaped, and the remainder of the warriors were taken captive, including Memeskia.

Langlade, despite his promises of quarter, ordered the old chief executed. Memeskia was tomahawked to death; Langlade cut out the chief's heart and ate it as his warriors looked on. The warriors then ritualistically dismembered Memeskia's body, dumped it into a large kettle, boiled and consumed it.

As the French had supposed, Memeskia's death broke Britain's brief dominance over Indian trade in the region. Attempts to revive Pickawillany failed. Within the next few years following Memeskia's death in 1752, the village was all but deserted. Pickawillany's former residents fled back to their original tribal homes in what have become the states of Indiana, Illinois, Michigan and Ohio. French influence was restored – but only for a short time.

In little more than a decade, by the end of the French and Indian War in 1763, France would permanently relinquish to the British all claims to lands northwest of the Ohio River. By the end of the American Revolution in 1784, the British would also relinquish the same area; three years later, it would become the Northwest Territory, established through the Northwest Ordinance of 1787.

Ironically, during America's Revolutionary War, Memeskia's son, also known as La Demoiselle, served as a scout and interpreter for American general George Rogers Clark during his successful expeditions against British forts in what is now Indiana and Illinois.

Today the historic village of Pickawillany, once home to Memeskia - the Old Piankashaw King, La Demoiselle, Old Britain – is currently undergoing reconstruction through the efforts of the Ohio Department of Natural Resources, Division of Historic Sites.

Menominee
[Me-nomie-na, Menomni, Menomnik;
"Wild Rice Eater;" also Alexis]

Potawatomi?
b. 1790? – d. 1841

Adapted from a pencil drawing by Daniel McDonald,
History of Marshall County, Page 102, dated 1837.

"The President does not know the truth. He, like me, has been imposed on. He does not know that you made my young chiefs drunk and got their consent and pretended to get mine. He does not know that I refused to sell my lands and still refuse. He would not by force drive me from my home, the graves of my tribe, and my children who have gone to the Great Spirit. My brother the President is just, but his young chiefs lied. I have not sold my lands. I will not sell them. I have not signed any treaty and will not sign any. I am not going to leave my lands. I do not want to hear anymore about it."
    – Chief Menominee, to Colonel Abel C. Pepper, interpreted by
    a man named Wise, August 6, 1838.

"Great Father – We undersigned Indian Chiefs of the Potowatomie tribe residing in the State of Indiana beg leave to state That by a [solemn] treaty in date 28 [October] 1832 a reserve of 22 sections of land was granted to us and our bands that by a letter of the Secretary of War [Lewis Cass] on date 26 [January] 1836 we were assured _that the land was our own that we should be no more disturbed by the general_[government] that we may stay on it as long as we Shall wish_ a copy of the treaty and a copy of the map of [survey] was given to us as evidences of our title that we have never sold consented to, or signed any treaty for [sale] of our reserve That inaswithstanding all this Gen. Tipton the Senator of Indiana has given a letter in date 25 March by which he Says that our reserve is sold and the treaty ratified and that the [white] people may go [and settle] upon it. We feel distressed Great Father [during] two years we have worked very hard on the said land and were resolved to have it divided amongst us and live as White people and now they take [it] from us against our will is this right? We respectfully ask you Great Father to let us know your mind about this as soon as possible and we shall be satisfied. Therefore, we have Signed Me-nomie-na X his mark; et. al.
    – Letter to President Andrew Jackson, dated April 6, 1837.

Menominee's [*Wild Rice Eater's*] early life, like so many other American Indians of the period, is filled with as many unknowns as his later life was filled with hardships. His place of birth is not known, nor is his tribal origin certain. He was most likely born around the year 1790, possibly in Wisconsin, since his personal name is also that of a tribe living there; and some of his descendents continue to reside in Wisconsin.

Menominee was considered a *Neshnabeck* or *Bode'wadmiyuk Pasigwin* [a Potawatomi chief], but Colonel Abel C. Pepper, the Indian Agent sent to round up Menominee and his band at their reservation at *Ni-jo-de sa-ga-ig-an-og* [Twin Lakes, Indiana] in 1838, noted in a letter that the chief "did not properly belong to the Potawatomis," although Pepper did not speculate on any other possible origins.

Some sources say Menominee converted to Christianity at an early age and became a minister of the Gospel among Potawatomi warriors during the War of 1812. He may have been known at first as simply "the Menominee," but was adopted into the Potawatomi, and later, through respect, received the title of chief.

Menominee become a notable part of Indiana Indian history when he and his band peacefully resisted forced emigration to the West during the period of Indian removal in the late 1830s.

By signing the 1832 Treaty of Tippecanoe near Rochester, Indiana, Menominee, along with three other Potawatomi chiefs, received a shared reservation of twenty-two sections [twenty-two square miles] southwest of the present-day city of Plymouth near two connected lakes, now known as Lawrence and Cook, in north central Indiana. But in 1836, Menominee and the three other chiefs, Mar-kah-tah-mo-wah, Pe-pe-no-wah and Wekgoma, the son of original treaty signer No-taw-kah, refused to sign a second Treaty of Tippecanoe, which required them to return possession of the land to the United States.

Three treaties were signed with the Potawatomi in 1836. The second treaty, one Menominee refused to sign, required the Potawatomi to cede their Indiana reserves to the government and move *wetth-bgeshmok* [west] within three years of its ratification by Congress. Memominee and his three Potawatomi allies maintained that they had made many improvements to the land during their four years of ownership, and all rights to the land should remain theirs.

A second treaty with the Potawatomi was signed later that same year. Menominee was not among "the Proper Chiefs of the Wabash Potawatomi" at the 1836 Yellow River treaty council, which authorized several land cessions, including his own reservation. However, his fellow chiefs No-taw-kah, Muck-kah-tah-mo-way [Black Wolf] and Pe-pin-oh-waw capitulated and signed the document. Menominee continued to maintain that he "… never sold our lands," adding that "… we have worked very hard upon the land."

Menominee had been greatly influenced by the teachings of the Catholic Church. In August 1834, he had received Catholic instruction and was baptized into the Church by Father Louis Deseille. In 1835, under the supervision of Father Deseille, Menominee had built a *nume'wgumuk* [church building] near his village, along the shores of Twin Lakes in what is now Marshall County.

Soon after the log chapel, which he called Chi-chi-pi Outi-pe, was built, Menominee felt the call of *Kshe'mnito* [The Great Spirit] to minister among his own people and neighboring tribes. The newly confirmed Catholic Potawatomi leader would become known as "The Potawatomi Preacher." However, Menominee had two wives who were sisters, a custom common among the Potawatomi. Menominee asked The Great Spirit for a vision as to which wife he should "put away." The sisters did not want to be separated, but in order for Menominee to be baptized into the Catholic Church, he evidently made a choice. Only one wife, Angelique Sagike, and a daughter, Mani, or Mary Ann, born 1835, are mentioned in historical accounts, although other historical accounts reveal the chief also had grown children at the time of his baptism.

Father Deseille, a Belgian missionary, gave Menominee his Christian name, Alexis, because of Father Deseille's association with South Bend, Indiana, land speculator Alexis Coquillard. From his Twin Lakes pulpit, Alexis Menominee's main message included abstinence from liquor and strict avoidance of Ten Commandment aberrations, such as theft, murder and bearing false witness. Menominee's non-violent Christian beliefs and teachings and, especially, his refusal to sign the 1836 Tippecanoe Treaty and abdicate his reservation, made him a local "Prophet" among the Potawatomi of the area. The result was that hundreds of Potawatomi relocated to his village.

Beginning with only four *wigwamuk* [houses], the village grew to more than one hundred residences within two years. Menominee's proselytes, made up mostly of scattered Potawatomi, arrived and settled in the belief that, by adopting Christian values and acculturating into the dominant Euro-American lifestyle, they would be allowed to remain in their homeland and live with Menominee on his fourteen thousand acre reservation. They were mistaken.

Although Menominee's band of Christian Potawatomi laid claim to the *sugmuk* [earth] in which their ancestors were buried, scores of American squatters were already lurking at the edges of the reservation. They clamored for more land and urged government intervention by the United States and the State of Indiana to open up for settlement the land on which Menominee and his people lived. Uneasiness between the two cultures soon grew into conflict and confrontation.

Since he had not signed the 1836 treaty along the Yellow River and was not among the signers of a treaty prepared in Washington, D.C., the following year, Indian Agent Pepper declared that Menominee was not a real leader among the Potawatomi. Working under the premise that some of Menominee's Potawatomi were preparing an armed defense of their treated reservation, Pepper contacted Governor David Wallace for permission to form a militia and remove Menominee and all Potawatomi living within a fifty mile radius of the reservation "by any means necessary."

When the deadline for Indian removal arrived in August of 1838, Abel acted on his premise of Menominee's leadership of an armed Indian resistance. Governor Wallace appointed Indiana State Senator— and general of the militia-- John Tipton to gather troops and head to the Twin Lakes reservation and escort, by force if necessary, Menominee and his band off the reservation and out of Indiana.

Tipton and his *shmakneshuk* [soldiers] arrived at Twin Lakes on August 30. Some eight hundred sixty Potawatomi, including their *okama* [leader], The Potawatomi Preacher, were rounded up and held in the church Menominee had built. Menominee's village and the fields of corn surrounding it were burned.

Menominee was taken into captivity. He was bound "like a dog" and, along with two other resistance chiefs, locked into a horse-drawn, wooden-wheeled, steel-barred cage. Resulting hardships from a long, forced march would become known in Indiana history as the infamous "Trail of Death."

On the journey of some six hundred sixty miles, through Indiana, Illinois, Missouri, and finally into Kansas, drought, disease, and death plagued the eight hundred fifty-nine Potawatomi captives. Some forty children, along with several elderly and some already ill adults, died along the way; but nearly one hundred escaped and returned to Indiana before the tribe reached Potawatomi Creek in eastern Kansas, November 4, 1838.

Menominee survived the Trail of Death, but after witnessing the forced removal of his people and the resulting deaths and privations along the journey, his heart was broken. At the age of fifty years, The Potawatomi Prophet died April 15, 1841, at St Mary's Mission, Sugar Creek, south of the modern-day town of Osawatomie in what would become Linn County, Kansas.

September 4, 1909, some seventy years after Menominee's band was forcibly evicted from the treated reservation he refused to relinquish to what he felt was unfair governmental demands, the State of Indiana dedicated a monument in his honor. Seventeen feet high, including its base, the granite statue is of an Indian in full regalia. The statue remains, located on South Peach Road, six and a half miles southwest of Plymouth, south of Twin Lakes.

Additionally, an Indiana Historical Bureau Marker, commemorating the Trail of Death, is located along Indiana State Road 17, near Menominee's former Twin Lakes reservation. Recently, the entire length of the Trail of Death has been signed with historical markers.

Me-no-quet

[Mo-no-quet, Manauquet, Man-o-quett, Menucquett,
Me-nuok-quet, Minoquet; *"Banked Cloud,"*
"Stormy Weather"]

Potawatomi
b. 1775? – d. 1836-1837?

Illustration adapted from an original portrait painting by James Otto Lewis,
watercolor, circa 1826-28.

"Here in his village, I first saw Monoquet. He was a thin, sparse
man, about 50 years of age, stood five-feet seven inches in his
moccasins. His forehead was high and rather square, his eyes
small and bright, his big nose was aquiline, his voice was tenor,
clear and sharp. He touched his forehead with the index finger
of his right hand and thus addressed me, 'Nin Monoquet,' then
brought the hand down with a clap on his right thigh and said,
'Cheep,' meaning chief."

*— Metcalf Beck, local historian, Leesburg, Indiana, during a
visit in the fall of 1835, published 1873.*

"He was a man of great leadership qualities and
remained faithful to resisting the white invasion. He
was defeated because of the size and strength of his foes.
It is difficult to see how he might have acted honorably
in any other manner. Placed in the frame of context
and frame of his time, he remains a heroic character."
— Waldo Adams, Kosciusko County Historian.

Me-no-quet [*Banked Cloud, or Stormy Weather*] was a *pasigwin*
[chief] of the upper Wabash River *dodem* [clan] of *Neshnabeck* or
Bode'Wadmiyuk [Potawatomi], according to some sources. However,
in some treaty notations, he is considered *a pasigqin of the St. Joseph
River dodem*. Local Indiana historians recall his fondness for brightly
colored, ruffled shirts, his frequent use of whiskey and some mysterious
tales surrounding his life and his death.

Me-no-quet was born sometime during the American Revolutionary
War. There is no record of his parentage or his actual birthplace, but the
otam [village] where he lived-- and died--was located at the headwaters
of *Ke-top-e-kon* [Buffalo Fish Stream, or the Tippecanoe River] in
northern Indiana. With an estimated population of between one
hundred to three hundred people, Me-no-quet's Potawatomi village is
thought to have been the largest in the area.

Me-no-quet's village site was a few miles south of Leesburg, Indiana,
in present-day Kosciusko County, Plains Township. Atop a northern
rise, it overlooked the river, just west of a well-traveled north-south path,
now designated as Indiana State Road 15. Most Indiana road maps of

today indicate a modern village named "Monoquet," which is at the original village site.

Leesburg store ledgers of the 1830s note that Me-no-quet preferred to wear brightly colored cloth shirts rather than deerskin, which was hot to wear in the summer and cold to wear in the winter. A storekeeper at the nearby village of Clunette, Joseph Smith, notes that Me-no-quet, while on his way to Fort Wayne to collect his clan's annuity, stopped by his store. He had just enough money in his possession to purchase an inexpensive black, broad brimmed hat. Smith writes that Me-no-quet's purchase visibly "raised his spirits."

Some local historians have written that Me-no-quet insisted he had never left the area of his village, but this claim seems doubtful.

Me-no-quet adamantly maintained that he had fought with The Shawnee Prophet and his followers against Indiana Territorial Governor and General William Henry Harrison and his American *shmakmeshuk* [soldiers] at the Battle of Tippecanoe in November of 1811, near modern-day Lafayette, Indiana. He most likely visited other tribal chiefs in the region of *Me-sheeh-weh-ou-deh-ik* [the Elkhart River] before being confined to his two thousand five hundred sixty acre Kosciusko County reservation, which the 1832 Treaty of Tippecanoe set aside for him.

Smith's account indicates that the chief traveled at least once to the Indian agency at Fort Wayne to receive a treaty-negotiated annuity payment. And, documentation also shows he was present at many treaty negotiations between the Potawatomi and the United States. His name, spelled in numerous ways, appears on several treaties.

As "Menauquet," the Potawatomi chief endorsed the Treaty of Mississinewa, signed near present-day Peru, Indiana, in 1826. In 1828 "Me-non-quet" marked the Treaty of Carey Mission, signed along the eastern shores of Lake Michigan, at St. Joseph's, Michigan. His mark is on the 1828 Treaty of Chicago, this time as "Man-o-quett."

Man-o-quett also was present a treaty council along the Tippecanoe, at "Camp Chippe-way-naung" in present-day Fulton County, Indiana, in 1832. Me-no-quet was "granted and guaranteed" four sections of land, "including his village," in October that year when he signed the first Treaty of Tippecanoe at Chippewanunk Creek, a tributary which flowed into the Tippecanoe, three miles north of the present-day city of Rochester.

According to the terms of that agreement, the United States government presented large grants of land to several Indian signers. The U.S. government also agreed to pay a total of more than five thousand dollars in horses and nearly ninety-five thousand dollars in merchandise as annuities. Terms also provided for construction of a sawmill, including payment of a salary for an operator for the mill.

In December of 1835, "Men-o-quet," and several other Potawatomi chiefs signed a second series of treaties along the Tippecanoe. This second set of treaties rescinded all Indian rights to lands received in the previous treaties of 1832. He may have returned to Chippe-way-naung again in 1835 for these negotiations. Although his signature does not appear on this second series of treaties, he is listed among the Potawatomi principal chiefs as "Mi-no-quet."

Signatures on this document indicated agreement by the Potawatomi to relinquish their claims to all lands in northern Indiana, including Me-no-quet's four sections, and move to reservations west of the Mississippi within two years of ratification by the United States Congress.

Congress' ratification of the 1835 treaty took place in the spring of 1836, meaning the Indians would be forced to vacate their lands by 1838; however, Me-no-quet would never leave his home for this journey to the *wetth-bge-shmok* [west]. He died while this treaty was in the process of ratification.

Me-no-quet's death occurred sometime during the spring of 1836. Local histories tell that a large supply of whiskey, a partial payment of his clan's annual annuity, had arrived in his village. A drunken frolic ensued and lasted for several days.

According to local historian Burnell, it appears that for some time Me-no-quet had been involved in an on-going quarrel with another Potawatomi chief named Wahbememe, [*White Pigeon*]. Wahbememe's village was located just south of today's Indiana-Michigan state line, near present-day Howe, Indiana, along the Pigeon River, several miles northeast of Me-no-quet's village.

Burnell records that a woman from Wahbememe's village was a visitor in Me-no-quet's village during the time that most residents, including Me-no-quet, were busy imbibing their partial annuity payment. Me-no-quet became attentive to the attractive young woman. Unfortunately for her, sometime during her visit, Me-no-quet died. Some members of Me-no-quet's tribe accused the young woman of having caused his demise by means of witchcraft - or possibly by poisoning him.

According to the accounts of journalist Metcalf Beck, a contemporary of Me-no-quet, the aging chief had been in failing health for some time. Beck speculates that Me-no-quet actually expired from chronic respiratory illness, most likely tuberculosis, which was noted at the time as "lung fever." Still, many of Me-noquet's followers held the young woman responsible for his death. She was taken into custody and held captive; but she escaped. She headed *wetth-kse-nyak* [north], back toward her home village, but never completed the journey.

Two of Me-no-quet's warriors followed her trail and found her hiding in some bushes near present-day Leesburg. They dragged her from the bushes, pulled her to the middle of the road and tomahawked her to death. Her body was left lying along the trail, but, later, fearing reprisal from the woman's relatives and Wahbememe's clan, Me-no-quet's followers returned and secretly buried her body. Shortly afterward, Me-no-quet's remains also were "buried" according to Potawatomi tradition.

According to James W. Armstrong in his *History of Leesburg and Plains Township*, Me-no-quet's body was taken to a tree about a half-mile south of the village, an area known today as "Monoquet Meadows." A blanket was ceremoniously placed across his shoulders, and he was left sitting upright, facing *wetth-gsha-tak* [south], against the tree. His horse and dog were killed and placed beside him along with the rest of his worldly goods. Me-no-quet's remains, his animals and his earthly belongings were encompassed in this traditional Indian burial site, surrounded by a fence of poles, constructed horizontally, four feet high.

Following Me-no-quet's death, his son, "Jim" Monoquet, was designated chief of the village. Despite the conditions of the 1836 Treaty at Tippecanoe, Me-no-quet's band remained in Kosciusko County for another ten years before being removed under the direction of Alexis Coquillard. Coquillard, an affluent South Bend land speculator, had received a governmental contract for removal of Me-no-quet's people from northern Indiana in the late 1840s. Jim Monoquet remained chief after the clan's removal to Kansas.

Me-no-quet's remains were retrieved later, and his bones buried, according to Potawatomi tradition. The location of his final resting place is not known.

Me-she-kin-no-quah

[Meshekinnaquah, Mih-sih-kin-aah-kwa, "Little Turtle"]

Miami – Mahican?
b. 1752 – d. 1812

Adapted from a portrait painting by Gilbert C. Stuart, dated 1797.

"General Wayne — I hope you will pay attention to what I now say to you. I wish to inform you that where your younger brothers, the Miamis, live, and also the Pottawatomis of St. Joseph's, together with the Wabash Indians, you have pointed out to us the boundary line between us and the United States; but now I take the liberty to inform you that that line cuts off from the Indians a large portion of country which has been enjoyed by my forefathers, time immemorial, without molestation or dispute. "The prints of my ancestors' houses are everywhere to be seen in this portion. I was a little astonished at hearing you and my brothers, who are now present, together heretofore at [the] Muskingum [River, Ohio], concerning this country. It is well known by all my brothers present, that my father kindled the first fire at Detroit; from thence he extended his lines to the headwaters of the Scioto; from thence to his mouth and from thence to Chicago, on Lake Michigan. At this place I first saw my elder brothers, the Shawnees. "I have now informed you of the boundaries for the Miami Nation, where the Great Spirit placed my forefather, a long time ago, and charged him not to sell or part with his lands, but preserve them for posterity. This charge has been handed down to me. I was much surprised to find that my other brothers differed so much from me on this subject, for their conduct would lead me to suppose that the Great Spirit and their forefathers had not given them the same charge that was given to me, but, on the contrary, had directed them to sell their lands to any white man who wore a hat, as soon as he should ask it of them. "Now elder brother, your younger brothers, the Miamis, have pointed out to you their country, and also to other brothers present. When I hear your remarks and proposals on this subject, I will be ready to give you an answer. I came with an expectation of hearing you say good things; but I have not yet heard what I expected."

– *Me-she-kin-no-quah, speaking at the Treaty of Greenville council, 1795.*

"... [S]ince they [the whites] first set foot in this country ... and they already cover it like swarms of flies and gnats ... while we, who have inhabited this country no one knows how long, are still as thin as deer ... it is no wonder the whites have driven us year after year from the borders of the seas to the banks of the Mississippi. They spread like oil upon a blanket; we dissolve like the snow before the vernal sun. If we do not change our course, it is impossible for the race of red men to subsist."
— *Me-she-kin-no-quah, speaking at Philadelphia, Pennsylvania, 1797.*

Me-she-kin-no-quah, or Little Turtle, sometimes translated as Great Turtle Mother, is among the most notable Indians of the Old Northwest. He became the central figure of Indian resistance to American expansionism during the late 1780s and first half of the 1790s. Through military successes and careful diplomacy, during a period of armed conflict between Indians and Americans that became known as the "Little Turtle War," he was able to establish and maintain a military alliance among most Algonquin-speaking tribes in the territory, which now includes the present-day states of Ohio, Michigan, Illinois and Indiana.

Me-she-kin-no-quah was born prior to a series of conflicts that erupted while European powers England and France struggled for possession of their American colonies and the control of the lucrative fur trade with Indians living in the area of the Great Lakes. Called the Seven Years War in Europe, in North America this conflict is known as the French and Indian War [1755-1763].

Me-she-kin-no-quah's birthplace was along the upper *Kineepikomeekwa Siipiiwi*, or Eel River, east of present-day Columbia City, Whitley County, Indiana. His Miami father, A-que-nack-que [*The Turtle*] was a noted Miami chief. Some sources indicate his mother may have been Mahican or Mohican, a tribe that originally lived in what is now the upper Hudson River Valley of present-day New York State. Eastern tribes were the first to be pushed from their homelands by European settlement. Many emigrated west, crossing the Allegheny Mountains, eventually settling in western Ohio and eastern Indiana.

However, twentieth century Miami elder, Kiilhsoohquah, [*Sun Woman*] said that her father, Mak-e-shen-e-quah [*Crescent Moon*], one of Me-she-kin-no-quah's sons, maintained that his grandmother, Little Turtle's mother, was full blood Miami.

More than a decade before the outbreak of the French and Indian War, when Me-she-kin-no-quah was an infant, his father allied himself with the powerful Piankashaw chief, Memeskia [*Dragonfly*]. Memeskia, known as the "Old Piankashaw King," was caught up in the economic and political struggle between France and England. In an effort to lure Memeskia away from the French, the British persuaded him to establish a village where he would be closer to British traders. Memeskia attracted many followers who moved to the area and, likewise, allied themselves with the British and their cheaper yet superior quality trade goods.

Me-she-kin-no-quah's family moved to Memeskia's village of Pickawillany [Ohio], where, acting as Memeskia's second-in-command and agent, A-que-nack-que, signed the Treaty of Lancaster [Pennsylvania]. This agreement between the British and the Indians simultaneously halted the aggression of the powerful Five Nations of the Iroquois Confederation against the tribes of the Old Northwest and afforded the residents of Pickawillany the military protection of the British. Many Miami joined Memeskia, but in 1752, the French attacked the British post at Pickawillany and assassinated the "Old Piankashaw King." After this event, A-que-nack-que returned with his family to the area near the main Miami village of *Cecaahkonki*, or Kekionga [*Blackberry Patch*], at modern-day Fort Wayne, Indiana.

Although A-que-nack-que was a chieftain, Miami ascendancy to positions of power was matrilineal. Me-she-kin-no-quah, who became the Miami's most powerful war chief of his time, earned and maintained his tribal position through merit. His genius was in his tactical military leadership, which was admired by his allies, feared by his enemies and respected by both. He was also a skillful diplomat.

Me-she-kin-no-quah grew up amid conflict. Just a toddler when the French attacked Pickawillany, he grew to adolescence during the French and Indian War. At the war's beginning, a majority of Miami sided at first with the French, who had a longer presence among them. The French were the traders in the area and had constructed Fort des Miamis near Kekionga sometime before 1720.

After the French surrendered Fort des Miamis to the British in 1760, the Miami changed allegiance. However, they soon became dissatisfied with their new British allies and joined the Ottawa chief Pontiac in his efforts to drive English influence from Indian country by seizing all the forts in the region and returning them to French control. In 1763, as part of Pontiac's Rebellion, the Miami captured the British-held fort at Kekionga, but the French never came to reclaim it. Without French support, Pontiac's Rebellion failed.

By the time Me-she-kin-no-quah was entering adulthood, the Miami had switched allegiance a second time. They joined the British in their fight against the American colonies during the Revolutionary War [1775-1783]. This change of allegiance was an effort to halt the increase of American settlements in traditional Miami hunting grounds south of *Oyo* [the Ohio River] in what would become the State of Kentucky.

Little Turtle cemented his reputation as a fearless warrior and artful leader during a Revolutionary War skirmish, November 5, 1780, along Aboite Creek, not far from his village. With little experience in warfare, the young Little Turtle, leading an outnumbered group of warriors, defeated a French-Creole cavalry detachment under the command of Colonel August de La Balme.

La Balme's French troops, allies of the fledgling United States, were en route through Indiana to the British-held fort at Detroit. Part of La Balme's mission was to "punish" all pro-British Indian tribes, including the Miami. La Balme forces raided the British warehouses at Kekionga and sought further booty from the Miami along the upper Eel River. West of Kekionga a few miles, Little Turtle, employing effective military tactics in his first command, was able to surprise, outmaneuver, trap and annihilate the superior mounted force while leading his warriors on foot.

After the French and Indian War, the British king had issued the Royal Proclamation of 1763. King George, in this largely symbolic proclamation, declared that resident Indians retained all rights to lands northwest of the Ohio River. However, after the Revolutionary War, the victorious Americans ignored the British-issued declaration. Throngs of American war veterans, taking advantage of land grants and cheap land prices offered by speculators, crossed the Ohio and flooded into the Indian-controlled frontier.

Although the new American government discouraged "squatters" from invading Indian land, debts from the recent war of liberation from Britain were crushing, and the new United States needed money. Congress' passage of the Northwest Ordinance of 1787 seemed to be a financial solution to abating its heavy debts. This ordinance provided much-needed funds through the division and sale of Indian land, which the new government considered the spoils of war. Additionally, it was thought that American settlement of the region would thwart English annexation of the region now called the Northwest Territory into Canada.

However, the Northwest Ordinance did not deter the British government, headquartered in nearby Canada, from maintaining a military and commercial presence in what the United States considered newly acquired territory. The British continued to occupy several forts, offer military assistance to, and trade guns and ammunition with the Indians.

From 1783 to 1790, Indian war parties--assisted by British arms and sometimes manpower--carried out a series of raids against the growing number of American frontiersmen and their settlements in Kentucky and southern Indiana. Settlement of these lands threatened Indian access to these traditional hunting grounds that were shared by several tribes. Over the next seven years Miami raiders and their allies, mostly Shawnee, were recorded as having killed as many as fifteen hundred to two thousand American settlers.

In response to these harassing raids, the United States planned retaliatory military action. A "scorched earth" policy was put into effect. Mounted American militia systematically destroyed entire Indian villages in Ohio and Indiana territories. Fall crops that would sustain the Indian in winter were burned and as many Indians as possible were killed or captured.

In what was hoped to be a "final solution" to the Indian problem in the Northwest Territory, President George Washington ordered that a standing army be assembled on the north bank of the Ohio River at Fort Washington, now Cincinnati, Ohio. Washington put Revolutionary War general Josiah Harmar in command. Assisted by Kentucky Militia colonel John Hardin, Harmar's ultimate goal was to move north and seize the main Miami village at Kekionga. Along the way, he would destroy as many Indian villages as possible. But Harmar's preparations for his citizen army were hastily and poorly conceived.

An American force of fourteen hundred fifty men, comprised mostly of militias from Pennsylvania, Virginia and Kentucky, marched north in late fall. Eager to reach Kekionga, Harmar hurried his troops, became isolated from his supply base and his under-fed militia became disorderly.

In what is known as the Battle of Kekionga, the Americans were twice ambushed and defeated, once at a crossing on the Eel River on October 18 and again on the *Taawaawa Siipiiwi* [Maumee River] near Kekionga, October 22, 1790. The Battle of Kekionga was America's first military campaign since the American Revolution--and its first defeat.

During this battle, Little Turtle led a coalition of Indian forces, sometimes known as the Miami Alliance or the Wabash Confederacy. However, Little Turtle and his Miami warriors were not alone. Combined Indian forces included warriors under the command of Shawnee war chiefs Weyapiersenwah [*Blue Jacket*] and Catahecassa [*Black Hoof*], Delaware war chief Buckhongahelas [*Breaker to Pieces*], Wyandotte war chiefs Tarhe [*Crane*] and Half King. The combined Indian forces routed the American army and inflicted losses of more than two hundred militia. The surviving American troops marched hastily south to regroup at Fort Washington.

The following year a second American expedition against the Indian villages in western Ohio and eastern Indiana was organized at Fort Hamilton [present-day Hamilton, Ohio], just north of Fort Washington. To lead this expedition, President Washington chose another Revolutionary War veteran, General Arthur St. Clair, who was also governor of the newly formed Northwest Territory. Once again, the Miami and their allies under Little Turtle's overall leadership surprised the Americans.

St. Clair and his two thousand troops were attacked eleven miles from what is now Portland, Indiana, just east of what would become the Ohio State Line. In the resulting battle, facing twelve hundred Indian warriors, St. Clair lost more than one-third of his force. Six hundred men were killed and, counting some four hundred wounded, casualties amounted to nearly half of St. Clair's army. The defeat remains the worst in the history of all the wars fought by the United States against the

American Indian. St. Clair and the survivors fled the field in disarray, leaving their artillery, many of their wounded and most of their dead.

Despite two over devastating defeats and increasing national opposition to this campaign of annihilation, subduing the Indians of the Northwest Territory and seizing control of Indian lands became a top priority to President Washington. Washington ordered a third American army be assembled and trained; this time he placed celebrated Revolutionary War hero General "Mad" Anthony Wayne in command. Wayne was resolved not to fail. His success lay in his preparation of his troops, based on knowledge of the determined enemy.

Wayne took two years to raise his legion and drill them to become Indian fighters. Wayne was aided in part by Little Turtle's own son-in-law, Apekonit [*Carrot*], the Miami-adopted American captive William Wells. Wells, who had fought with the Miami during the first two American defeats, had left the Miami to join Wayne's army.

Early in 1794, Wayne and his professionally trained army of some three thousand men started their venture north from Fort Washington. Along the way, in order to protect his supply lines and guard the rear of his columns, Wayne built a series of forts and manned each with a small garrison. One of those forts was erected near the site of St. Clair's defeat in western Ohio, at the headwater of the Wabash. He called the log stockade Fort Recovery and armed it with a few of the cannon that St. Clair had left behind during his hasty retreat.

Me-she-kin-no-quah called Wayne "the general that never sleeps with both eyes closed." The Indians had lost their element of surprise, perhaps the greatest factor in their first two victories. In an effort to protect his people from what he supposed would be military defeat and possible annihilation, Me-she-kin-no-quah counseled negotiations with the Americans and a peaceful settlement. Reluctantly but realistically, the Miami war chief predicted the unlikelihood of a third Indian victory in the face of a technologically superior military force.

Little Turtle was mocked by several followers and even accused of cowardice for his dire predictions. He gave up overall command of the Indian alliance, passing that role on to Shawnee leader Blue Jacket. Often indicated as having been its main war chief, Little Turtle's role in the confederacy, while significant, may have been exaggerated by the historians of the time through the influence of his son-in-law,

Apekonit or William Wells, who went on to become Indian Agent at Fort Wayne.

Blue Jacket, who, according to some historians, may have had the most significant overall leadership role all along, took over as central commander. Me-she-kin-no-quah agreed to continue with the alliance and fight as a coalition warrior under Blue Jacket, despite his premonitions of defeat.

Leading a small command of Miami warriors, Little Turtle led an attack on Fort Recovery, but Wayne's garrison was able to repulse the attack from behind the walls of the stockade, using St. Clair's recovered cannon.

Finally, on August 20, 1794, General Wayne's army engaged the combined Indian forces under Blue Jacket at the Battle of Fallen Timbers, a location where a tornado had leveled a forest grove along the Maumee River, near present-day Toledo, Ohio. As Little Turtle had predicted, Wayne's tactics succeeded.

Fasting before battle was an Indian tradition. Instead of heading directly into battle, Wayne, on the advice of Wells, waited three days before attacking the now-famished warriors. During the pitched battle, Wayne's troops were able to flank the Indians, who were aided by a few British regulars. A frontal bayonet charge finally routed the Indians. The resulting victory ended four years of hostilities, 1790 through 1794, the period sometimes designated by the Americans as "Little Turtle's War."

Little Turtle pledged lasting peace with the Americans by signing the Treaty of Greenville [Ohio] 1795. He passed the remainder of his sixty-year life working for Indian causes, from introducing smallpox vaccine, to promoting agricultural pursuits and abstinence from alcohol among his people.

Little Turtle sired four children by his first wife, and by his second wife, he had a daughter named Manwangopath, also Wah-man-go-path, or "Sweet Breeze." It was Sweet Breeze who married William Wells, a white captive raised Miami.

Me-she-kin-no-quah's post-war political stance made him many enemies among the followers of Shawnee chief Tecumseh [*Panther Passing Across*] and his brother Tenskwatawa [*The Open Door*], The Shawnee Prophet.

During his remaining years, the United States government frequently recognized Me-she-kin-no-quah for his peacetime role among his people. He visited Washington, D.C., on several occasions, meeting with three presidents: George Washington, John Adams and Thomas Jefferson. The United States government built a spacious home for him at the Eel River Trading Post. From this base, he visited Fort Wayne often.

Me-she-kin-no-quah died July 14, 1812, of complications resulting from gout and Bright's disease, at his son-in-law's Fort Wayne home. He was buried in Fort Wayne.

In 1912, almost one hundred years to the day from the date of Me-she-kin-no-quah's death, workmen digging a cellar for a new house along the Maumee River accidentally discovered his grave. Among the many artifacts found buried with the famous war chief was the ceremonial sword presented to him by President George Washington. His remains were reburied on that same site and the house built at a different location.

Me-she-kin-no-quah's gravesite, along with a memorial, is located at 634 Lawton Place, Fort Wayne, Indiana.

Meshingomesia
["Large Leaf Burr Oak"]

Miami
b. 1782? – d. 1879

Illustration adapted from a photograph by L.F. Craven, dated circa 1870.

"Some of my band have been attending the schools of the whites and are disposed to engage in agricultural pursuits. They desire to make permanent improvements upon the land for themselves and their children to enjoy, as do the more successful white neighbors. But they are reluctant to build houses and barns and make other permanent improvements unless they have the title to the land upon which they make such improvements and are guaranteed that they can hold and enjoy the same."

— Meshingomesia, from a letter to the Commissioner of Indian Affairs, dated November 21, 1867.

Meshingomesia [*Large Leaf Burr Oak*] is believed to have participated in the last armed confrontation between the Miami and American forces at the Battle of the Mississinewa, fought December 18, 1812. He presided over the last Miami tribal reservation in Indiana, oversaw its fragmentation and witnessed confirmation of United States citizenship bestowed upon his Miami band.

Meshingomesia's mother was Chakapeah; his father, Metocinyah, was an influential chief. Several years prior to Meshingomesia's birth, Metocinyah had led his band westward from the Great Miami River in southwest Ohio to settle on the banks of the *Nimacihsinwi Siipiiwi* [Mississinewa River] in north central Indiana.

Metocinyah's new village was located at the confluence of Metocinyah Creek, also called Jocinah Creek, and the Mississinewa in present-day Liberty Township, southeastern Wabash County, Indiana, hear the Grant County line.

Several sources indicate that Meshingomesia was born in this village near the end of the American Revolutionary War [1776-1784], possibly around 1782.

About 1815, Meshingomesia married a Miami woman named Tak-e-no-quah, daughter of So-a-nah-ke-kah. Together they raised two sons, Po-con-ge-ah, also spelled Pecongah, and Aw-taw-waw-tah, or Au-taw-wah-tah.

Prior to Metocinyah's death, the Forks of the Wabash Treaty with the United States government was signed in 1838 and reaffirmed in 1840. That treaty created the last Miami Indian reservation in

Indiana; a reserve of some six-thousand four hundred acres set aside for Meshingomesia and his two brothers, Dixon and Flour. Provisions state that the Mississinewa band was to share the reserve "forever." After his father's death, Meshingomesia assumed the position of village chief and, as chief, made many trips to Washington, D.C., on behalf of his tribe.

The Meshingomesia band of Miami remained a cohesive tribal unit on the ten-square mile reserve located along the Mississinewa River for forty years. Known as the Mississinewa Reserve, it was located in present-day southeast Wabash County and northwest Grant County.

In 1852, Chief Meshingomesia paid sixty-five hundred dollars in gold for a six hundred forty acre section on Treaty Creek outside the reserve for the purpose of creating a Quaker boarding school for Indian boys. The school, named White's Institute, still exists.

New property laws were enacted by the State of Indiana in 1861. The conveyance law, as it was titled, granted the right of purchase and sale of property to alien residents, African-Americans, and those of mixed blood. Determined to be among these racial categories, Indians, original owners of the land and the land's residents of longest tenure, were finally allowed to apply for American citizenship.

By 1870, one thousand acres of the reserve had been cleared for agricultural purposes. By this time, Meshingomesia had become a Baptist convert and commissioned a Baptist church to be built on the reserve. A strong believer in educating the youth of the tribe, Meshingomesia encouraged the State of Indiana to build a school, which it did, locating it near his home.

As tribal chief, Meshingomesia was under pressure from a number of the members to divide the large reserve of more than six thousand acres into smaller tracts. He eventually yielded in 1872, when the government interceded. The next year, in 1873, the last Miami reserve in Indiana was surveyed and subdivided into private farms, ranging from seventy-five and one-hundred ten acres. These private farms were distributed among the rapidly acculturating sixty-three inhabitants who remained. Meshingomesia personally received two farms, totaling one hundred sixty acres.

Meshingomesia lived to the age of ninety-five on his one-hundred sixty acre portion of the reserve. He died, December 16, 1879, three months after his wife, Tak-e-no-quah, who preceded him in death on

September 15. They are buried together in Meshingomesia Cemetery, also known as Indian Village Cemetery. This is the largest Indian cemetery in Indiana and is located near the site of the 1812 Battle of the Mississinewa. An Indiana Historical Bureau marker identifies the site.

All remaining Miami residents of Meshingomesia's former reserve received federal and state citizenship in 1881.

Metea

[Meteya, Metba, Metawa; "The Sulker," "One Who Sulks," "He Sulks," "Kiss Me," "Prophet"]

Potawatomi – French?
b. 1760-1775? – d. 1827

Illustration adapted from a portrait painting by Samuel Seymour, dated 1823.

"I would rather have lost my life. Had I returned from battle without my gun, I should have been disgraced; but had I died with my face toward my enemy, my young men would have said that Metea died like a brave."

— Metea, his response to a question to a friend of Colonel McKenney, regarding his returning to retrieve his rifle after having been wounded by American soldiers, September 11, 1812.

"My Father: a long time has passed since first we came upon our lands; and our people have all sank into their graves. They had sense. We are all young and foolish, and we do not wish to do anything that they would not approve, were they living. We are fearful we shall offend their spirits if we sell our lands; and we are fearful we shall offend you if we do not sell them. This has caused us great perplexity of thought, because we have counseled among ourselves, and do not know how we can part with the land. My Father: Our country was given us by the Great Spirit, who gave it to us to hung upon, to make our cornfields upon, to live upon, and to make our beds upon when we die. And he would never forgive us should we bargain it away. When you first spoke to us for lands at St. Mary's, we said we had a little, and agreed to sell you a piece of it; but we told you we could part with no more. Now you ask us again. You are never satisfied. We have sold you a great tract of land already; but it is not enough! We sold it to you for the benefit of your children, to farm and to live upon. We now have but little left; and we shall want it for ourselves. We know not how long we shall live, and we wish to leave some lands for our children to hunt upon. You are gradually taking away our hunting grounds. Your children are driving us before them. We are growing uneasy. What lands you have you may retain forever; but we shall sell no more. My Father: You think I speak in anger; but my heart is good toward you. I speak like one of your children. I am an Indian – a redskin, and live by hunting and fishing. My country is already too small and I do not know how to bring up my children if I give it all away."

*— Metea, at the 1821 Treaty of Chicago signing near Lake
Michigan, after the Potawatomi ceded five million acres on
the east [Michigan] side of the lake.*

**"We behold in him [Metea] all the characteristics of the
Indian warrior to perfection."**
*— From the writings of Stephen H. Long, his observations
during a conference at Fort Wayne, 1827.*

Metea [*The Sulker*], a *pasigwin* [chief] and a member of the large
o'dodam dodem [Eagle Clan], was considered one of the finest orators
among the *Neshnabe*, or *Bode'wadmiyuk* [True People, or Potawatomi]
in the years of treaty negotiations following the War of 1812. Although
biographer Andrew Hartsock writes that Metea "was not an especially
powerful clan elder," he rose to prominence as a warrior and later as the
main advocate of Potawatomi interests.

Metea's father was Wapakitch, [*White Tailed Eagle*]; his mother was
a French woman named Jeanette de la Hourrau. Several writers claim
Metea was full-blood Potawatomi, but this seems doubtful.

Metea had four wives and many children. Several of his children
perished from starvation and disease, but at least one son survived.
Named Wapakitch after Metea's father, this son, also known as
Alexander, was born in 1826, a year before Metea's death.

Metea likely was a member of the Wabash Confederacy or Miami
Alliance, a military coalition of Algonquin-speaking tribes, formed
during the late 1780s to offer armed resistance against American
encroachment into Indian Territory. American historians have given
many titles to this period between 1790 and 1794, including the War
of the Wabash Confederacy. The Treaty at Greenville [Ohio] was signed
in 1795, but Metea, like his anti-American ally, the Shawnee leader
Tecumseh [*Panther Passing Across*] was not among the signatories.

After the treaty was finalized, Metea moved from his location on the
Sohq-who-si-be [the St. Joseph River of Lake Michigan], near present-
day South Bend, Indiana, to a site at the confluence of *Muskwawasibe*,
or Cedar Creek, and *Kochisohsibe*, or the St. Joseph River of the Maumee
[*Miowmik*, or Miami]. His new village of *Muskwawsepeoton*, or Red
Cedar Town, was located some ten to twelve miles upstream, north of
the location of the newly erected Fort Wayne.

There is no evidence that Metea played a major role in the pan-Indian tribal movement of the early 1800s headed by Tecumseh and his brother, Tenskwatawa [*The Open Door*]. But, during the War of 1812, many Potawatomi, including Metea, allied themselves with Tecumseh and the British in their fight against the Americans.

Metea served as a war chief and has been documented as one of Tecumseh's closest aides. Metea may have been one of the leaders of the attack on American troops and evacuees during the Fort Dearborn Massacre at *She-gog-ong* [present day Chicago, Illinois], which occurred along the south shores of *Mischigonong* [Great Lake, or Lake Michigan], August 15, 1812.

A few weeks after the Fort Dearborn Massacre, Metea, while spying for British forces, encountered General William Henry Harrison's large army in western Ohio. During a skirmish in a large boggy area known as Five Mile Swamp, south of besieged Fort Wayne, September 11, 1812, Metea was struck in the elbow by an American musket ball. Although his elbow was shattered, he escaped, but only after returning to retrieve his rifle. He carried the effects of this bullet wound the rest of his life and usually wore a blanket draped over his nearly useless right arm to disguise his disability.

However, his shattered elbow was just one of some seventeen wounds Metea received during the War of 1812, including one which left him with a noticeable and documented facial scar. As the result of these wounds, Metea received a yearly pension from the British for the remainder of his life.

Despite his British loyalties, Metea warned *Wamtagozhi* [French] trader Joseph Bondie, about an impending attack on Fort Wayne. Metea trusted Bondie an adopted Potawatomi, and didn't want him to be injured during the siege. However, Bondie betrayed Metea's trust and warned the garrison. Forewarned, the Americans at Fort Wayne were able to prepare for the siege and repel the allied tribal forces led by Potawatomi chief Winamac [*Catfish*].

Metea served with Tecumseh's forces during the Battle of the Thames along the Thames River, Ontario, Canada, in October of 1813. Tecumseh was killed during the battle, also known as the Battle of Moraviantown, and the *Sagnash* [British] surrendered. After the American victory in the War of 1812, peace was negotiated with the

Potawatomi. During these negotiations, Metea became known as the most eloquent orator and skillful diplomat among the Potawatomi delegations.

Metea became the main voice of Indian resistance to land cessions. He allied himself with defiant Potawatomi chieftains and British sympathizers Patasha [*Stutterer*, or Pierre Moran] and Winibiset [*The Crafty One*, or Main Poc]. These three Potawatomi attempted to rally remaining tribal members to resist Indian land cessions to the Americans. A trusted British ally for many years, Metea seemingly became resigned to American dominance and seemed to change his political stance after the death of Winibiset and in light of Patasha's numerous treaty cessions.

Metea signed a land cession treaty known as the Rapids of the Miami Treaty in 1817 and the St. Mary's Treaty of 1818, which ended all Potawatomi-American hostilities. He also signed land cession treaties during councils held at Washington, D.C., and at Chicago, Illinois, in 1821. However, angry about having to travel to Detroit [Michigan] to receive his annual American treaty annuities, Metea traveled to Ontario, Canada, where he also received gifts from the British.

By signing the 1826 Treaty of the Wabash [River] at Paradise Springs, near current-day Wabash, Indiana, Metea and other leaders ceded all Potawatomi rights to their Indiana lands to the United States. An Indiana Historical Bureau marker near the river at the park site of Paradise Springs commemorates this event.

In later years, Metea became a strong advocate of Indian education and assimilation into American culture. He sent several youth from his tribe to be educated at the Choctaw Academy in Kentucky.

However, following the Treaty of the Wabash at Paradise Springs, Metea returned to his anti-land cession sentiments. He informed American governmental officials that he would not sign any further treaties nor barter away any more Indian land. Not long after stating his resistance to further land cessions, he died.

Circumstances surrounding Metea's death remain mysterious. At least three separate documented versions contain one constant thread - Metea died from ingesting some type of poison.

One account says that, during an Indian council held at St. Joseph, Michigan, in the fall of 1827, Metea was intentionally poisoned by drinking a concoction of mayapple or mandrake root [*Podophyllum peltatum*]; administered by person or persons unknown. Some American writers adhere to this account and portray the perpetrators as resentful Indians, who blamed Metea for signing away Potawatomi lands. This story must be dismissed, however, because all records confirm that Metea died in Fort Wayne.

Some writers claim that the Indian agent at Fort Wayne, Benjamin Stickney, was Metea's killer. These accounts hold that Stickney was either a willing tool for Indians angry about Metea's role in treaty land cessions, or that perhaps Stickney was acting on behalf of an American government unhappy that Metea had refused to sell any more Indian lands without complete agreement of all Potawatomi. Regardless, either version points the finger at Stickney as having served Metea a poisonous, fatal drink while he was on a peace mission at Fort Wayne.

A third account claims that Metea's death was accidental, that he mistakenly drank a bottle of poison, possibly nitric acid, which he mistook for liquor, while visiting Stickney at Fort Wayne.

Metea's warriors buried his body near the present-day section of Rockhill at the west end of the City of Fort Wayne, along the St. Mary's River. His body was later exhumed by a Fort Wayne surgeon and examined to determine the cause of death, then reburied. No documented conclusions regarding his death were reached.

Despite his vocal resistance to any further sales of Indian land, the Potawatomi leaders sold Metea's village site in 1828, the year following his death.

Pacanne
[*Pacan, Pecanne, Paccan, Pucan, Pecon, Pikawn, Pecahn; "Nut"*]

Miami-French
b. 1745? – d. 1814-1816?

Adaptation of a line drawing sketch by Henry Hamilton, dated 1778; also based on an etching by Elizabeth Simcoe, dated circa 1790's.

"I give that man his life. If you want to go to Detroit, or upon the lake, … you'll find enough [British soldiers]; what business have you with this man who is come to speak to us?"
– Journal notation by British Captain Thomas Morris of Pacanne's speech to Morris' Ottawa captors at Kekionga, 1765.

"Father – Here are your own words, in this paper you promised that you would consider the Miamies as owners of the land on the Wabash, why then are you about to purchase it from others [the Potawatomi and Delaware]?"
– Pacanne, quote from "Journal of the Proceedings," of the treaty council at Grouseland (Vincennes, Indiana), September 27, 1805.

Pacanne [*Nut*] was a principal civil chief among the Miami for some fifty years until his death around 1815. He was a contemporary of Waspikingua [*Young Dappled Fawn*], or Le Petit Gris, another prominent civil chief. As civil chiefs, Pacanne's and Le Petit Gris' had considerable influence on Miami history in Indian Territory. However, because of their less militant roles both men have been overshadowed historically by their more documented associate, the celebrated Miami warrior and statesman, Meshekinnoquah [*Little Turtle*] – possibly Pacanne's brother or brother-in-law.

Considered principal war chief of the Miami nation, Little Turtle rose to prominence during the American Revolution. He was the most documented figure in the formation the confederacy of Algonquin-speaking tribes of the Great Lakes – sometimes known as the Miami Alliance or Miami Confederacy. This coalition offered armed resistance during the late 1780s and early 1790s against the attempts of a fledgling United States to annex all Indian lands northwest of the Ohio River to the Great Lakes. These years of armed conflict came to be known by American historians as the Little Turtle Wars [1790-1794].

As a result of his prominence among the several tribes forming this coalition of tribes, Little Turtle was documented as a major influence in treaty councils, although civil chiefs, such as Pacanne and Le Petit Gris, traditionally handled such negotiations.

Several historians consider Le Petit Gris to be principal civil chief of the Miami, but that opinion mostly likely stems from Pacanne's absence from the main Miami village of *Cecaahkonki* [Blackberry Patch], or Kekionga [Fort Wayne, Indiana] during much of the armed conflict between the Alliance and the United States. Still, Pacanne was considered by the American government as a key figure during and following the formation of the Territory of the United States Northwest of the Ohio River, as the United States officially designated the region in 1787.

During this time, Pacanne was considered by the government in Washington, D.C., as one of the most influential Indians in the entire territory, which included the modern-day states of Indiana and Ohio, Michigan, Illinois, and Wisconsin along with eastern Minnesota.

Pacanne, for the most part, advocated peaceful solutions to conflicts, dating from the time of Pontiac's Rebellion [1763-1766] until the conclusion of the Little Turtle Wars [1790-1794]. For a brief time, following a personal tragedy, Pacanne supported the Miami Alliance in its battle against American intrusion into Indian Territory. But in 1794, following the Indian defeat at the Battle of Fallen Timbers, near present-day Toledo, Ohio, Pacanne returned to his earlier philosophy of Indian neutrality and pressed for diplomatic solutions to the ongoing struggle between two conflicting cultures.

Considered Miami, Pacanne's bloodline had ties to French royalty. His grandfather was the French trader Pierre Roy, who had married a Miami woman, [Margaret] Ouabankikoue, at Detroit, around 1702. Pacanne's father was also named Pacanne, sometimes spelled Pecan or Pacan. He was commonly called Pacanne Andre. However, the younger Pacanne most likely became a principal civil chief because of the influence of his great uncle, his grandmother's brother, Wisekaukautshe, or Le Froid Poid, [*Cold Foot*].

Cold Foot was a civil chief of the most prominent of six Miami clans, the Atchatchakangouen. He had remained loyal to the French and was one of the few chiefs who not did leave the Miami's most populous village of *Cecaahkonki*, or Kekionga for the British-established trading center at the village of Pickawillany [Ohio] in 1749.

After Pickawillany's founder, the powerful *Peeyankisia*, or Piankashaw chief Memeskia [*Dragonfly*] was killed by French forces in 1752, most Miami returned to Kekionga and renewed their allegiance with France. However, realizing the importance of Kekionga's location and the political and financial power of Pacanne's family, the British were determined to keep the Miami in their fold.

Pacanne receives his earliest historical mention stemming from an incident that occurred in 1764 at Kekionga, sometimes documented as "Pacanne's Village."

Pacanne's Village was located near the confluence of the *Mahmaiwahsiipiiwi* and *Kociihsaiipi* [the St. Mary's and St. Joseph's rivers] that forms the *Taawaawa Siipiiwi* [the Maumee River]. A portage from Kekionga took travelers southwest through the "Golden Gate" to the *Pawwekomsepe* [Standing Still River] that connected to the *Waapaahsiki Siipiiwi*, or the Wabash River.

This trade and communication route not only linked Canada with important French trading centers at Fort des Miamis [Kekionga], Fort Ouiatenon, near modern-day Lafayette and Fort Vincennes, Indiana on the lower Wabash River. The route ultimately, by way of the Ohio and Mississippi rivers, flowed to the port of New Orleans on the Gulf of Mexico.

The recent war between France and Britain, known in North America as the French and Indian War [1775-1763], had ended in defeat for the French. The British victory interrupted the important trade route through Kekionga, the most important key to the control of Indian Territory. The British wanted to gain and maintain influence in the area and keep friendly relations with the Indians living along this fluvial route. A major stumbling block for the British was the influential Ottawa leader, Pontiac.

Pontiac had been allied with the French before and during the recent war. Almost immediately after the French defeat, he planned an uprising against the British. Pontiac had formed a coalition of Great Lakes tribes; his plan was to seize all British-held forts and return them to the French. The British certainly did not want the powerful and numerous Miami to join Pontiac's coalition.

At the height of Pontiac's Rebellion against British forts in the region, the British government in Canada sent Captain Thomas Morris to Kekionga. Morris' mission was to dissuade the Miami from joining forces with Pontiac. By the time Morris arrived, Pontiac and a group of followers were already at Pacanne's Village attempting to gain the Miami's support.

Morris, with an interpreter and several Indian guides traveled via canoe across Lake Erie; then they followed the Maumee River upstream to Pacanne's. Upon arrival, Morris immediately was taken into custody by Pontiac's followers, despite the protests of his Indian guides and interpreter.

Morris' Indian captors threatened him with torture and death, but he was rescued and hidden by several friendly Miami. After a search of the village, Pontiac's warriors discovered where the British officer had been hidden. They dragged Morris from his hiding place, tied a rope around his neck and secured him, by his neck, to a post in the middle of the village. Helpless in this position, Morris could do nothing but listen as two rival Indian factions, Pontiac's pro-French followers and the Miami British faithful, argued over his fate.

Morris notes in his diary that he was finally released when a young chief rode into the village on a white horse, untied him and spoke on his behalf. Morris' narration reveals this young chief – Pacanne - was "king of his village, though still a minor."

With customary Miami maturity arriving at the age of twenty-three or twenty-four, Pacanne was obviously younger than twenty-three at the time, and perhaps, according to some accounts, possibly as young as seventeen years old. Being a village chief at such a young age was a rarity among the Miami and also speaks to young Pacanne's evident charisma and talent for leadership. These two factors would help keep him in power for nearly fifty years.

Although Pacanne's primary village was Kekionga, he also lived in other locations. A British sympathizer during the American Revolution, he and Le Petit Gris guided General Henry Hamilton's troops down the Wabash River, to reclaim Fort Gage near Vincennes, a British fort that had been conquered by American forces commanded by Colonel George Rogers Clark in 1779.

By the end of the American Revolution, Pacanne switched allegiance, serving as a scout and interpreter for the American army. Pacanne and a few followers established a village along the western banks of the Wabash. He resided there among the *Peeyankisia* or Piankashaw, another of the six Miami divisions. His military position and this location gave him opportunities to keep an eye on both the Americans and some of the more hostile western tribes, such as the *Kiwigapaw* [Wanderer], or Kickapoo and *Muskuta* [Little Prairie People], or Mascouten.

During the time of the Little Turtle Wars, Pacanne regularly returned to Kekionga with military intelligence for Little Turtle and the Confederacy. His constant council at this time was to maintain peaceful relations between his people and the Americans. But in 1787, while serving as a scout and hunter for American Major Josiah Harmar on his expedition against the Kickapoo villages along the *Osanamon* [Vermillion River], a tragic event changed his mind about his relationship with the Americans.

While Pacanne was away from his village along the Embarrass River in August of 1788, an unauthorized force of some sixty Kentucky militiamen, under the command of Major Patrick Brown, raided two "friendly" Indian villages. One of these two settlements belonged to the son of Memeskia, a Piankashaw chief, who was, like his father, known to the French as La Demoiselle [*Dragonfly*, or *The Lady*]. He, like Pacanne, was working for the Americans. Pacanne's village was the other one destroyed.

During the raid, some of Pacanne's relatives were killed and several horses stolen. The regular American army stationed at Fort Knox near Vincennes claimed to be totally unaware of this unauthorized attack. Upon learning of the attack, Major John Francis Hamtramck, the American commander at Vincennes, openly condemned the acts of the militia, but neither he, nor Harmar, were able to make amends to Pacanne.

Returning from his scouting duties with Harmar, Pacanne found the survivors of his village camped north of Vincennes, along the eastern banks of the Wabash, near *Kaawinsaahkionki*, the location of modern-day Terre Haute, Indiana. When he heard the story of the attack, Pacanne appeared to take the news calmly, but the event changed his mind about peaceful relations with the ever-encroaching Americans.

Without reporting again for military duty, Pacanne and his remaining followers quickly left the area and returned to Kekionga. Once there, he no longer advocated peace but voiced his active support of Little Turtle's military alliance against the Americans.

It is likely that Pacanne's forces helped defeat American troops led by his former commander, Harmar, now a general with the American army, in 1790 and again under the command of the Northwest Territorial Governor, General Arthur St. Clair in 1791. However, Pacanne was most likely not there in person, as civil chiefs rarely went into battle.

In 1794 Pacanne more than likely sent warriors to be with his relative, Little Turtle, who was now under the overall command of Weyapiersenwah, or Blue Jacket, at the Battle of Fallen Timbers.

After the defeat of the Indian forces by General Anthony Wayne, Little Turtle became one of the so-called "peace chiefs." It appears that Pacanne also returned to his original opinion that American settlement of his homeland was inevitable. From this time on, he once again advocated peace and worked in the best interests of the Miami during treaty negotiations with the Americans.

Pacanne attended treaty councils at Greenville [Ohio] in 1795. Although he refused to sign this treaty, he pledged to keep its provisions and encouraged his followers and contemporaries to do the same. He represented the Miami during several treaty negotiations, including the Treaty of Grouseland in 1805, which relinquished Indian claims to lands in southern Indiana and Illinois territories. During this council, Pacanne spoke openly against American land acquisitions from tribes who had no clear claim to the lands they were selling.

Despite his protests against sale of Miami lands by tribes with no clear claim, from 1805 through the War of 1812, Pacanne - like Little Turtle - opposed the Shawnee-based, pan-Indian resistance movement of Tecumseh [*Panther Passing Across*] and Tenskwatawa [*The Open Door*]. Through the efforts of Pacanne and Little Turtle few Miami warriors enlisted in the Shawnee brothers' movement of tribal unity and resistance of American advancement into Indian lands. As a result, Pacanne was one of the peace chiefs marked by the Shawnee brothers for assassination.

After the War of 1812 ended, although never a clear ally of the United States, Pacanne continued to advocate Miami neutrality. As the main Miami civil chief during this time, the American government considered him an Indian leader of great importance.

By 1814 Pacanne had been principal Miami civil chief for fifty years. That year he initiated plans for a village to be built along the *Kineepikomeekwa Siipiiwi*, or Eel River. Pacanne projected this new village to be a place where all Miami could live peacefully. His plans were never brought to fruition. He died before his village of peace could be completed.

Upon Pacanne's death his nephew, Pe-she-wa, [*Wildcat*, or Jean Baptiste Richardville], the son of his sister Tacumwah [*The Other Side*] and the French trader Antoine Joseph Derouet de Richerville succeeded him as civil chief of the Miami.

Pacanne's burial place is unknown.

Pa-lons-wah
[Palonzwah, "Big Bird?"; or, possibly a corruption of his Christian name, Francois or Francis Godfroy]

Miami – French
b. 1787? – d. 1840

Illustration adapted from a painting by James Otto Lewis, at the Treaty of Fort Wayne, 1827, and from a watercolor and ink painting by George Winter, sketched in 1839 and executed circa 1863-71.

"Personally Chief Francis Godfroy was a remarkable, fine-looking man. His tout en semble would attract the attention of the observer were he [Godfroy] among a large congregated number of indians (sic).

– George Winter, from his Journal, after sketching Francis Godfroy in 1839.

"Brother, the Great Spirit has again taken to himself another of our once powerful and happy, but now declining nation. The time was when these forests were filled with red men. But the same hand whose blighting touch has withered the majestic frame that lies before us and caused the noble spirit that animated his body to seek another abode has in like manner dealt with his fathers and with ours. And so it will deal with us. Such occasions as this have become so common recently that we scarcely notice them. But when the brave and generous are stricken, our tears of sorrow flow freely."

– Wa-pa-pin-cha [*Black Raccoon*], from his funeral eulogy for Pa-lons-wah, May, 1840.

"'The Oak has fallen and the forest is in mourning.' Departed this life on the eve of the 1st of May, after a lingering illness, which he bore with philosophical resignation, Francis Godfroy, chief of the Miami Tribe of Indians, in the 53rd year of his life. It is with feelings of deep regret that we record the notice of chief Godfroy's death, for if ever a man deserved the title of the 'forest's noblest nobleman,' that man was Francis Godfroy."

– From Chief Francis Godfroy's obituary, published in the Niles National Register, Baltimore, Maryland, June 20, 1840.

Pa-lons-wah [*Big Bird*], or Francis Godfroy, was the son of French trader Jacques Godfroy and an unidentified *Myaamiaki* [Miami] woman. He was born and raised in the area of *Cecaahkonki* [*Kekionga*, or Blackberry Patch], near present-day Fort Wayne, Indiana.

Pa-lons-wah had two Miami wives; they gave birth to a total of twelve children.

His first wife, Sac-a-quah-tah, mothered six children. She died sometime after February of 1840. His second wife, Sac-a-che-quah, [Catherine Coleman] was the daughter of an American settler and had been raised as a Shawnee captive. Tradition has it that she was "won" in a horse race. She also bore six of his children, including Wah-pah-nah-ki-ka-kah-owah [*White Blossom*, or Gabriel Godfroy], who later became a Miami tribal chief in the area of Peru, Indiana. Sac-a-che-quah died in February of 1869.

Pa-lons-wah became war chief of the Miami in 1812, following the death of Me-she-kin-no-quah [*Little Turtle*]. He was a close associate of civil chief Peshewa, [*Wildcat*, or Jean Baptiste Richardville].

Pa-lons-wah allied with Tecumseh's [*Panther Passing Across*] pan-Indian movement and sided with the British during the War of 1812. Under orders from General William Henry Harrison, American troops destroyed several pro-British Miami villages along the *Nimacihsinwi Siipiiwi*, or Mississinewa River, in December of 1812. As war chief and defender of those villages, Pa-lons-wah led the last armed conflict between the Miami and American forces known as the Battle of Mississinewa.

With the onset of winter weather, General William Henry Harrison had ordered Lieutenant Colonel John B. Campbell and six hundred American troops to march from Ohio and destroy all the Miami towns along the Mississinewa. Harrison thought this tactic would protect his rear guard as he marched north to engage the British at Detroit. Campbell was also ordered to protect the Delaware village of Silver Heels and other pro-American or neutral Indian chiefs living in the area. But, Campbell disobeyed those orders.

On the cold, winter morning of December 17, Campbell ordered his troops to attack Silver Heels' village. The Americans surprised the Delaware, killed eight warriors and took forty-two prisoners, men, women and children. Campbell's troops then burned two more villages, this time Miami, along the river. However, with the element of surprise gone, the Miami resisted and counterattacked. Campbell retreated back to a location near Silver Heels' burned-out village and set up camp for the night.

Just before daybreak on the morning of December 18, Pa-lons-wah, with the support of Joseph Richardville and Little Thunder, led three hundred warriors against Campbell's troops near present-day Jalapa, Indiana, in Grant County. At the time, nearly half of Campbell's force was unfit for duty as a result of frostbite, illness and battle wounds. Pa-lons-wah's early morning attack routed the Americans. As winner of the last armed conflict between the Miami and Americans in Indiana, Pa-lons-wah later agreed to peace terms with the Americans.

Pa-lons-wah's wealth and influence grew following the War of 1812. His trading post, which he acquired through a treaty with the Americans, was located in present-day Blackford County, Indiana, along the *O-sah-mo-nee* [Yellow Paint], or Salamonie River. It flourished; and he later inherited his father's trading post at *Nan-matches-sin-wa*, [Mount Pleasant], near the *Waapaahsiki Siipiiwi*, or Wabash River, east of present-day Peru, Indiana.

Pa-lons-wah was elected civil chief of the Miami about 1830, following the death of Peshewa [*Wildcat*]. His wealth, his rapport with the well-liked Peshewa and his charisma among his people had much to do with his election. As a former war chief and now civil chief, Pa-lons-wah signed several Miami land cessions between 1818 and 1840. For his signature, he received money and several large grants of land from the U. S. federal government.

As a result of signing a treaty at *Paawikami Siipiiwi*, [the Forks of the Wabash] on November 28, 1840, Pa-lons-wah and his family received fifteen thousand dollars a year in annuities, payable at the Indian Bureau at Fort Wayne. Terms of the treaty allowed his children to share in the annuity until the youngest son reached the age of twenty-one. Since his family had to be present to receive their annuity, Pa-lons-wah's relatives were given special dispensation to stay in Indiana following the removal west of most Miami in 1846.

In 1836, Pa-lons-wah sold his home and Salamonie River trading post. Until his death, he centered his attention on *Nan-matches-sin-wa*, with its large two-story structure, which housed both the trading post store and Pa-lons-wah's living quarters. The post also included a storehouse, a springhouse, and several log outbuildings.

Pa-lons-wah died on May 7, 1840, at fifty-three years of age, at his Mount Pleasant home. He was buried in the adjacent Godfroy Cemetery, located along present day Indiana Highway 124, east of Peru. An Indiana Historic Bureau marker identifies the site.

Pa-ta-sha
[Perig, Peereesh, Parish, Parrish, Peerish, Peannish,
"The Stutterer;" Peter Morin, Pierre Moran,
Pier Moran]

French – Kickapoo – Potawatomi
b. 1780? – d. 1826? - 1830s?

*Adapted from a wall mural painting by Kelby Love, located at 200 E. Jackson Blvd.,
at the YMCA in Elkhart, Indiana. No known authentic image exists.*

Pa-ta-sha [*The Stutterer*] was born a metis, a person of mixed Indian and French descent, who, despite a speech impediment and facial scarring, rose to become a tribal chief in two separate Indian nations. Throughout his life, he assumed a variety of names.

Patasha was born sometime around the year 1780. His birthplace was between the confluence of Big Pine and Kickapoo creeks, north of modern-day Attica, Indiana, in what would become Warren County. His mother was a *Kiikaapoi* [Wanderer, or Kickapoo] named Un-kno-un-won. His father was a French trader named Constant Morin. [The spelling was changed to Moran by the British following the French and Indian War [1754-1762].

Constant Morin had come to Indian Territory and settled first at Ouiatenon, a thriving French trading center along the Wabash River, near modern-day Lafayette, Indiana. Ouiatenon was established during the 1750s across the Wabash from an area known as Wea Plains. In that area a tribe of Kickapoo lived among the Wea and Piankashaw, tribal divisions of the Miami nation. Most likely, this is where Pa-ta-sha's parents met.

Given the Christian name, Pierre, by his French father, Pa-ta-sha was reared as a Kickapoo by his Indian mother. Pa-ta-sha is described as a natural leader. Through his father's influence, he was a lifelong Roman Catholic; through his mother's lineage, he became a tribal chief among the Kickapoo at a young age.

Like many Indian personal names, Pa-ta-sha's reflected a notable physical characteristic. In his case, the characteristic was a speech impediment. His Kickapoo name translates as "The Stutterer," also as "Speaks as a Wagon Mired in Mud Which Cannot Proceed." But, over the years, Pa-ta-sha became known by a variety of names. Both his Christian name and his many Indian variations remain a part of Indiana Indian history.

Among the Kickapoo he became known as Perig. He married a Kickapoo woman, whose name is not known. They had at least two children. Physically, Perig is described as tall, about six-feet, and as having a disfigured face, possibly the result of a wound received in battle.

In early adulthood, Perig became a disciple of Tenskwatawa [*The Open Door*], The Shawnee Prophet. He lived for a time at *Kithtippecanunk*

[The Clearing], the center of a pan-tribal movement based on the spiritual message of The Prophet and the political tenets advocated by his brother, Tecumseh [*Panther Passing Across*].

Prophetstown, as the village was known among American settlers, was located near the confluence of the Tippecanoe and Wabash rivers, near modern-day Battle Ground, Indiana. Unfortunately for the pan-Indian cause and his own future among the Kickapoo, Perig was not present at the Battle of Tippecanoe.

The Battle of Tippecanoe, fought between an American army under the command of Territorial Governor William Henry Harrison and a coalition of pan-tribal forces led by The Prophet, occurred November 7, 1811. The Indian defeat crippled the Shawnee brother's coalition of resistance to American expansionism. Although some accounts put Perig among the Indian combatants, according to one historical source, he was not present because of faulty intelligence provided him.

Perig and more than five hundred of his Kickapoo warriors were encamped along the Wabash, not far from the site of the battle on the evening of November 6. Perig's best intelligence was that Harrison's troops were still a week's march away, when in fact they already were encamped just outside Prophetstown. He did not find out that he and his Kickapoo warriors might have been able to turn the tide of battle until after the outcome had already been decided. Following this logistical blunder, an immediate council of Kickapoo warriors was convened; Perig was dismissed as chief - then banned from the tribe.

After banishment from the Kickapoo, Perig resided among the *Neshnabe*, or *Bode'wadmiyuk* [True People, or Potawatomi], in their *otan* [village], located at Black Rock, along the Wabash River in western Indiana Territory. He married a *kwe* [Potawatomi woman] named An-Cosh [*Little Deer Tracks*], the daughter of their *pasigwin* [chief]. Through this marriage, he was adopted into the tribe. To his credit, and despite his documented verbal speech impediment, Perig had an obvious gift for leadership. He quickly rose to the rank of *okama* [tribal leader], this time as a Potawatomi. Over the remainder of his years, under many names, Perig signed several treaties, listing himself as Potawatomi.

Following the American victory at the Battle of Tippecanoe, during the War of 1812, Peereesh, as his descendents prefer he be called, remained loyal to the *Sagnash* [British]. After the *megatkiwin* [war] had ended in 1815, Peereesh, along with fellow Potawatomi chiefs, Metea [*Sulker*] and Winibiset [*The Crafty One*], continued to advocate resistance to American expansionism into Indian Territory. For his loyalty, he received pensions and payments from the British, possibly throughout the rest of his life.

According to some accounts, British-sympathizer Peereesh worked as a double agent following the War of 1812. During this time, he became widely known by the more Anglicized name of Peter [also Pierre or Pier] Moran. Regardless of his English affiliation, the United States government also rewarded him for his signature on several treaties with a variety of gifts, annuities and property in Indiana and Michigan. Possibly because of interpretation variations – possibly because Peereesh changed his own name – the name listed on official documents vary widely.

In 1817, listed as "Perish" on the Treaty of the Maumee, or Miami Rapids at Lake Erie, he received one full section of land at the mouth of *Me-sheh-weh-ou-deh-ik* [the Elkhart River] in what would become the center of the modern-day city of Elkhart, Indiana. The following year, at the 1818 Treaty of St. Mary's, this time noted as "Perig," he received another section of land "where he now lives," along Flint Creek in present day Tippecanoe County, Indiana.

At Chicago in 1821, he signed a third treaty, this time as "Peannish." In this treaty, he received three additional sections of land, again near current-day Elkhart. Later he sold all his treaty land at the mouth of the Elkhart River to his brother-in-law, Zachariah Cicot [Cicott], also a French and Indian metis, married to Peannish's sister, Pe-Say-Quot.

This transaction complete, Peannish returned south and lived near his birthplace on the north bank of the Wabash River, across from Cicot's trading post at the town of Independence, Indiana, in eastern Warren County, upstream from the town of Attica.

Some five years later, in 1826, Peannish, now known as Parish, moved again to what is now Benton County, Indiana. He set up camp in a huge stand of native timber—an island in the prairie - some seven miles southwest of the present-day county seat of Fowler. In those days, Parish's Grove, his final *e'camotmowot* [sanctuary], covered an estimated 1,000 acres and contained numerous native species "of immense size."

Parish, according to one historic account, selected a giant walnut tree and built a sleeping platform in the very top, in order to escape mosquitoes. Whatever his reasoning, his prairie grove was his home until his death.

Possibly because of his continued defiance of American settlement of the Old Northwest, his continued vocal anti-American sentiments and his noted weakness for whiskey, Parish was known among the *cmokmaken* [American] settlers as a "contrary and combative Indian."

All accounts report that his death was the result of injuries related to a fall. One account says that he fell from his pony and broke his neck. Another more widely accepted story, maintains that he awoke from an alcoholic stupor while in his treetop perch and fell to his death.

Some accounts date Parish's death as having come in 1826, but his descendants put it around 1830. However, documents show that Pierre Moran signed a bill of sale for his Elkhart land in 1831; and, listed as "Re-Re-Mo-Sau, alias Panish" on the 1832 Treaty of Tippecanoe, he was provided with a section and a half of land "along the River Raison" in Michigan.

Regardless of the year of his death, all accounts agree his remains are buried in central Benton County, on the western edge of the grove that bears his name.

Peshewa
[Pechewa, Pinjewah, "The Wildcat," "The Lynx;" or
Jean Baptiste Richerville (also Richardville)]

Miami – French
b. 1761? – d. 1841

*Adapted from a portrait painted at Fort Wayne by James Otto Lewis, dated 1827. Also
adapted from a portrait by George Winter, sketched c. 1830's, executed 1860's date uncertain.*

"Father, we think our answer is good - You point to the West and ask us to go there-There I shall never go, nor will my people. They are all opposed to leaving here. They will not sell their lands. I speak not for myself, but for my people - What you hear from me is the voice of the Miami. We have answered more than once that we will not sell, and still you ask us for land. You tell us again that our Great Father loves us - His acts do not show it - If he loved them he would clothe and feed them - He would not send them into the western wilderness. You go about like the fox in the night to gather information, to steal our opinions. We know the value of our soil as well as the White Man can tell us - Here the Great Spirit has fixed our homes - Here are our cornfields and cabins - From this soil and these forests we derive our subsistence, and here we will live and die - I repeat, we will not sell one inch of our lands."

– Peshewa to the United States; selected excerpts from the proceedings of treaty negotiations at Forks of the Wabash, September 25-26, 1832.

Peshewa, [*Wildcat*] or Jean Baptiste Richardville, like his parents, became a very financially successful trader. By the time of his death in 1841, he was thought to be among the richest men in the United States.

Local legend recalls that Peshewa was born under an ancient apple tree, reputed to be more than one hundred years old at that time of his birth. This tree was located along the *Kociihsaiipi*, [St. Joseph's River of the Maumee] at *Cecaahkonki* [Kekionga or Blackberry Patch], present-day Fort Wayne, Indiana.

Peshewa's birth came sometime near the end of the French and Indian War [1755-1763]. He was the second of four children born to Antoine Joseph Derouet de Richerville and a Miami, or possibly mixed Miami-French, mother, Tacumwah [*The Other Side*], also known as Maria Louisa.

His French father, known by the shortened name of Derouet de Richerville [later, Richardville], was a fur-trading merchant living at Kekionga. Tacumwah was also involved in his trade and together they passed on lessons to their son about success in the fur trading business. Peshewa's birth came about the time the French surrendered Fort Miamis, the fort at Kekionga to the British.

In 1763, during Pontiac's Rebellion, the predominately pro-French Miami massacred the British garrison at Fort des Miamis. In 1770, Peshewa's parents divorced. Tacumwah stayed at Kekionga, where she ran the family business; Peshewa's father moved to Trois Rivieres [Three Rivers, or possibly Quebec City, in French Canada. Peshewa spent time with both parents, immersing him in two cultures. He would reside periodically in Canada throughout the rest of his life, attending school and adding a fluent knowledge of the French and English languages to his Miami tongue.

Peshewa is believed to be related to influential Miami war chief Meshekinnoquah [*Little Turtle*] and civil chief Pacanne [*Nut*]. During his early manhood, he was present with Little Turtle during most of the Miami-American armed conflicts during President Washington's military aggression into Indian-held lands of the Northwest Territory.

Many accounts designate Little Turtle as the leader of a coalition of Algonquin-speaking tribes, known as the Miami Alliance or Wabash Confederation, which offered military resistance against American expansionism during the period from 1789 through much of 1794. As a member of this coalition of tribes and Little Turtle's constant companion, Peshewa also participated in subsequent treaty negotiations and signed the Treaty of Greenville [Ohio] in 1795. By this time, he was in his early thirties.

In 1800 Peshewa married Natoequah, a Miami woman. They reared a son, Miahqueah, also called Joseph, and three daughters: Susan, Catherine and La Blonde.

During the early 1800s, Peshewa avoided involvement in Tecumseh's [*Panther Passing Across*] pan-tribal resistance to American expansionism into what remained of Indian Territory and the subsequent War of 1812, by seeking refuge in Canada.

Peshewa returned to Fort Wayne after the War of 1812 had ended and, upon Pacanne's death in 1816, succeeded him as the elected civil chief of the Miami. His unanimous election followed the commission of an act similar to one accomplished by his predecessor, Pacanne.

As a young chief in 1765, Pacanne was credited with single-handedly saving the life of an English officer by defying a large, hostile group of followers of the Ottawa chief and anti-British organizer, Pontiac.

According to one account from early American settlers, the Miami council had decided to burn a prisoner at the stake. Peshewa's mother, Tacumwah, gave him a knife and instructed him to cut the prisoner lose and "proclaim your chieftainship." Peshewa obeyed and in the confusion, Tacumwah helped the prisoner escape. Following the incident, which demonstrated his individual bravery and leadership, Peshewa was unanimously declared principal chief.

As principal civil chief, Peshewa guided his people through many difficult times, up to and including Miami removal from Indiana in 1846. He was known as a skilled negotiator, working to protect the interests of a now-declining Miami nation. He won many important concessions during treaty negotiations with the United States from 1815 through 1840, including procurement of the Great Miami Reserve, a reservation of some seven hundred sixty thousand acres in north central Indiana, during the council at the Treaty of St. Mary's [Ohio] in 1818.

However, some also accused Peshewa of using his political position for his personal financial gain as well as lucrative considerations for his family and close friends. During his lifetime, he received large grants of money and land and was awarded several homes from the United States government. He became the richest Indian in Indiana and possibly "the most wealthy man of the native race in America," according to historian Henry Schoolcraft. His net worth was estimated at one million dollars at the time of his death in 1841.

Three of Peshewa's treaty houses still stand. One is located in Fort Wayne at 5705 Bluffton Road. The house was built in 1827 and is the oldest Indian treaty house still standing east of the Mississippi River. A second treaty house is located near present-day Huntington at *Paawikami Siipiiwi*, or the Forks of the Wabash, at the junction of Indiana Highway 9 and U.S. 24. A third treaty house is privately owned and is located near the former *Wahshahshie* [Osage] village site, southeast of present-day Peru. His third house, a refurbished brick structure, sets near the confluence of *Nimacihsinwi Siipiiwi* and *Waapaahsiiki*

Siipiiwi, or Mississinewa and Wabash rivers, along Seven Pillars of the Mississinewa Road near the former Osage Village site.

Peshewa died at his treaty home in Fort Wayne on August 13, 1841. He is buried in historic Cathedral Square at the intersection of Lewis and Calhoun streets.

Leopold Pokagon
[Pe-ge-gen, Pugagun, Pocagin, Pugegin, Pocagin; "Rib"]
also,
[Saqoquinick, Sakekwinik; "The Man of River's Mouth"]

Chippewa? – Ottawa? – Potawatomi?
b. 1775? – d. 1841

Adapted from a watercolor portrait by Van Sanden dated 1838.

"Father, I implore you to send us a black robe to instruct us in the word of God. If you have no case for us old men at least have pity on our poor children, who are growing up in ignorance and vice. We still preserve the manner of prayer as taught our ancestors by the black robes who formerly resided at St. Joseph. Morning and evening, with my wife and children, we pray together before the crucifix in the chapel. Sunday we pray together oftener. On Fridays we fast until evening, men, women and children, according to the traditions handed down to us by our fathers, for we ourselves have never seen a black robe. Listen to the prayers he taught them and see if I have learned them correctly."
– *Leopold Pokagon, personal plea to Father Gabriel Richard, at Detroit, 1830.*

"I understand this and I understand perfectly what you are about to do, but I think you have forgotten something. And it is something very important to your self and to your people. You must consider it or the tide will turn against you too."
– *Leopold Pokagon's response to General Zachary Taylor, after Taylor expressed the thought that the tide had turned against the Potawatomi, Fort Dearborn, Michigan, September 26, 1833 [from Gilbert, pages 77-78].*

Although no historically recorded evidence exists of Leopold Pokagon until 1825, it is believed he was born in the vicinity of the current-day town of Bertrand, Berrien County, Michigan, at the beginning of the American Revolutionary War, sometime around 1775 or 1776.

According to legend, he may have been of Chippewa or Chippewa-*Wdawa* [Ottawa] extraction, or he possibly may have been fully *Neshnabek,* or *Bode'wadmiyuk* [Potawatomi]. Alone and abandoned as a child, the Potawatomi of *Sohq-wah-sebe* [Saint Joseph River of Lake Michigan] found him, took him in, and reared him as their own son. He was given the personal nickname of Pe-ge-gen, meaning "Rib." This name came from a conspicuous human rib, which adorned his topknot at the time he was first found. His name later came to be spelled Pokagon and pronounced "Poe-kay-gun."

Recognizing his potential, Pe-ge-gen was adopted into the powerful and numerous *Kitchigumi dodem,* or Great Sea Clan. The clan members gave him the personal name of Saqoquinick, also spelled Sakekwinik [*Man of the River's Mouth*].

Saqoquinick married a Potawatomi medicine woman named Acuarie or Kitisse. Later, he married a daughter or possibly a niece of Topenebee [*Quiet Sitting Bear*], a *wkama* [leader] of the Potawatomi Bear Clan. His second wife, known by the Christian name of Elizabeth, gave birth to three sons: Paul, Francis and Simon.

In 1825, Territorial Governor Lewis Cass ordered a census of Indian villages in southwestern, lower Michigan. According to the census, an *otan* [village] of one hundred occupants, the third largest of forty-seven Potawatomi villages along the St. Joseph River of Lake Michigan, was "headed by a man named Pugagun."

Pugagun's village was located south of the Sauk Trail, six miles northwest of present-day South Bend, Indiana, along the west bank of the St. Joseph River, in Berrien County, Michigan. It was opposite the trading village of Bertrand, established by metis [French and Indian] trader Joseph Bertrand at a place the French called *Parc-aux-Vaches* [Buffalo Cow Pasture]. In this census comes the first historical mention of Saqoquinick; it names him as a tribal leader.

During this time, Saqoquinick was friendly with a Baptist missionary, the Reverend Issac McCoy. Rev. McCoy was active in helping the Potawatomi learn agricultural techniques. Saqoquinick became known as a "Baptist sympathizer." In 1827 Rev. McCoy became a governmental employee in the Indian Service and an advocate of President Andrew Jackson's Indian removal policy. Jackson's political stance called for the emigration of all Indians to reservations west of the Mississippi River. Saqoquinick did not agree.

Since missionaries of the Catholic Church did not support the Indian Removal Act, Saqoquinick, known to be a highly spiritual man, converted to Catholicism in 1830. He was baptized into the Church and given the Christian name of Leopold Pokagon. Leopold Pokagon did not have any position of influence or leadership among the St. Joseph River Potawatomi bands until 1826, following the death of Topenebee, the band's primary *wkama*. Shortly after Topenebee's death, Pokagon rapidly assumed the role of principal chief. Pokagon's sudden rise to leadership is attributable to several events.

Pokagon's marriage into Topenebee's family and clan is probably the most important factor in his assuming leadership of the entire St. Joseph Valley Potawatomi. To add to this, Topenebee's daughter, Madeline, had married the wealthy and influential metis trader Bertrand, who advocated Pokagon's leadership. Also, Pokagon's defense of Topenebee's twenty-eight-year old son, known as Topenebee the Younger, helped his leadership status.

Topenebee's son was considered ineligible to take over his father's role as *wkama*, since he had killed one of his own kinsmen. Pokagon took him into his home and protected him after Topenebee's death.

Furthermore, no other leader of significance came forward to champion the cause of the declining Potawatomi. His conversion and alliance with the Catholic Church, which did not favor Indian Removal, and Pokagon's personal, political and social philosophies, which met the approval of American governmental officials of the time, helped to keep his band in Michigan.

During the early 1800s, Pokagon had rebuked the Shawnee leader, Tecumseh [*Panther Passing Across*], and his plans during the early 1800s for a pan-tribal Indian nation. Pokagon supposedly did join the British during the War of 1812, and supposedly aided the survivors of the 1812 Fort Dearborn Massacre; and, he did not support the Sauk leader, Makataimeshekiakiah's [Black (Sparrow) Hawk] War against the Americans in 1832.

As a friend to the Americans, Pokagon saw the future of his people as one of removal to the west or possible extinction by the land-greedy *cmokman* [white men] unless the Potawatomi became totally acculturated. Pokagon was quick to accept American demands, which included Christian conversion, abstinence from alcohol, formal education of Indian children, ownership of private property and involvement in a capitalist economy. By publicly espousing these views, Pokagon took American officials by surprise, and he subsequently was able to avoid removal to the west.

By signing the Carey Mission Treaty of 1828, Pokagon gave up the last large blocks of Potawatomi lands in southwestern Michigan and northern Indiana; however, through political maneuvering, his village and some other villages, were designated in the treaty as Indian reserves. Unlike another Catholic convert, " The Potawatomi Preacher," Chief Menominee [*Rice Eater*], who refused to sell his reservation at *Ni-jo-de sa-ga-ig-an-og* [Twin Lakes] in northern Indiana and was forced west, Pokagon and his band were permitted to remain, although they would have to move to a new Michigan location.

In 1832 numerous Potawatomi leaders, including Pokagon, signed the Treaty of Tippecanoe at Chippewanuck, near present-day Rochester, Indiana. This treaty ceded claims to all remaining Potawatomi land in northern Indiana - once again some individual reserves were exempted, including Pokagon's.

On September 26, 1833, Pokagon was one of the chiefs who signed the second Treaty of Chicago. In this treaty, the Potawatomi gave up claims to all lands west of Lake Michigan, some five million acres. In return they were given reservations of similar size west of the Missouri River. However, Pokagon again requested that he be able to stay in Michigan. This request was granted, although Pokagon's people were required to remove from the St. Joseph River of Lake Michigan.

Pokagon and his band moved from the St. Joseph River valley in 1837 and relocated to adjacent Cass County, Michigan, settling six miles northwest of nearby Dowagiac, in the area of Silver Creek. However, continuing efforts by Michigan settlers and politicians to remove Pokagon and his tribe forced the chief to seek legal intervention at Detroit in 1840. Judge Epaphroditus Ranson's ruling at Detroit in August of that year favored the Catholic Potawatomi's land ownership rights and halted American efforts to remove Pokagon's band from its Michigan reserve.

Leopold Pokagon died July 8, 1841, at age sixty-six. He and his wife are buried beneath the Catholic *au-naw-ma-we gaw-ming* [chapel] that he helped build near Dowagiac.

In 1994, Pokagon's tribal descendents finally received official federal recognition as the Pokagon Band of the Potawatomi.

Simon Pokagon
["Rib"]

Chippewa? – Ottawa? – Potawatomi
b. 1830? – d. 1899

Adapted from two portrait paintings, one by E.A. Burbank, dated 1898; the other by M.O. Whitney, dated 1893.

"In early life, I was deeply hurt as I witnessed the grand old forests of Michigan, under whose shades my forefathers lived and died, falling before the cyclone of civilization as before a prairie fire. In those days, I traveled thousands of miles along our winding trails, through the unbroken solitudes of the wild forest, listening to the songs of the woodland birds as they poured forth their melodies from the thick foliage above and about me. Very seldom now do I catch one familiar note from those early warblers of the woods. They have all passed away ... I now listen to the songs of other birds that have come with the advance of civilization ... and, like the wild wood birds our fathers used to hold their breath to hear, they sing in concert, without pride, without envy, without jealousy – alike in forest and field, alike before wigwam or castle, alike before savage and sage, alike before chief or king ..."
  – Simon Pokagon, from his speech at the Columbian World Exposition, Chicago, 1893.

"The world's people, from what they have so far seen of us on the Midway will regard us as savages; but they shall yet know that we are human as well as they ... The Red Man is your brother, and God is the Father of all."
  - Simon Pokagon, spoken at the Columbian Exposition, Chicago, 1893.

"[T]he pale-faces came by chance to our shores, many times very needy and hungry. We nursed and fed them, fed the ravens that were soon to pluck out our eyes, and the eyes of our children; for no sooner had the news reached the Old World that a new continent had been found, peopled with another race of men, then, locust-like, they swarmed on all our coasts; and, like the carrion crows in spring, that in circles wheel and clamor long and loud, and will not cease until they find and feast upon the dead, so these strangers from the East long circuits made, and

turkey-like they gobbled in our ears, "Give us gold, give us gold;" "Where find you gold? Where find you gold?"
– *Simon Pokagon from The Red Man's Greetings, a birch-bark book, published 1893.*

"[In the War of 1812] our cause was far more sacred to us than was the Americans' to them. They had drawn the sword in defense of one of their [property] rights; we for all of ours; for our very existence, for our native lands, and for the graves of our fathers, most sacred to our race."
– *Simon Pokagon, from The Future of the Red Men, a birch-bark book, published 1898.*

Simon Pokagon was known by white America during his lifetime as the "best educated, full blood Indian in North America." A *Neshnabe* or *Bode'wadmiyuk pasigwin* [True People or Potawatomi, chief], he was an acclaimed writer, philosopher and lecturer. He wrote many poems, hymns and magazine articles, but perhaps he is best known for his "birch bark" booklets. These short books, written by hand on birch bark, recorded stories of Simon Pokagon's personal life, along with the history of the North American Indian and his views for the future of his race.

Simon was born about 1830 in his *nin-noss* [father] Leopold Pokagon's *otan* [village] along the *Sohq-wah-se-be* [St. Joseph River of Lake Michigan], near present- day Bertrand, Berrien County, Michigan. His birth took place at nearly the same time as his father's conversion to Catholicism.

Simon was baptized at birth as a member of the Catholic Church and was given his Christian name. His last name, Pokagon, is derived from his father's nickname, given to him by his adopted Potawatomi family.

According to legend, as a youth of ten or eleven, Simon's father, whose origins may be Chipewa, Ottawa and/or Potawatomi, was found wandering alone by a band of Potawatomi. At the time of his discovery, he was wearing a human bone woven into his hair. He was given the nickname of Pokagon, meaning "Rib." He was later given the personal Indian name of Saqoquinick, also spelled Sakekwinik [*Man of the River's*

Mouth], but Pokagon was the name by which he would become known to American settlers of the area. After his conversion to Catholicism, he took the Christian name Leopold. He was the first chief of the Pokagon Band of Potawatomi, which is today a nationally recognized band, living in Michigan.

Simon's early years were passed at his father's *otan* in the St. Joseph River Valley of lower southwestern Michigan. As tribal chief, Leopold Pokagon, also spelled Pe-ge-gun, signed the 1833 Treaty of Chicago. The Chicago treaty ceded all Potawatomi lands in Michigan to the United States. Most signatories were required to move to tribal reservations in the west within three years of the treaty's ratification by the United State Congress; however, through Leopold's political maneuvers, the Pokagon Band was granted a concession, which allowed Leopold and his band to remain in Michigan. Although they were not required to move west of the Mississippi, the Pokagon Band was forced to move from the St. Joseph River Valley to other sites within southwest Michigan.

When Simon was about three or four years old, the Pokagons moved first a few miles north and east of their former village and settled close to present-day Sumnerville. A few years later, they moved a second time and settled near present-day Dowagiac, Michigan, in Silver Creek Township, Cass County. Leopold's *gi-nib-owin* [death] came when Simon was eleven years of age. Simon eventually would assume the hereditary role of civil chief of the Potawatomi following his father's death, but only after the death of Leopold's two older *ni-gress*, or *o-gwis-san* [sons], Paul and Francis.

Paul Pokagon, Simon's oldest brother, was the first to succeed Leopold; Paul died in 1841. The second son, Francis Pokagon, then assumed the role of chief until his death sometime around 1850; and, Simon, the youngest of the brothers, succeeded Francis. At the time, Simon was about twenty or twenty-one years old.

Until the age of twelve, Simon spoke only Algonquin. His mother and the "Black Robes," or Catholic *me-kat-e-wik-wan-e* [priests], encouraged him to pursue a formal education. At age 14, on the recommendation of the priests, Simon entered the recently founded College of Notre Dame du Lac in South Bend, Indiana. After four years of studies at Notre Dame, Simon continued his education in Ohio, attending Oberlin College for one year and Twinsburg College for two more years. During this period of time, Simon became fluent in five languages, including English, Latin and Greek. He also became an accomplished pianist, poet and writer.

After returning from college, upon the death of his brother, Francis, Simon became civil chief of the Pokagon Band. Besides holding the title of chieftain, Simon also acted as interpreter and mediator for his tribe. By 1865, tribal clan structure had changed, as did the role of chieftain. With the tribe now more democratically organized as an entity, tribal chieftains took the title of "secretary" of the tribe and played a less autocratic leadership role. Although Simon rightfully no longer held the title of chief, he was elected secretary of the Pokagon Potawatomi for many consecutive terms.

While on a hunting trip into the wilderness near the Black River in northern, lower Michigan, Simon met Lonidaw Sinagaw, also known by her Christian name of Angela. She would become his wife.

Lonidaw was born in 1838, during the time of forced Indian removal, at Menominee's [*Rice Eater's*] village near *Ni-jo-de Sa-ga-ig-an-og* [Twin Lakes], in present-day Marshall County, Indiana. At this time Menominee, another Catholic convert also known as "The Potawatomi Preacher," was being pressured by the Indiana government to sell his reserve and move west. When Menominee refused to sell the four-section reserve he had received at the Treaty of Tippecanoe, signed near Rochester, Indiana, in 1832, he and his band were attacked by Indiana *shmakneshuk* [militia].

Under the command of Colonel Abel Pepper, the militia burned Menominee's village and crops, and then rounded up the aging chief and most of his band. They were forced to march some six hundred sixty miles from northern Indiana to a Kansas reservation. During the march, some forty elderly and children died, giving the trek the title "Trail of Death." Lonidaw's parents eluded capture at the village but became separated when trying to escape the militia.

Lonidaw's *o-gaw-shi-maw* [mother] was pregnant at the time, and she fled into a nearby *mash-kig* [swamp]. While hiding in a hollow sycamore tree, Lonidaw's mother gave birth to Simon Pokagon's future wife.

Simon and Lonidaw were married in 1851. They established their first home along Long Lake in Michigan. Later, they moved to Rush

Lake, near present-day Hartford, Van Buren County, Michigan. Simon Pokagon would continue to live there most of his adult life, even after the untimely death of his beloved Lonidaw at the age of thirty-five.

By the time Lonidaw died in 1871, the couple had four children: Cecilia, William, Charles and Jerome. Her death left Simon with the responsibility of raising their young family. He later married a second *ikwe* [wife], Victoria. Victoria had been divorced, and marrying her kept Simon from being in full compliance with the rules of the Catholic Church.

Over the years, Simon Pokagon grew into a writer, speaker and lecturer of great note. His articles were published in many magazines of the day, including "Arena," "Forum," "Harper's Weekly," "Chatauquan" and the "American Review of Reviews." Although professionally successful, as tribal secretary, Simon's devoted his life to his people.

During the American Civil War [1861-1865], Pokagon met twice with President Abraham Lincoln and, in the next decade, "smoked a pipe of peace" with President Ulysses S. Grant. As a result of these meetings, he was able to obtain the delayed annuity payments due the Potawatomi from the United States for lands ceded by the Treaty at Chicago in 1833. According to Simon's writings, by the time the remainder of these treaty annuities, some three hundred ninety thousand dollars, was received at the end of the Civil War in 1865, the Potawatomi were still owed "between one hundred and two hundred thousand dollars."

During the 1893 Columbian Exposition, held in Chicago, Simon became outraged when he discovered that no American Indians had been chosen as dignitaries for this event. However, Simon was asked by the Mayor of Chicago to be the "keynote speaker on Chicago day" during the Columbian Exposition. After delivering his speech to a large, receptive crowd, he presented Chicago's city fathers with a deed for the land on which the Exposition was being held, the land which had been undersold by the Potawatomi, at three cents an acre, nearly sixty years before. Finally, in 1896, the Pokagon Potawatomi received one hundred fifty thousand dollars for these land cessions, but Simon kept only four hundred dollars for himself, requesting the remainder be distributed among the Pokagon Band.

These events inspired Simon to write a long series of articles chronicling the history of Indians in America. This series was later compiled into a collection known as *The Red Man's Greeting,* which was later retitled as *The Red Man's Lamentations.*

Originally written on birch bark, *The Red Man's Greeting* gained national and international attention. The work not only made Simon Pokagon famous in the United States, but also in Europe. He was able, from this time on, to support himself entirely as a lecturer and author.`

Following a fire at his cabin, Simon Pokagon died in *Mkokisis* [The Month of the Bear], January 28, 1899, at his home in Lee Township, Allegan County, Michigan. The fire not only destroyed his *e-camotmowot* [home], but all his papers and manuscripts.

Two years after his death, his semi-autobiographical work of fiction, *O-gi-maw-kwe Mit-i-gwa-ki: Queen of the Woods,* a romantic, fictionalized account of his courtship with Lonidaw, was published. Considered his most famous work, it was written many years before, while the young couple was still living at their cabin on Rush Lake. The book is dedicated to her.

Simon Pokagon and Lonidaw are buried side-by-side in the church cemetery at Rush Lake, Michigan.

Pontiac
[Ponteach, Pontiak, Pontiague, Obwandiyag; "Stopping Up the Pathway"]

Ottawa? – Ojibwa? – Miami?
b. 1720? – d. 1769

Adapted from a portrait painting, based on historical research and artist's intrepretation; no known authentic image exists.

"My children, you have forgotten the customs and traditions of your forefathers. Why do you not clothe yourselves in skins, as they did, and use the bow and arrow, and the stone-pointed lances, which they used? You have bought guns, knives, kettles and blankets from the white men, until you can no longer do without them; and what is worse, you have drunk the poison firewater, which turns you into fools. Fling all these things away; live as your wise forefathers who lived before you."

– Pontiac, reiterating the philosophy of the Delaware Prophet, Neolin, at a war council along the Riviere a l'Ecorce, April 27, 1763, prior to the siege of Fort Detroit.

"For I warrant you, when the English shall be driven from here or killed, we shall all retire to our villages according to our custom, and await the arrival of our father the Frenchman. These, you see, my [French] brothers, are my sentiments. Rest assured, my brothers, I will watch that no more wrong shall be done to you by my people, nor by other Indians."

– Pontiac, from his speech to the French, presenting reasons for making war against the English, May 25, 1763.

"It is important to us, my brothers, that we exterminate from our lands this nation which seeks only to destroy us. You see as well as I that we can no longer supply our needs as we have done from our brothers, the French. The English sell us goods twice as dear as the French do, and their goods do not last ... they do not want to give us any credit as our brothers, the French do. When I go to see the English commander and say to him that some of our comrades are dead, instead of bewailing their death, as our French brothers do, he laughs at me and at you. If I ask anything for our sick, he refuses with the reply that he has no use for us. From all this you can well see, that they are seeking our ruin. Therefore, my brothers, we must all swear their destruction and wait no longer. Nothing prevents us; they are few in numbers, and we can accomplish this ... [t]here is no more time to lose. When the English are defeated we shall

then see what there is left to do, and we shall stop up the ways hither so they may never come again upon our lands."
— *From Pontiac's Council Speech, May 5, 1763, recorded by the French Chronicler, Peckham.*

Pontiac, or Obwandiyag [*Stopping Up the Pathway*], was a member of the Odawa or Ottawa tribe. He is especially noted for his having organized a pan-tribal Indian rebellion at the end of the French and Indian War [1756-1763]. Between 1763 and 1765 Pontiac's forces, which encompassed many tribes of the Great Lakes area, threatened or captured all British fortifications in Indian Territory, the area that eventually would become known as the Old Northwest. Despite nearly universal recognition of his personal name, clearly documented evidence of his early life is varied and conflicting.

Recorded birth dates for Pontiac vary by some twenty years, listed as anywhere from 1703 to 1725. Historical accounts also differ greatly regarding his exact birthplace. Some historians believe Pontiac to have been born in Canada, while others put his birthplace along the Detroit River in the present-day State of Michigan. Other accounts note his birth as being at the confluence of the Auglaize and Maumee rivers at present-day Defiance, Ohio, while others write that he was born along the Ottawa River, near the boundary of the present-day states of Michigan and Ohio. His parentage is also obscure.

His father may possibly have been either Ottawa or Miami, and his mother, either Ojibwa or Ottawa. It is known, however, that he had one wife, named Kantuckeegan, and two sons, Otussa and Shegenaba, and that the famed Potawatomi chieftain, Shabbona [*Burly Shoulders*], a trusted aide of the Shawnee leader Tecumseh [*Panther Passing Across*], was his grandnephew. And it is known that, as a youth, Pontiac lived along the Detroit River, on the Canadian side, near the French fort of Detroit. It is also clearly recorded that the Ottawa were strongly allied with the French in their struggles with Britain.

Although Pontiac had no hereditary claims to tribal leadership, by 1755 his skills as a speaker and his bravery as a warrior had elevated him to the status of war chief among the Ottawa. That same year, he was at the head of his Ottawa warriors during the first battle of the French and Indian War, a successful French-led ambush of British colonial forces under General Edward Braddock in Little Meadows, Western Maryland. This battle ended in defeat for Braddock and his British troops, who had been sent to capture Fort Duquesne, a French outpost where the confluence of the Susquehanna and Allegheny rivers form the Ohio River at modern-day Pittsburgh, Pennsylvania.

After the final defeat of the French and their Algonquian-speaking allies by the British in early 1763, English troops quickly took control of most former French forts in the Indian Territory of the Great Lakes wilderness. As British forces were en route to garrison the former French stockade of Fort Detroit, Pontiac encountered their commander, the British frontier scout, Major Robert Rogers, along the southern shore of Lake Erie.

Rogers, leader of a British colonial scouting unit known as Rogers Rangers, informed Pontiac that the French had been defeated, and all territory that once had belonged to France, now belonged to England. Pontiac replied that, although the French had surrendered, the Ottawa had not and would not capitulate.

Despite their differing political views, Pontiac provided Rogers safe passage to Detroit, where the major took command of the fort. As long as Rogers was in residence and in command of the fort, the Indians were treated with dignity and respect. However, when Rogers departed, British military attitudes changed. Subsequent commanders had little respect for Indians, turning a blind eye to unscrupulous British traders, who began plying Indians with liquor in order to cheat them in business dealings.

In stark contrast to the French, who had little interest in owning Indian land and often intermarried with Indian women of the region, British governmental leadership claimed Indian land for the British Crown and sold it without regard to tribal ownership. British commanders also discouraged the practice of giving gifts, a universal practice that the Indians had come to expect from the French.

Amid this change in political climate, the words of the Delaware Prophet, Neolin, became the inspiration for Pontiac and many other Indians. Neolin, who said his message came directly from the Master of Life, preached that if the British were allowed to live among the Indian, the Indian would surely die.

"Maladies, smallpox and their poison will destroy you totally," he said.

Neolin believed the Master of Life wanted the Indian to return to traditional ways, to wear skins rather than cloth, to hunt with traditional weapons, such as spears and the bow and arrow, and especially to avoid the use of spirituous liquor.

Pontiac became a strong proponent of Neolin's teachings. These teachings, coupled with Pontiac's mistaken belief that the French would return to the area and once again become their allies, made him determined to drive the English forces from the region and re-establish Indian autonomy and trade with the French.

Pontiac sent beaded belts of red wampum, meaning war throughout Indian Territory. Soon, he was successful in uniting several of the tribes between Lake Ontario in the east to the Mississippi River in the west – much of the area that would become the Old Northwest. With co-conspirator Guyasuta, a Seneca chief who may have been with Pontiac during the Braddock ambush of 1755, the Ottawa leader assembled warriors from the Ottawa, Chippewa, Kickapoo, Illiniwek, Miami, Wea, Mascoutens, Potawatomi, Huron, Delaware, Missasauga, Seneca and Shawnee.

A secret war council of tribes was held along the Riviere a l'Ecorce, ten miles southwest of Fort Detroit, April 27, 1763. A week later, May 5, a second council was held at a Potawatomi village on the Canadian side of the Detroit River. Through these councils, the tribes were induced to attack the British fort nearest to each tribe's home territory.

Less than a week later, May 9, 1763, simultaneous attacks began on fourteen British forts. In a brief time, all but four British forts, three in western Pennsylvania, and the main western British outpost of Fort Detroit, had been captured by the tribes of Pontiac's coalition. His personal efforts were less successful. Despite a personally led, six-month siege on Fort Detroit, Pontiac failed to capture it.

Initially, Pontiac's plan had been for his warriors to enter the fort under a guise of friendship, but would be secretly armed, carrying sawed off shotguns hidden under their blankets. Once inside, Pontiac and his men would surprise the British soldiers and win victory quickly and easily. However, an Ojibwa woman, a mistress of a British officer, warned British commandant, Major Gladwin, of Pontiac's strategy ahead of time.

Now aware of Pontiac's plan, the soldiers were prepared and the scheme was foiled. Instead of a small detachment of guards, Major Gladwin increased the number of soldiers at the gate. Entering the fort a second time and encountering too many adversaries to overtake, easily or quickly, Pontiac's men left the fort without a confrontation.

Two days later, Pontiac tried to enter the fort again, but this time he was simply denied admittance. His original plan of surprise thwarted, Pontiac was left with no alternative but to lay siege to the fort and attempt to starve out the garrison.

For success in his battle against the British, Pontiac had relied heavily on promised military assistance from the French. Despite his expectations, the French never delivered on their promises. In fact it was a letter from the French commander at Fort du Chartes, an outpost along the Mississippi River in western Illinois, which prematurely ended Pontiac's siege on Fort Detroit.

Overall, Pontiac's Confederation had many military successes, killing more than two thousand British settlers and soldiers, but after his failure to defeat the British at Detroit, most members of his confederation melted away to their homes in the face of a coming winter. Pontiac's Confederacy and his dream of liberating all Indians from British domination began to crumble. Although individual skirmishes between factions of the confederacy and British soldiers and settlers continued, further attempts to revive the confederacy failed. After two years, Pontiac finally gave up the struggle.

On July 25, 1765, along the Wabash River at Fort Ouiatanon, near modern-day West Lafayette, Indiana, Pontiac agreed to peace terms with British envoys, although the final formal treaty of peace was not signed until the following year, July of 1766, at Oswego, New York.

After signing a treaty with the British, Pontiac received a pardon from the English king and returned to his Maumee River village in Ohio. From then on, he counseled peace with the British among his people. In 1768, because of his political stance of peaceful coexistence, he, his family and several close followers were banished from the village by a group of militant younger warriors.

Following his expulsion, Pontiac and his family moved west into Illinois Territory. According to some historical accounts, the British, fearing the possibility of more organized Indian uprisings, hired a Peoria warrior named Black Dog to assassinate Pontiac.

On a trip to the trading post at Cahokia [East Saint Louis, Illinois], on April 20, 1769, Black Dog killed the Ottawa leader. In retaliation for Pontiac's murder, a combined force of the "Three Fires" [Ottawa, Potawatomi, Objiwa], Sac and Fox nearly annihilated the Illiniwek at a high rocky bluff along the Illinois River, known today as Starved Rock.

Pontiac's Rebellion, sometimes called the Pontiac-Guyasuta War, or also the Indian War of Liberation, was the first and, for a time, the foremost successful Indian resistance to European invasion.

Some thirty years later, The Shawnee Prophet, Tenskwatawa [*The Open Door*], also would echo Neolin's teachings: a return to Indian traditions and spirituality, along with avoidance of all European products, especially liquor. Some forty years after Pontiac, between 1805 and 1811, The Prophet and his brother, Tecumseh, would form the final Indian coalition in Indian Territory.

Shabbona

[Shabonee, Shabonier, Shaubena, Shay-be-nay, Shab-e-nai, Shau-bon-ni-agh, Chamblee, Chambley, *"Built Like a Bear," "Broad Shoulders," "Burly Shoulders," "Head and Shoulders Like a Bear," "Coal-Burner."*]

Ottawa-Seneca-Potawatomi
b. 1775 – d. 1859

Adapted from an Ambrotype photograph, taken by H.B. Field, dated 1857.

123

"Perhaps your people do not know that the battle of Tippecanoe was the work of white men who came from Canada and urged us to make war. Two of them who wore red coats were at the Prophet's Town the day that your army came. It was they who urged Elskatawwa [The Prophet] to fight. They dressed themselves like Indians, to show us how to fight. They did not know our mode. We wanted to attack at midnight. They wanted to wait until daylight ... The fight had begun too soon. They were not all ready. The plan was to creep up through the wetland where the horses could not run, upon one side of the camp and on the other through a creek and steep bank covered with bushes. So as to be ready to use the tomahawk upon the sleeping men as soon as their chief was killed. The Indians thought white men who had marched all day would sleep. They found them awake. In one minute from the time the first gun was fired I saw a great war chief mount his horse and begin to talk loud. The fires were put out and we could not tell where to shoot, except on one side of the camp, and from there the white soldiers ran, but we did not succeed as the Prophet told us that we would, in scaring the whole army so that all the men would run and hide in the grass like young quails. I never saw men fight with more courage than these after it began to grow light. The battle was lost to us by an accident, or rather by two. A hundred warriors had been picked out during the night for this desperate service, and in the great council house the Prophet had instructed them how to crawl like snakes through the grass and strike the sentinels; and if they failed in that, then they were to rush forward boldly and kill the great war chief of the whites, and if they did not do this the Great Spirit, he said, had told him that the battle would be hopelessly lost. This the Indians all believed ... I think that I could have shot [General Harrison], but I could not lift my gun. The Great Spirit held it down. I knew then that the great white chief was not to be killed, and I knew that the red men were doomed. As soon as daylight came our warriors saw that the Prophet's grand plan had failed – that the great white chief was alive riding fearlessly among his troops in spite of bullets, and their hearts melted ... It was my last fight. I put my body in the way. It was strong then, but it was not strong enough to stop the white men. They pushed it aside as I do this stick. I have never seen the place since where we fought that night. My heart was very big then. Tecumseh had filled it with gall. It has been empty ever since."

– Shabbona, excerpts from his eyewitness account of the Battle of Tippecanoe, Nov. 11, 1811, recorded in Me-Won-I Toe, an 1864 book by Solon Robinson.

"[Tecumseh was] engaged with a foot soldier: the soldier having run his bayonet through Tecumseh's leather coat near his hips, and the latter, trying to disengage himself from the bayonet with his sabre in his hand when a horseman rode up and shot [Tecumseh] through the head."

– Shabbona, from his eyewitness description of Tecumseh's death at the Battle of Thames, Ontario, Canada, Sept. 1813, as told to Thomas Forsyth in 1816.

Shabbona [*Built Like a Bear*] is said to have been the grandnephew of the great Ottawa chief and Indian organizer, Pontiac, who formed a coalition of Great Lakes tribes to fight against the British takeover of Indian Territory after the French defeat in 1763. Some forty years later, Shabbona would become an integral part of another pan-tribal coalition movement, led by the Shawnee brothers, Tecumseh [*Panther Passing Across*] and Tenskwatawa [*The Open Door*], the Shawnee Prophet.

Despite not being known as an orator, Shabbona was, nevertheless, noted by American historians as one of the five most influential chiefs of his time when he visited Washington, D.C., in 1845.

A physically imposing figure, Shabbona is described as standing more than six feet in height with a thick, stocky, powerful build. He is also described as having a very large head, and he may have had a spinal deformity which gave him a "bear-like" appearance; hence his personal name, also translated as "Head and Shoulders Like a Bear."

However, the Potawatomi word for bear is *makwa*, giving rise to speculation concerning the origin of Shabbona's personal name. Four separate spellings are documented as Chamblee, Shab-eh-nay, Shab-e-nai and Shau-bon-ni-agh, plus more than a dozen variations, found in historical writings and recorded on various treaties.

Juliette Kinzie, the wife of a Chicago trader of the time, said that his name, spelled Chamblee, was in recognition of his birthplace at Chambly, Canada, near Montreal. Other theories note possible corruption of the French words *chevalier* and *Camp-de-ble,* meaning "field of wheat."

While Kinzie states that Shabbona was born in Canada, other accounts put his birthplace as being along the Maumee River in what is now northwestern Ohio; other accounts say he was born in lower southeastern Michigan and yet, other writings record his birthplace as being along the Kankakee River in current-day Will County, Illinois.

Regardless of his place of birth, documentation shows that Shabbona was born to an Ottawa father, often thought to be the nephew of Pontiac, and a Seneca mother. In adulthood, Shabbona married a Potawatomi woman, the daughter of Chief Spotka. Through this marriage, he became a leader among a clan of the Mascouten, also known as the Prairie Potawatomi or "Little Prairie People."

When his father-in-law died, Shabbona assumed the role of chief over several mixed tribes of Chippewa, Ottawa and Potawatomi living in the prairies of northern Illinois, southern Wisconsin and northwestern Indiana. After Spotka's death, Shabbona married twice more, first, to Miomex Zebequa, and later to a woman named Pakonoka. He is known to have fathered many children.

By 1807, Shabbona had become a disciple of Tecumseh and The Shawnee Prophet. The Shawnee brothers espoused the idea of a pantribal coalition, with ownership of all Indian lands held in common by Indians within an Indian Nation, not by individual tribes, chiefs or clans. The brothers moved from western Ohio in 1809 to establish a new village at *Kithtippecanunk [The Clearing],* an area at the confluence of the Tippecanoe and Wabash rivers in north central Indiana. Populated by Indians from many tribes, this new village became known to the American settlers of the region as "Prophetstown."

Now closer to Shabbona's villages, the Mascouten leader visited the Shawnee brothers often over the next two years. He was known to adhere fervently to the teachings of the Shawnee Prophet, most notably practicing abstinence from alcohol.

At the Battle of Tippecanoe, near modern-day Battleground, Indiana, in November of 1811, Shabbona was a main leader among the Indian combatants. After the Americans under Indiana Territorial Governor William Henry Harrison defeated the Prophet's forces and put the pan-Indian movement in temporary disarray, Shabbona remained loyal to Tecumseh. He became one of Tecumseh's closest aides and fought with the British during the War of 1812.

According to his personal testimony, Shabbona was at Tecumseh's side when the great Shawnee warrior fell at the Battle of Thames [Ontario, Canada] in 1813. Shabbona later gave an eyewitness account of Tecumseh's death, and it may have been he who carried his leader and comrade from the battlefield. However, Shabbona's eyewitness account of Tecumseh's death changed form in his later years.

During one of his many trips to Washington, D.C., he gave credit to Kentucky Militia Colonel Richard Mentor Johnson, by then a United States Senator, for killing the Shawnee leader. Many theories of how Tecumseh fell and the disposition of his body arose after his death, none proved above the others, so the historical accuracy of Shabbona's story has come into question.

Regardless, disheartened by Tecumseh's death, Shabbona became resigned to the idea that the invading Americans could not be stopped from settling on Indian lands. In the aftermath of the War of 1812, he decided to work for peaceful relations between the two conflicting cultures. Because of his peaceful interventions on behalf of the Americans, he was derided by many of his former Indian allies, who referred to him as a "friend to the *cmokman* [white man]."

When the so-called "Winnebago Uprising," led by Red Bird in 1827, threatened early settlers in and around the growing village of Chicago, Illinois, Shabbona, along with several other chiefs with American affiliation, traveled around the countryside warning settlers of possible attacks by hostile Indians. He also visited many Indian villages in an attempt to keep his own tribal members, as well as the Sauk and Fox, among others, from going to war against the Americans.

While visiting the village of Big Foot, a Sauk chief still hostile to the whites, Shabbona was taken prisoner and threatened with death.

He was released the following day, but from that time on, his reputation as being "the white man's friend" kept him in constant danger of retaliation from anti-American Indian factions.

Many Indians, especially the Sauk and Fox, detested Shabbona and marked him for death. His son, Pypeogee, and his nephew, Pyps, were both assassinated, and Shabbona escaped ambushes and other attempts on his life several times over the next several years.

In 1829 Shabbona signed the second Treaty of Prairie du Chein [Wisconsin], which ceded an area in northwestern Illinois and southwestern Wisconsin as well as the area including the modern day cities of Wilmette and Evanston in Illinois. For his signature, Shabbona was awarded a two-square mile reserve along the Illinois River in Grundy County [Illinois], southwest of Chicago. At the center of his holdings was a "prairie island" of trees, which became known as Shabbona's Grove.

Makataimeshekiakiah [*Black (Sparrow) Hawk*], the noted Sauk chief, visited with Shabbona at least twice before declaring war on the United States in 1832. Shabbona refused to join Black Hawk. Instead, he sided against Black Hawk by warning settlers of possible impending attacks. He also joined the American army as a guide and scout and was instrumental in Black Hawk's capture at the Battle of Bad Axe Creek near present-day Sauk City, Wisconsin.

Black Hawk later said, if not for Shabbona, all the Potawatomi would have joined his cause and his uprising could have lasted for years.

During Indian removal from Illinois in 1836, Shabonna led his people to their new reservation at Council Bluffs, Iowa, but he soon returned to his Illinois prairie grove. Twice more he visited his people who were by then now living in Kansas. After his second trip, he returned to find that his treaty lands had been determined through Illinois courts as having been abandoned, and the property was put into forfeiture. All of his two hundred acres had been confiscated and sold by white land speculators.

This unfairness done, local settlers, remembering all Shabbona's good deeds and assistance, used their personal funds to buy twenty acres surrounding Shabbona's Grove and presented it to him as a gift.

The chief lived there until his death at the age of eighty-four, July 17, 1859, in Morris, Illinois.

Shabbona is buried at Evergreen Cemetery in Grundy County, Illinois, near Morris. A large boulder bearing his name marks his final resting place.

Shup-she-wah-no

[Ship-she-wa-non, Ship-she-wa-no, Shipshewanoe,
Shipshewana, Shuw-a-aw-no, Ship-shewanee, Ship-She-
Wahn-O, Shipshe Wano, Shep-She-Wa-No, Shuv-A-Aw-
No, Ship-She-Wah-No, Shep-Shau-Wah-No, Cup-Si-
Wah-No, Shav-C-Aw-No, Shep-She; *"Vision of a Lion"*]

Potawatomi
b. 1760? – d. 1841-1845?

Adapted from the sculpted relief on the monument at Shipshewana Lake. No authentic
image is known to exist.

"In memory of Chief Shipshewana and his band of Pottawatomie (sic) Indians removed from this reservation, Sept. 4, 1838, and escorted to Kansas by a company of soldiers. One year later the heart-broken chief was allowed to return to his old camping grounds on the banks of beautiful Shipshewana Lake where he died in 1841. Shu-she-wah-no in Indian language means 'Vision of a Lion.'"

— Inscription on a monument plaque located along the southeast shore of Shipshewana Lake, dedicated May 30, Memorial Day, 1931.

Shup-she-wah-no once dreamed that he saw an animal unlike any he had ever seen before. He described this animal as a large, tawny-colored cat-like creature, having a large head covered with long hair – a *Shup-she*, or cougar, in the Potawatomi language. For this description of his vision, he was given his name, which means "Vision of a Lion."

Shup-she-wah-no was a minor *Nashnabe*, or *Bode'wadmiyuk pasigwin* [Potawatomi chief], documented as living with his tribe in northeastern Indiana, along a lake near the Michigan-Indiana state line in present-day Lagrange County, Indiana, in 1838. Other than a few documented pieces of history - the origin of his personal name and his forced removal from his home along the Indiana lakeshore that he loved - solid facts concerning Shup-she-wah-no remain elusive.

No record of his birthplace or the date of his birth is known to exist, neither is documentation, or even stories, of his parentage, possible marriages or children, or any other facts of his early life are known to exist.

Shup-she-wah-no's name appears on the Treaty of Carey Mission, signed at St. Joseph, Michigan, September 20, 1828. The Carey Mission treaty ceded Potawatomi claims to remaining lands in the northeastern corner of Indiana. On this treaty, his name appears as "Ship-she-wa-non" and lists his residence as being at the "head of Tippecanoe," presumably the river which begins at the border between what is now Whitley and Noble counties, at a body of water now known as Crooked Lake.

His name again appears, this time as Ship-she-wa-no, on the Treaty of Tippecanoe, signed near Rochester, Indiana, in 1832. In this treaty, several prominent Potawatomi *pasigwin* were guaranteed reservations, each containing several sections of land, from the United States government. However, no mention is made in either treaty, Carey Mission or Tippecanoe, regarding any such reserve being provided for Shup-she-wah-no.

Most local historians claim that, "the old chief" and his small band of Potawatomi was one of several "scattered tribes" rounded up by Indiana militia or *shemakneshuk* [soldiers] in 1837 and forced to relocate onto a consolidated reservation in Lagrange County. The following year, Shup-she-wah-no and his family "joined" the infamous Trail of Death, a forced march from Indiana to a Kansas reservation along the Osage River. Accounts of the six hundred sixty mile journey, on which at least forty Potawatomi elders and children died, record that "Shuw-a-aw-no" was "bowed down in grief" at having to leave his Indiana home.

After just one year, according to local historical writings, the chief had grown so melancholy that he and his family were allowed to leave Kansas and return to his beloved Indiana lake country. Although differing accounts indicate he may have died in Kansas, possibly in 1845 or 1848, local tradition maintains that he died of a heart attack at his lakeside village in 1841, some two years after his return to Indiana.

Despite this local legend, documents from Washington D.C.'s National Archives reveal two letters sent from Kansas, dated November and December of 1841, signed by a chief of the same name, Shup-she-wah-no. One letter requested government funding for construction of a grain mill and additional money for improvements to existing farmland. The other letter objected to continued governmental sale of Indiana lands without the consent of all Potawatomi. These letters provide some evidence that Shup-she-wah-no actually may have lived out his life in Kansas.

Shup-she-wah-no's name also appears among the signatures on a letter dated 1843, sent by the Prairie Band of Potawatomi in Kansas to the United States Government. This communication registers a protest against land grants being given to *cmokman* [white] men married to Potawatomi women. However, this letter may have been signed by a descendent or by someone of the same name, as local Indiana legends and traditions staunchly maintain that a homesick Shup-she-wah-no came back to Indiana and died of a "broken heart" along the shores of the lake that now bears his name – Shipshewana Lake.

To add weight to this legend, several well-documented descendents of the same family, known now by the name "Ship-she," are mentioned in several Lagrange County records of the mid-1800s. One Ship-she descendant is documented as having become a federal marshal and was famous for his tracking abilities and his frequent apprehension of fugitives. Some of Shup-she-wah-no's descendants still live in and around the nearby town of Shipshewana.

Hezikiah Davis, the first American settler in the area, founded the village that was to become the town of Shipshewana in 1889. Davis, a successful farmer and businessman, arrived in Lagrange County from Ohio in 1832. After several years of financial success, he built a small rail station along the route between Sturgis, Michigan, and Lima, Ohio, known as the Lakeshore and Michigan Southern. He wanted to name the station and the adjacent three-building business district he also had built for himself - Davistown.

However, prior to the final platting, Davis' wife, Sarah Reynolds Davis, suggested the town, now located along Indiana highway 5, just north of U.S. 20, be named for "a Potawatomi Indian Chief who had befriended the early settlers." Her husband honored her wishes and Americanized the name as Shipshewana.

Historical documentation of early Shipshewana settlers' stories confirms that Shup-she-wah-no was a man of honor and *e'tokmite'k* [peace]. Shup-she-wah-no lobbied settlers against selling liquor to certain Indians, and according to many accounts, he was called upon to defuse potentially volatile confrontations between early settlers and Indians living in the area.

One early setter claimed that once a problem was brought to Shup-she-wah-no's attention, no such problem occurred again. But Shup-she-wah-no's desire for peaceful solutions may have come to him later in life.

There is no way of knowing whether or not the proud Potawatomi chief was involved in the militant Indian-American *megatkiwin* [wars] of the 1780s and 1790s, but according to one account written by Professor R. L. Case in 1931, Shup-she-wah-no, a young warrior in those days, was a likely participant.

Case depicts Shup-she-wah-no as a member of the Wabash Confederacy, also called the Miami Alliance. This coalition brought together many Algonquin-speaking tribes of the Old Northwest for the purpose of halting American incursion into Indian Territory through armed resistance. Under the command of several war chiefs, most notably, though possibly incorrectly, the Miami war chief Meshekinnoquah [*Little Turtle*], this coalition decisively defeated two numerically superior groups of American forces; one led by General Josiah Harmar in 1791 and the other under the command of General Arthur St. Clair in 1792. However, the confederacy lost a decisive battle to General Anthony Wayne at Fallen Timbers, along the Maumee River in Ohio Territory, in 1794. This defeat effectively ended the coalition.

Case writes that Shup-she-wah-no may have been present at these three battles and most likely was present at the signing of the resulting treaty of peace at Greenville [Ohio] in 1795, although his name does not appear among the Potawatomi signatures of that document.

Following the end of President Washington's Indian War in 1794, Case writes that Shup-she-wano, "now a middle aged man with a family," came to the lake country of northern Indiana to live a peaceful life; but a few years later, he was called upon by Chief Pokagon [*Rib*] to help defend Potawatomi lands against an invasion by the *Shawanoe* [Shawnees], led by Chief Elk Heart. Case writes that Shup-she-wah-no assisted Pokagon in organizing an orderly retreat, avoiding an all-out war and keeping most of northern Indiana and southern Michigan in possession of the Potawatomi.

Furthermore, Case writes that after the Shawnees were gone, leaving Shup-she-wah-no's destroyed village in their wake, the Potawatomi chief returned home and was greatly saddened by the loss of his village. Unable to eat and weakened by hunger, Shup-she-wah-no fell into a deep sleep and had the vision for which he gained the personal name by which he was known to early white settlers.

Although Shup-she-wah-no personally did not fight in the War of 1812, he sent family members and warriors to *Kithtippecanunk* [Prophetstown] to defend the center of a pan-Indian movement led by the Shawnee brothers, Tecumseh [*Panther Passing Across*] and Tenskwatawa [*The Open Door*], The Shawnee Prophet, from advancing American forces. According to Case, Shup-she-wah-no was saddened by the subsequent defeat of the Indians at the hands of American forces under Indiana Territorial Governor William Henry Harrison at the

Battle of Tippecanoe in November of 1811. It is said that when his relatives and warriors returned with wounds, and he learned some had been killed during the battle, he lost any desire to continue fighting against the overpowering advancement of American incursion.

On May 30, 1931, a day designated as "Chief Shipshewana Day," a ceremony was held along the shores of Lake Shipshewana. A monument, consisting of a large boulder, which had been moved some four miles to a site along the southeast shore of the lake, was dedicated in honor of Shup-she-wah-no. The monument, along with a sculpted profile relief and an engraved plaque, noting the local history of the chief, still stands.

Spemica Lawba
[Spencialawbe, *"High Horn"* or *"Big Horn;"* also, James or Johnny Logan, Captain Logan]

Shawnee - Creek?
b. 1774? – d. 1812

Illustration based on historic descriptions and artist's conception.
No authentic image is known to exist.

"My dear Sir: I proceed to ... give you the particulars of the death of Logan, a distinguished Shawnee chief and a nephew of Tecumseh. I was ... reading ... and all was silent and still in camp ... Suddenly, I was surprised by ... Logan's voice ... he said, "My friends, we have had a bloody battle, and I am badly wounded."... He suffered the most acute agony without a groan and calmly provided for [the] safety of his wife and children ... When it was announced that the great chief was dead, a deep gloom settled over the army, as if a dire calamity had befallen each individual officer and soldier. At the time of his death, Logan could not have been over forty years of age; perhaps he was not over thirty-five."

– From the eyewitness account of a soldier, identified only as L.C., who was present at the death of Spemica Lawba, printed in "Daily Indiana Journal," 1852.

Spemica Lawba [*High Horn*, or *Big Horn*] is better known to history by his Anglicized name of Logan. Most sources add the military title of captain, although some sources report that, despite his service to the United States Army during the War of 1812, Logan never received a military commission.

During the war, while serving as a scout and spy for General William Henry Harrison, Logan died as the result of a gunshot wound received in a firefight with a small British force near Fort Defiance [Ohio] in the fall of 1812. According to some accounts, Spemica Lawba is the only Indian during the war to have received full military honors at his burial.

Logan's physical description varies from his being extremely tall, nearly seven feet in some accounts, "with a large, barrel chest and very homely features", to his being a "splendidly formed, fine-looking fellow," about six feet tall and weighing between 240 and 250 pounds.

This descriptive confusion possibly results from differing accounts by various sources citing Spemica Lawba's adopted Christian name. He is sometimes noted as "James" Logan and sometimes as "Johnny" Logan. However, there was another noted Indian named Logan from the same area, although not from the same era or tribe.

Tachnechdorus, a Mingo [Seneca] chief also living in Ohio, also was given the Anglicized name of James Logan by a Quaker missionary of the same name--James Logan. This Logan was described as a physically large man and could have been confused with Spemica Lawba.

Also, confusion when referring to Logan could arise from another Shawnee warrior, named Captain Johnny, who was a close friend and possible relative [cousin] of Spemica Lawba. Some physical attributes from all three may have been rolled into one.

And, another of Spemica Lawba's companions possibly another cousin, was named Bright Horn, a personal name very similar to High Horn and Big Horn, the translations of Logan's Shawnee name.

Regardless of confusion over physical features and personal names, Spemica Lawba was noted among his contemporaries, Indians as well as Americans, as possessing uncommon bravery, loyalty and sense of duty.

Spemica Lawba was born in what is today designated as Logan County, Ohio, around 1774. His parents lived in a village located along the *Hathepnnithiipi* [the Mad River], near modern day Piqua. His father was a village chief named Moluntha. His mother was Tecumpease [*Crossing the Water*], also known as Grenadier Squaw, a sister of Tecumseh [*Panther Passing Across*]. Tecumpease's mother possibly may have been Shawnee, Creek or possibly Cherokee.

In 1786 when Spemica Lawba was about twelve years old, a party of Kentucky militia, seeking retaliation for Indian attacks against American settlements south of the *Pelewathiipi* or *Spaylaywithiipi* [the Ohio River], raided several Ohio Shawnee towns, known as the Macochee Towns. Spemica Lawba's village was one of the Macochee Towns attacked and burned during this retaliatory expedition. Most inhabitants of Spemica Lawba's village were killed or captured. Some managed to escape into the surrounding woods.

While searching the woods for survivors, the militia's leader, Colonel Benjamin Logan, and some of his men were "ambushed" by arrows fired from the underbrush. Charging their hidden attacker, the mounted militiamen found the village's only remaining defender - a young Spemica Lawba.

Colonel Logan was so impressed by the Shawnee boy's bravery and sense of honor that the Kentucky officer took Spemica Lawba into his home and reared him as his own son. Some years later, he "gave [Spemica Lawba] his name of Logan." Some accounts say the militia commander endowed his newly adopted son the first name of James, others say he was christened as John. To further add confusion to Spemica Lawba's anglicized name, some accounts also note his adopted father as "General James" Logan, others as "Colonel Benjamin" Logan.

Named either James or John, the young Logan adapted well to Anglo-American life. Living with the Logan family in Kentucky over the next several years, Logan learned to speak fluent English and studied a variety of subjects. A few years later, as part of an exchange of American and Indian prisoners, he was returned to the Shawnee in Ohio. At some point, either prior to the exchange or possibly after, he married a young woman named *Pskipahcah Ouiskelotha*, or Blue Bird. Blue Bird, like Logan, was a Shawnee, captured during the Macochee Town raids and reared in an American home.

Blue Bird had lived with one of Colonel Logan's neighbors, a fellow militia commander named Colonel John Hardin. She was also returned to her native home in Ohio around the same time as Spemica Lawba and lived with him as his wife until his death. Together they had at least three children.

After his release, Spemica Lawba reoriented easily into the Shawnee way of life. Despite his Anglo-American upbringing, his formal education and his avowed loyalty to his adopted family, he quickly gained the trust and respect of the Shawnee.

Adept at languages, Spemica Lawba learned the tongues of all the neighboring Algonquin-speaking tribes. Given his mastery of dialects and his equal fluency in English, the United States Army hired Logan as a mediator, interpreter, scout and spy. He served with the American forces against his own people.

Although some sources adamantly maintain Logan never held the rank of captain, or any rank at all, most historic sources have Logan receiving honorary rank and commonly refer to him as "Captain" Logan. Regardless, his notation on the payroll of the Americans did not go unnoticed by his uncles, Tecumseh and Tenskwatawa [*The Open Door*], The Shawnee Prophet, leaders of the anti-American, pan-tribal movement, or their followers and supporters.

In the days leading up to the War of 1812, Logan tried in vain to persuade Tecumseh and The Prophet to desert their British allies, give up their pan-tribal resistance movement and join the Americans. Following The Prophet's defeat by American forces, led by Indiana Territorial Governor William Henry Harrison, at the 1811 Battle of Tippecanoe, "Captain" Logan's adamant pro-American political stance – and his service to Harrison – increased his fervor of his detractors among the loyal remnants of Tecumseh's pan-tribal movement. Both his uncles, along with their militant ally and disciple, Potawatomi war chief Winamac [*Catfish*], became avowed enemies of the traitorous Spemica Lawba.

By the beginning of the war, Harrison had resigned his governor's office for a general commission in the American army. General Harrison considered Logan, along with Miami adoptee, Apekonit [*Carrot*, or William Wells], among his most trusted and active scouts. Both served together at the American outpost of Fort Wayne [Indiana], the fort constructed at the confluence of the St. Mary's, St. Joseph and Maumee rivers in northeastern Indiana Territory following the 1794 Indian defeat at the Battle of Fallen Timbers near present-day Toledo, Ohio.

Despite Harrison's trust and confidence in Logan, the Shawnee scout came under scrutiny from a few of General Harrison's officers. Logan, along with his cousins, Captain Johnny and Wautheeweela [*Bright Horn*], were sent on a spying mission along the *Hotaawathiipi* [Maumee River] in an attempt to determine if British military strength at Fort Miamis at the Rapids of the Maumee could threaten Fort Wayne. The reconnaissance mission failed when a "superior force" of British regulars and Indian allies discovered the three American scouts.

British forces pursued Logan, Captain Johnny and Bright Horn back to the fort. Afterward, some of Harrison's officers muttered among themselves that Logan and his Shawnee friends most likely had not only exaggerated the story of their near capture, but probably had voluntarily provided information to the British regarding American positions and numbers. To allay these suspicions, Logan volunteered for a second – and his last - dangerous mission.

Offended by these challenges to his credibility, Logan vowed that he would return with a prisoner or a scalp, or he would die in the attempt.

Logan, Captain Johnny and Bright Horn, left Fort Wayne for Fort Miamis a second time in November of 1812.

To avoid detection, the trio of American spies followed a little-traveled trail through *miskekopke* [low, swampy ground]. On November 22, while taking a mid-day rest, they were surprised by an armed group of mounted men headed along the same trail, but going in the opposite direction.

The group was made up of five British-allied Potawatomi, an Ottawa chief's son under the command of a British metis [mixed Indian and white] officer, Captain Matthew Elliott. This chance encounter immediately put Logan's life in danger.

Some accounts claim the British had offered as much as one hundred fifty dollars for Logan's scalp. And, among the Potawatomi under Elliott's command was Logan's avowed enemy, the militant war chief Winamac.

Winamac, reportedly one of the leaders of Indian forces during the failed Battle of Tippecanoe, had vowed to kill the traitor Logan on sight; now it seemed he had his chance. The two enemies recognized each other immediately. Logan, realizing he could not out run the mounted patrol during an escape attempt, used his wits.

Instead of standing to fight or attempting to flee, Logan and his outgunned and out-manned comrades advanced toward the mounted column with smiles on their faces and waving their hands in the air. Logan spoke in English with the British officer, explaining to Elliott as sincerely as possible that he and his friends had deserted the Americans and were now on their way to join British forces.

Logan's feigned sincerity convinced the British captain of his intentions, but not Winamac. Winamac argued that Logan was an American spy and should be killed immediately, but he could not sway Elliott. Elliott told Winamac that, if the prisoners tried to run, they would be shot or rundown by the horses; however, as a precaution, he did allow Winamac to seize their weapons. Now unarmed, the trio of American spies was forced to walk among the horses as the entire entourage headed back to British-held Fort Miamis.

According to Logan's contemporary, Kentucky militiaman and historian Robert McAfee, Logan's continuing friendly demeanor finally convinced Elliott there was no danger to come from the trio of spies.

He ordered their weapons returned to them; although other accounts say that Logan and his two companions were only able retrieve their weapons by stealth when the party stopped to rest.

Logan, McAfee writes, had planned to make his escape after the group stopped to camp that evening. But now, with their weapons returned, Logan decided an escape attempt should come as soon as possible. According to McAfee's account, written in 1815, Logan signaled his companions as to his intentions, then suddenly turned and shot Winamac, killing him instantly; a later account claims that it was Captain Johnny who killed Winamac in the ensuing gunfight.

Outnumbered two to one, Logan, Captain Johnny and Bright Horn continued firing at their captors. Running and reloading with bullets they had concealed in their mouths, the trio of American spies ducked behind trees and kept up the intense firefight. In the second volley, the British officer and the Ottawa were killed. In the course of the skirmish, all the remaining members of the British party were killed or wounded or had escaped into the woods. Although now free of their captors, their daring escape had not left the American spies unscathed; both Logan and Bright Horn had been wounded.

Bright Horn had been shot in the leg, but Logan was hit just "below the breastbone." Bright Horn would recover; Logan's wound would prove fatal.

Captain Johnny, who escaped the battle uninjured, rounded up two British horses, strapped Logan to one and helped Bright Horn mount the other. Logan and Bright Horn rode away while Captain Johnny stayed behind to act as a rear guard - and to take the scalp Logan had promised to deliver upon on his return.

It took nearly four hours for Logan and Bright Horn to ride the twenty miles to Fort Winchester, the former site of Fort Defiance [Ohio]. Captain Johnny arrived at the fort early the next morning carrying a scalp, which satisfied Logan's vow to the Americans. Whether the scalp belonged to Winamac or to the young Ottawa chief also remains a matter of conflicting historical accounts.

Logan had been bent over when struck by the British ball. The ball had entered his lower chest and passed downward, traversing entirely through his midsection, eventually lodging against his spine. The outline of the ball was visible through the skin on his back and was easily removed; but despite surgery and subsequent medical attention, a stoic Captain Logan died two days later, November 24, 1812.

By all accounts, Logan accepted his suffering and imminent death with resolve and without complaint. Before he died, he requested that all money due him from his army service be paid to his family, and that the Americans escort his wife, Blue Bird, and his children to Kentucky. It was his hope that his family could live in safety with Colonel Hardin, Blue Bird's adopted American family. There they could escape any possible retaliatory vengeance from the clansmen and relatives of the enemies he had killed. Logan also requested his children be reared with all the educational advantages he had been given.

Although Hardin was willing to honor the scout's request, Logan's wife was not. Despite her husband's request, Blue Bird and her children continued to live Indian lives. She refused to leave Ohio and remained among the Shawnee until she and Logan's children were forced west of the Mississippi River during Indian removal and lived among the Shawnee in what is now the State of Missouri. Eventually, they would settle on a reservation in Kansas.

According to most accounts, Captain Logan was accorded full military honors in a ceremony at Fort Wayne – the only Indian of that time to be so honored. Following that ceremony, his remains were transported some sixty miles by sled over snowy ground and buried near the site of the old fort at Defiance, located at the confluence of the Auglaize and Maumee rivers. But, in this account, Defiance was not his final resting place.

Reportedly, Logan's body was later disinterred and moved to his former village at Wapakoneta, Ohio, the home of his son, Aqueshka, and his daughter, Cageshe. Two large boulders, one at his head with the simple inscription, *Captain John Logan,* and another at his feet, mark his original burial site at Fort Defiance.

However, other accounts say that no such military ceremony took place. Instead these accounts maintain that Captain Johnny and Bright Horn took Logan's body directly to Wapakoneta, where he was honored and buried according to Indian tradition.

Logan's name is remembered through several townships, counties and towns in Ohio and Indiana. The City of Logansport, Indiana, located at the confluence of the Eel and Wabash rivers, was named in his honor in 1828 after Colonel John B. Duret used his muzzleloader to win a shooting contest and the right to name the community. The community agreed with the name Duret chose, providing that no apostrophe be used and the two words, Logan(s) and port, were combined into one.

Tecumseh

[Tecumthe, Tecumtha, Tecompse; *"Panther Passing Across," "The Panther", "He Moves From One Place to Another," "Goes Through One Place to Another," "The Shooting Star"*]

Shawnee – Creek? – Cherokee?
b. 1768? – d. 1813

Adapted from a pencil sketch by Pierre Le Dru, Vincennes, Indiana, the only known authentic likeness, dated 1808.

"Brothers – We all belong to one family, we are children of the Great Spirit; walk on the same path; slake our thirst at the same spring; Brothers – We are friends; we must assist each other to bear our burdens. The blood of many of our fathers and brothers has run like water on the ground to satisfy the avarice of the white man. We, ourselves, are threatened with a great evil; nothing will pacify them but the destruction of all red men. Brothers we must be united; we must smoke the same pipe; we must fight each others' battles; and more than all, we must love the Great Spirit; he is for us; he will destroy our enemies, and make his red children happy."
 – *Tecumseh, excerpted from a speech to the Osage, 1809.*

"I am a Shawnee. My forefathers were warriors. Their son is a warrior. From them I take only my existence. From my tribe I take nothing. I have made myself what I am. And I would that I could make the red people as great as the conceptions of my mind, when I think of the Great Spirit that rules over all. I would not then come to Governor Harrison to ask him to tear the treaty. But I would say to him, 'Brother, you have liberty to return to your own country'."
 – *Tecumseh, from an address to Indiana Territorial Governor William Henry Harrison at Vincennes, 1810.*

"The way, the only way to stop this evil, is for all the red men to unite in claiming a common equal right in the land, as it was at first, and should be now – for it never was divided, but belongs to all. No tribe has a right to sell, even to each other, much less to strangers, who demand all, and will take no less ... Sell a country? Why not sell the air, the clouds, the great sea, as well as the earth. How can we have confidence in the White people? When Jesus Christ came upon the earth you killed Him and nailed him to a cross."
 – *Tecumseh, from an address to Indiana Territorial Governor William Henry Harrison at Vincennes, 1810.*

"Brother, I wish you to listen to me well. As I think you do not clearly understand what I before said to you. I will explain it again. Since the peace [Treaty of Greenville in 1795] was made the white people have killed some of the Shawnee, Winnebagos, Delawares and Miamis, and you have taken our land from us and I do not see how we can remain at peace with you if you continue to do so. You try to force the red people to do some injury. It is you that are pushing them on to do mischief. You endeavor to make distinction. You wish to prevent the Indian to do as we wish then, to unite, and let them consider their lands as the common property of the whole."

— Tecumseh, from a speech addressed to Territorial Governor William Henry Harrison at Vincennes [Fort Knox], August 20, 1810.

"... But what need is there to speak of the past? It speaks for itself and asks, 'Where today is the Pequot? Where the Narragansetts, the Mohawks, Pocanokets, and many other once powerful tribes of our race?' They have vanished before the avarice and oppression of the white men, as snow before a summer sun ... So it will be with you Choctaws and Chickasaws! Soon your mighty forest trees under the shade of whose wide spreading branches you have played in infancy, sported in boyhood and now rest your wearied limbs after the fatigue of the chase, will be cut down to fence in the land which the white intruders dare to call their own. Soon their broad roads will pass over the graves of your fathers, and the place of their rest will be blotted out forever. The annihilation of our race is at hand unless we unite in one common cause against the common foe. Think not, brave Choctaws and Chickasaws, that you can remain passive and indifferent to the common danger, and thus escape the common fate. Your people, too, will be driven away from your native land and ancient domains as leaves are driven before the wintry storms."

— Tecumseh, from his plea to the Choctaws and Chickasaws to join the pan-tribal movement, 1811.

"At the battle of the [Maumee] Rapids in the last war, the Americans certainly defeated us; and when we retreated to our father's fort [Miami] at that place the gates were shut against us. We were afraid that it would now be the case; but instead of that, we now see our British father preparing to march out of his garrison. Father you have got the arms and ammunition, which our great father sent for his red children. If you have an idea of going away, give them to us, and you may go and welcome for us. Our lives are in the hands of the Great Spirit. We are determined to defend our lands, and if it be his will, we wish to leave our bones upon them."

> – *Tecumseh, speaking to British General Henry Proctor prior to the Battle of Amherstburg Ontario Canada, 1812.*

Tecumseh [*Panther Passing Across*], in less than two decades, rose from relative obscurity to become the most legendary Indian figure in the Old Northwest Territory.

In the aftermath of the Little Turtle War [1790-1794] of armed Indian resistance against American expansionism, between the signing of the Greenville Treaty of 1795, which Tecumseh refused to sign, and his heroic death at the Battle of Thames in 1813, the politically oriented Tecumseh, along with his spiritually reawakened brother Tenskwatawa [*The Open Door*], called The Shawnee Prophet by Americans, stood at the center of a pan-tribal coalition, designed to stop American expansionism and keep lands east of the Allegheny Mountains in the common possession of all Indians. Tecumseh saw himself first as an Indian and only secondly as a tribal member.

Drawn by Tecumseh's message of common land ownership and the strength to be found in Indian unity, coupled with The Prophet's message of spirituality, Indian converts, ranging from the Allegheny Mountains to the trans-Mississippi west, from the Gulf of Mexico and as far north as Canada, joined the brothers' pan-Indian movement. The movement's physical center culminated in northern Indiana between 1809 and 1811, near the confluence of the Tippecanoe and Wabash rivers in a village that became known to the Americans as Prophetstown.

Tecumseh was born in 1768 at a *Shawanoe* [Southerners, or Shawnee] village along the *Hathepnnithiipi* [Mad River] in *Speh-leh-weh-sepe* [what is now Clark County, Ohio], near *Piquea* [*Men Rise From the Ashes*, also called Oldtown, or Old Piqua].

Tecumseh's father, Pucksinwah [also, Puckeshinwa, or Pukeesheno, *Hard Striker*], maintain that Tecumseh's mother, Methoataske [also written as Meetheetashe, *A Turtle Laying Eggs in Sand*], was of Creek or possibly Cherokee descent, perhaps a mixture of both. Pucksinwah and Methoataske had eight children, seven sons, including a set of triplets, and one daughter, Tecumpease [*Sky Watcher*, sometimes translated as *Crossing the Water*].

Legend holds that, on the night of Tecumseh's birth, Pucksinwah saw a comet pass through the sky. In honor of that event, Puckinswah named his second male child Tecumseh [more properly, Tecumthe], meaning "Panther Passing Across", also translated as "The Shooting Star."

According to Shawnee tradition, a comet passing through the sky signified that a child born under that sign would become a great leader. In Tecumseh's case, the tradition proved true.

Most accounts relate that Pucksinwah was killed in 1774, just prior to the American Revolution. His death came during the Battle of Point Pleasant, fought along the *Pelewathiipi* [Ohio River], in what is now the State of West Virginia, just prior to the American Revolution. The battle was one in a series of territorial border conflicts between the British colony of Virginia and Indians living in the Ohio Territory. This series of conflicts is known as Lord Dunmore's War, named after the governor of the Virginia Colony.

However, at least one writer maintains that Pucksinwah was "murdered in cold blood," by Ohio settlers. According to this second account, Tecumseh saw his murdered father's body and vowed revenge against all Americans.

Regardless of the circumstances, following Pucksinwah's death, Methoatakse left her eight children in the care of the Shawnee village and, according to differing accounts, either returned south to her original homeland or moved west of the Mississippi River and lived among the Shawnee in what is now the State of Missouri.

Methoatakse's departure left Tecumseh's older brother, Chicksika [also, Cheeseekau, *Chickasaw man*], to provide for his younger siblings. Chicksika had succeeded his father as war chief, and Tecumseh became

Chicksika's student. From the age of six years old, under Chicksika's tutelage, Tecumseh, said to have a natural aptitude for the tools of war excelled in learning the hunting and military tactics of the Shawnee. The two brothers traveled often together, visiting neighboring villages and various other tribes living in Indian Territory.

Some accounts add that Tecumseh also attended missionary school and learned to read and speak English very well. He studied world history, literature, and also studied the Christian Bible, which is said to been given to him by a teacher, Rebecca Galloway. Some accounts add that, at one time, he was engaged to marry an American girl, perhaps Galloway herself.

Several life events turned Tecumseh away from American civilization. Not only did he lose his father early in life, but he also lost two other father figures to *shemanese* [white men] violence. Chicksika was killed during the American Revolution, fighting for the British. And, in 1777, Cornstalk, the peace-seeking Shawnee chief and another of Tecumseh's mentors and possibly his uncle, was assassinated by Americans settlers after being lured into a council of peace.

Cornstalk's killing was followed by a war of retaliation against American settlements in Kentucky and Virginia. Some accounts say that, in 1780, a 12-year-old Tecumseh took an active part in these raids. Although in later years Tecumseh became known as a great warrior, it is said that during his first battle, he became frightened and ran away. These accounts say he was so ashamed that he vowed such an act would never happen again. True to his word, his courage in later battles – and his skills as a hunter - were often noted.

In adulthood, Tecumseh was described physically as being "finely proportioned" and as having a "regal bearing." Depending on accounts, Tecumseh's height was between "five feet nine or ten inches" to "about" six feet to "six feet-two inches." He is said to have been lightly complexioned with "bright hazel eyes." Some ethnically insensitive accounts say that he "could have passed for *waapa* [white], if he had not worn traditional Shawnee garb." Some historical accounts add that his face was "slightly pock marked;" others claim that during a buffalo hunt during his youth, he fell from his horse, breaking a leg, possibly both. This accident caused him to fear his days as a warrior were over, but he recovered from the fall. Although one of his legs reportedly remained shorter than the other, historical accounts make no mention of any sort of irregularity in his walk.

Tecumseh married twice, once to a metis [half-French, half-Indian] woman named, Mohnetohse. Mohnetohse was neglectful of Tecumseh's first-born son, Adjala, also called Mahyawwekawpawe, so he sent her home to her people; his sister, Tecumpease, took over the role of Adjala's mother.

Tecumseh's second wife was a Shawnee woman named Manete, also spelled Mamate or Namate [*White Wing*]. She died in 1792, while giving birth to Naythawaynah [*A Panther Seizing Its Prey*], also known as Pugeshashenwa, his second son. These half-brothers appear to be Tecumseh's only known children.

After the American Revolutionary War, Tecumseh was known to be present with the forces of the Wabash or Miami Confederacy, a successful military coalition of Algonquin-speaking tribes, during several battles against American forces between 1790 and 1794.

Because he was considered too young to take a leadership role, Tecumseh acted as an advance scout during the defeat of American general Josiah Harmar's troops in 1791. A year later, in 1792, he took part in the charge against Northwest Territorial Governor General Arthur St. Clair's troops in the worst recorded American defeat by Indian forces. These lessons in the success of Indian unity would not be forgotten.

Tecumseh also served as a *nenothtu* [warrior] under Shawnee war chief Weyapiersenwah [*Whirlpool*, or Blue Jacket] during the Battle of Fallen Timbers near modern-day Toledo, Ohio, in 1794. The resulting Indian defeat by General Anthony Wayne in that battle effectively ended the Wabash Confederacy.

Although Tecumseh developed a reputation as a *psaiwinenothtu* [great warrior], a fierce fighter and, later an *okema* [leader] in battle, following the dissolution of the Wabash Confederacy, he would become better known as a skillful orator, organizer and leader of the pan-tribal movement – and a humanitarian.

Tecumseh's intense hatred of American encroachment onto Indian lands is well documented; however as a leader, he did not tolerate traditional Indian methods of torture, such as burning at the stake. Not only did he refrain from these practices, he discouraged other

Indians from these practices as well. He reportedly treated all captives humanely, Indian or white, and later denounced the ritualistic killing of Indians accused of witchcraft by his brother, The Shawnee Prophet.

After the defeat of the Wabash Confederation at Fallen Timbers, Tecumseh refused to sign the 1795 Treaty of Greenville [Ohio]. This treaty ceded millions of acres of Indian land in most of what would become southern Ohio Territory, and southeastern Indiana Territory. It also established a new western boundary for the fledgling United States. Starting from the treaty site at Greenville, east to the Tuscarawas River and southeast to the Ohio River, this line, known as the Greenville Treaty Line, "guaranteed" Indian sovereignty in all lands to the west.

Following this treaty signing, Tecumseh became a vocal critic of all land sales by individual tribes. He insisted that all Indian land belonged to all tribes in common and declared any cessions or sales by individual tribes or tribal leaders to be invalid. With a few followers faithful to his pan-tribal message, including his younger brother Lalawethika [*He Makes A Loud Noise,* or *The Rattle*], he moved his village to the banks of Deer Creek in the Ohio country; but, over the next several years, few Shawnee expressed interest in Tecumseh's pan-tribal movement.

To be farther away from advancing American settlements, in 1797, Tecumseh and Lalawethika removed from the Deer Creek village. They settled along the banks of the Whitewater River, just west of the Greenville Treaty Line, near present-day Brookville, Indiana, in the area still known as Indian Territory.

Lalawethika was an inept warrior and hunter. Known as a drunkard and braggart, he was dependent on Tecumseh's hunting skills to feed his family. While the brothers and a few followers were living along the Whitewater, according to some accounts, they were visited by the prominent Delaware war chief Buckongahelas [*Breaker to Pieces*]. Buckongahelas, curious about Tecumseh's pan-tribal philosophy, invited the Shawnee brothers to move to his village along the *Wapahani* [West Fork White River].

Buckongahelas had been an active member in the now-disbanded Wabash Confederacy and had heard of Tecumseh's pan-tribal teachings. He may have invited the Shawnee brothers to join the Delaware living near modern-day Muncie, Indiana. Regardless, by 1805, Tecumseh and Lalawethika were living among the Delaware, although Tecumseh was often absent from Buckongahela's village on treks into the Ohio country.

At sometime during one of Tecumseh's absences, Lalawethika went into a coma so deep he was thought dead. He awakened with a spiritual message. Now calling himself Tenskwatawa, "*The Open Door to the Mystery of Life*," he began preaching a revival of traditional Indian ways. Like other Indian prophets before him, he preached that Indian salvation would come only through rejection of all things Euro-American – especially consumption of spirituous liquor – and a return to observance of traditional rituals and frequent prayers to The Great Spirit.

Tecumseh agreed with his brother's spiritual teachings, but his message was more political in nature. Espousing the principal that all Indians owned their lands jointly and that no single tribe or leader had the right to transfer possession of land without approval from all tribes, he began in earnest to urge all the tribes in the Great Lakes to unite.

Tecumseh also traveled among or sent messengers to tribes along the Mississippi River and as far south as the Gulf of Mexico. Over the next several years, the two brothers created the spiritual and political pan-tribal resistance movement that Tecumseh had been seeking.

Often using a bundle of green twigs as a visual example, Tecumseh demonstrated that strength lies in unity, that individual tribes, acting alone like a single stick, could easily be broken. As individuals, Indians could be pushed easily from their traditional homelands by the advancing whites into unknown lands west of the Mississippi. However, by joining together in a show of unity, the American usurpers could be defeated and driven out of Indian Territory, back across the Ohio River and Appalachian Mountains to the lands in the East.

At Buckongahela's Delaware village, the Shawnee brothers were, at first, well received. But eventually Tenskwatawa's message found few disciples among the Delaware. Now known as The Shawnee Prophet, his accusations of witchcraft among the Delaware, followed by several executions, aroused suspicions of his true intentions. Gradually, The Prophet's message became more political. As Tecumseh's leadership role in the pan-tribal political movement increased, so did the number of followers.

In 1807, the brothers moved back to Ohio, settling once again near Greenville. Tenskwatawa's spiritual preaching and Tecumseh's pan-Indian message attracted hundreds of visitors and devotees from many tribes. Many of these visitors became disciples of The Prophet and also allies of Tecumseh's confederation. As the population at their village grew – and the message of Indian unity continued to spread – the presence of so many Indians became a perceived threat to newly established American settlements in the area. Wary settlers petitioned the State of Ohio's government to remove the brothers.

In the spring of 1808, Tecumseh and his brother, with about sixty followers and permission from allied tribes, moved to a large prairie clearing [Kithtippecanunk] at the confluence of the Tippecanoe and Wabash rivers in northern Indiana. Outside the boundary of the newly formed state of Ohio and above the Indiana treaty lines of 1803 and 1805, the location was within an ever-shrinking Indian Territory. This new settlement near modern-day Lafayette, Indiana, became known among American settlers as Prophetstown.

Prophetstown continued to swell with new disciples and eventually stretched several miles along the banks of the Tippecanoe and Wabash rivers. Some population estimates were as high as three thousand, while other estimates put the number of residents considerably lower, perhaps as few as six hundred fifty.

Regardless of the exact numbers, just as in Ohio, settlers in the Indiana Territory, which at the time included what would become the states of Illinois and Wisconsin, viewed the concentrated settlement of so many warriors and their families as a threat to peace. Settlers took their concerns to Indiana Territorial Governor William Henry Harrison.

Harrison, after speaking briefly with The Shawnee Prophet at Vincennes early in the summer of 1809, invited the Indian mystic for a second visit to the territorial capitol the following year. But instead, it was Tecumseh and a large delegation that appeared to address the governor's concerns. The arrival of Tecumseh and nearly one hundred warriors made the citizens of Vincennes nervous; uneasiness on the American frontier grew. Verbal "parlays" between the Shawnee leaders and Harrison continued over the next two years.

During one of these meetings, Tecumseh, a master of example, sat next to Harrison on a bench. Tecumseh, angry over the land cession treaty that had been signed at Fort Wayne earlier that year, kept moving closer to Harrison as the two leaders spoke. Eventually the governor was forced to the end of the bench. When Harrison complained that he had no place left to sit, Tecumseh told him that he now knew "how the Indian feels."

Unlike the Prophet who professed all intentions regarding Americans as "peaceful," Tecumseh warned Harrison that violence was inevitable if settlers continued to encroach into Indian Territory. To increase the growing tension even more, Tecumseh told Harrison that he planned to kill any or all of the chiefs whom he felt had been swindled into signing the Fort Wayne Treaty and ceding rights to central Indiana lands in which they had no legal claim.

During another meeting, Harrison, seated on his veranda at his Grouseland mansion, offered Tecumseh a chair. Tecumseh refused the chair offered him by Harrison. He told the governor that "the sun is my father, and the earth is my mother. I shall repose upon her bosom."

While Harrison remained on his veranda with several soldiers standing guard, Tecumseh sat on the lawn, surrounded by a few warriors, and the conference continued.

Their third and final meeting between the two leaders came in that late summer of 1811. This council became the most heated of the three and nearly ended in violence. Tecumseh, who had arrived with some three hundred warriors, once again accused Harrison of swindling Indians out their lands. After an exchange of angry words, Tecumseh drew his tomahawk and Harrison began to unsheathe his sword. Fortunately, cooler heads prevailed and violence was averted.

After calming down, Tecumseh requested the meeting continue the following day. Harrison accepted, but went to meet Tecumseh accompanied by several regular army troops as well as a company of armed Indiana militiamen. Although the meeting was affable, once again, the two leaders could reach no peaceful solution.

After this final meeting, Tecumseh left on a proselytizing journey among several southern tribes. Often he sent messengers to spread his philosophy of a single Indian nation, but this time he went in person, hoping to attract additional supporters from among the Chickasaw,

Creek and Cherokee nations. Although some southern tribal leaders rebuffed Tecumseh's message, others, especially Creek leaders, joined the movement. Meanwhile back at Prophetstown, Tecumseh's confederacy was being threatened.

Harrison, taking advantage of Tecumseh's absence, marched against Prophetstown with an army totaling some twelve hundred regulars and militiamen in October of 1811. Despite strict orders from Tecumseh to avoid any type of confrontation until the confederacy was more solidified, a militant faction within Prophetstown – perhaps influenced by British agents - convinced The Prophet to attack the American encampment in an early morning raid.

Although The Prophet boldly predicted that "American bullets would be as rain" and Indian victory was inevitable, the attack was thwarted. Harrison and his *shemeganana* [soldiers] defeated the Indians during the bloody, early morning skirmish that became known as the Battle of *Kithtippecanunk* [Tippecanoe]. Afterwards, a victorious Harrison ordered the burning of a deserted Prophetstown, including all winter stores of food and grain.

On his return, Tecumseh found only a few faithful followers remaining at the village; Prophetstown was in ruins and his confederacy weakened. Disappointed and angry, Tecumseh blamed Tenskwatawa. Renewed efforts to unite members of the various tribes that formerly populated Prophetstown found little success. After an unsuccessful council to rally additional support was held along the *Nimacihsinwi Siipiiwi* [Mississinewa River], near current day Peru, Indiana, Tecumseh, along with his loyal comrades, joined with British forces during the War of 1812.

Even after the defeat at Tippecanoe, Tecumseh was still able to assemble more than two thousand Indian warriors and lead them against the Americans. During the first months of the war, Tecumseh, along with his Indian and British allies, was successful.

Tecumseh helped his friend, British General Isaac Brock, take the fort at Detroit; and he was instrumental in the victory over American forces at Maguaga, a Wyandot village near modern-day Trenton, Michigan. Despite his leadership abilities and the claims of many historians, Tecumseh was never officially commissioned into the British Army. For his role in the Battle of Maguaga, he was given a brigadier general's uniform, promised a general's pay and given command of an allied force of Indians and British sympathizers. Still, it wasn't long until the successes the early Indian-British coalition faded.

When Brock, Tecumseh's commanding officer and close friend, was killed at the Battle of Maguaga, British command was conferred on General Henry Proctor. Proctor, an inexperienced field officer, was neither liked nor respected by his troops. And, Proctor, unlike Brock and Tecumseh, allowed captives to be tortured and killed, acts that enraged both Tecumseh and the approaching American troops.

In May of 1813, Tecumseh led a large force of Indians in the siege of Fort Meigs along the Maumee River in northern Ohio. He nearly captured the fort, but Proctor did not provide the support the Indians needed; the British retreated from the field instead. The Shawnee leader and his men followed Proctor and covered his retreat east into Canada. Tecumseh and his men held off a superior force of thirty five hundred American troops commanded by Harrison, who had become commander of the American army after resigning his territorial governorship.

Once deep into Ontario, Canada, Tecumseh refused to retreat any farther. Near the Thames River, October 5, 1813, in what is known as the Battle of Thames or Battle of Moraviantown, Tecumseh urged Proctor to stand and fight as they held the higher ground away from the river. However, Proctor's inexperience or incompetence led to a poor deployment of his troops. Forced into fighting from a bad logistical location and faced with superior numbers, Proctor fled before the advancing American forces.

Without British soldiers to hold their flanks, Tecumseh and his small force were quickly overrun by Harrison's militia, which actually contained a greater number of Shawnee warriors than did Tecumseh's contingent. During the battle, Tecumseh, who earlier had a premonition of his impending death, was killed.

Some forty-five conflicting stories surround his death.

According to the Potawatomi chief, Shabbona [*Built Like a Bear*], who claimed to be Tecumseh's second-in-command and was near him on the battlefield, *"[Tecumseh] engaged with a foot soldier; the soldier having run his bayonet through Tecumseh's leather coat near the hips, and the latter [was] trying to disengage himself from the bayonet with his sabre in his hand when a horseman rode up and shot him [Tecumseh] through the head."*

Shabbona would later say that the man he saw shoot Tecumseh was a Kentucky militia colonel named Richard Mentor Johnson. Johnson rode a white horse with black markings into battle that day, the same type of horse described later by Shabbona. The colonel suffered several wounds during the battle, including a crippling one to his left hand, which was supposedly shattered by a ball from Tecumseh's rifle. By 1836, the Kentuckian had ridden the fame of being Tecumseh's killer into a United States Senate seat and later, in 1840, the vice-presidency of the United States. An aging Shabbona "positively" identified Johnson after being introduced to the senator, thereby confirming Johnson's "claim to fame."

Although Johnson had no problem in claiming that he had killed Tecumseh, his account of the action differed significantly from Shabbona's – and sometimes from his own. According to Johnson, Tecumseh's death came in at least two versions.

In one version, Johnson claimed that Tecumseh had shot his horse from under him, pinning him underneath. As Tecumseh rushed forward with a tomahawk to finish him, Johnson pulled a pistol loaded with "a ball and three buckshot" from a saddle holster and shot Tecumseh in the head.

In another account, after shooting Tecumseh from atop his mount that had been wounded seven times, Johnson rode the horse back to headquarters before it collapsed. In this version, Johnson claimed to have shot Tecumseh squarely in the chest.

However, in a letter published in the Louisville [Kentucky] Journal in October of 1859, another officer present at the Battle of Moraviantown, Captain James Davidson, refutes the Johnson and Shabbona stories.

In what is sometimes thought to be the most accurate and complete accounting of Tecumseh's death, Captain Davidson writes that he was present at the battle and saw Col. Johnson leave the field early in the battle after being badly wounded, adding that none of Johnson's pistols were fired that day. Although Johnson "was one of the bravest men I ever saw," Davidson concludes that Tecumseh was actually killed "by an old Indian fighter named Col. Whitley."

There are many other American accounts of Tecumseh's death, and Shabbona's is not the only Indian account. Several of Tecumseh's followers claimed to have been with him when the Shawnee leader fell.

One of those was the Sac war chief, Black Sparrow Hawk, who some twenty years later would lead his own insurgency against the United States. In his autobiography, Black Sparrow Hawk claimed to be protecting Tecumseh's right flank, but most historians agree that Black Sparrow Hawk, although a veteran of the 1812 war, was not present during the Battle of Moraviantown.

Other Tecumseh followers at Moraviantown, including Saganash, or Billy Caldwell, and Naiwash, related that their leader was wounded and eventually expired while urging his men into the fight. Still other accounts claim that, after being wounded,

Tecumseh requested to be left behind with a loaded pistol to end his own life. At least one account offers the notion that Tecumseh's fatal wound came from behind, the result of "friendly fire."

Regardless of how Tecumseh died, after he fell, most of the Indians quickly fled the battlefield. If they carried their leader off the field immediately or came back later – or at all – also invites historical investigation. Some accounts "positively" identify his body; others fail to.

If any Americans should have been able to recognize Tecumseh, it was Harrison. The two leaders had met face to face for long periods of time on several occasions. But on the battlefield, Harrison was reluctant to positively identify any of the fallen Indian bodies as Tecumseh; and, Harrison omitted any mention of the renowned Shawnee leader's death from his official reports.

Several other Americans present during the battle also were familiar with Tecumseh, including frontiersman Simon Kenton and interpreter Anthony Shane, a young man held prisoner in Tecumseh's village for several years. They, too, had trouble making positive identification. Several Indian veterans claimed another Shawnee resembling Tecumseh, possibly Tecumseh's brother-in-law, had fallen near where Tecumseh was fighting, causing a case of mistaken identity.

Others claimed that wounds to Tecumseh's head made it too difficult to make a positive identification – if his body was there at all. Some of Tecumseh's followers claim to have carried him from the battlefield before the Americans could mutilate him. Others said that they had returned the following day to find his body totally stripped, scalped and skinned.

For many years, another Kentucky senator and vice-president, Henry Clay, a veteran of the battle, would display a razor strop, which he claimed to have made of skin cut from Tecumseh's back.

Whether his body was carried off the battlefield by his loyal followers and buried secretly is still a topic of debate. For a time, rumors circulated that Tecumseh was still alive; while several others claimed to know the location, or locations, where the Shawnee leader's body had been buried.

Some accounts say Tecumseh was buried on or near the battlefield, between two trees, or by a log, or near a stump painted with an Indian totem. Other versions claim he was taken behind Indian lines and ritualistically buried later. Other accounts claim his bones were hurriedly buried, later unearthed and reburied in different locations.

Other accounts say that some of his followers buried him secretly on Walpole Island, Ontario. None of these accounts are verifiable and no one is sure where Tecumseh is buried, according to his biographer, John Sugden.

"An authentic Shawnee statement" from Ganwawpeaseka, also known as Thomas Wildcat Alford, the great grandson of Tecumseh, says that a group of tribal members returned to Canada from their Oklahoma reservation "some years" later to bring back Tecumseh's remains; however, the spot by a creek where he had been buried in a shallow grave had flooded and his remains were washed away.

Shawnee tradition states, "No white man knows, or will ever know, where we took the body of our beloved Tecumseh and buried him. Tecumseh will come again!"

Despite being one of the most enduring figures of fact and legend among American Indians, some modern historians believe that Tecumseh's leadership role has been overrated, and that his tenacity for Indian unity and emphatic resistance against American advance created a distrust and enmity between whites and Indians, which continued long after his death.

During a brief period from 1795 through 1813, when American incursion into a shrinking Indian frontier accelerated and led to a series of land cession treaties and tribal division, Tecumseh's pan-tribal coalition was the last bastion of united Indian resistance east of the Mississippi.

Several influential members of his coalition, including his brother Tenskwatawa, continued their military alliance with the British for a year and a half after Tecumseh's death, but gradually tribal unity unraveled. No other Indian leader since Tecumseh has been able to inspire such a cohesive pan-tribal coalition, a feat, which, as a young leader, he accomplished in only eighteen years.

Tecumseh's philosophy of life is summed up in his teachings:

"So live your life that the fear of death can never enter your heart. Trouble no one about their religion; respect yours. Love your life, perfect your life, beautify all things in your life. Seek to make your life long and of service to your people. Prepare a noble death song for the day when you go over the Great Divide. Always give a word or a sign of salute when meeting or passing a friend, or even a stranger, if in a lonely place. Show respect to all people, but grovel to none. When you arise in the morning give thanks for the light, for your life and strength. Give thanks for your food and for the joy of living. If you see no reason for giving thanks, the fault lies only in yourself. Touch not the poisonous firewater that makes wise ones turn to fools and robs the Spirit of its Vision. When it comes your time to die, be not like those whose hearts are filled with the fear of death, so that when their time comes they weep and pray for a little more time to live their lives over again in a different way. Live your life so that when you sing your death song, you will die like a hero going home with no shame to meet the Creator and your family."

– Teachings of Tecumseh, April 9, 1809. He was 44 years old at the time of his death.

Tenskwatawa
[Lalawethika, "The Rattle," "Rattling Bush;"
Tenskwautawa, Elkskwatawa, Lalawethika *"The Open
Door to the Mystery of Life,"* or *"The Open Door,"* "His
Mouth Is Open;" "The Shawnee Prophet"]

Shawnee – Creek/Cherokee?
b. 1775-78? – d. 1837

Adapted from a portrait painting by James Otto Lewis, dated 1824.

"I [Waashaa Monetoo, The Great Spirit, or The Master of Life] am the Father of the English, of the French, of the Spaniards and of the Indians ... But the Americans I did not make. They are not my children but the children of the Evil Spirit. They grew from the scum of the great water when it was troubled by the Evil Spirit and the froth was driven into the woods by a strong east wind. They are very numerous but I hate them. They are unjust – they have taken away your lands which were not made for them."
– *Tenskwatawa, The Shawnee Prophet, August 4, 1807.*

"The Great Spirit told me to tell the Indians that he had made them, and made the world; that he had placed them on it to do good and not evil ... that we ought to consider ourselves one man ... that they should not drink whiskey ... that it is the cause of all the mischiefs which the Indians suffer."
– *Tenskwatawa, excerpts from a speech to Indiana Territorial Governor William Henry Harrison, Vincennes, 1808.*

Tenskwatawa [*The Open Door to the Mystery of Life*], was known by the Americans during the early 1800s as The Shawnee Prophet. He was the younger brother of *Shawanoe* [Shawnee, or Southerners] leader Tecumseh [*Panther Passing Across*]. Together, these Shawnee brothers organized the last major Indian resistance to *shemanese* [white] encroachment into Indian Territory in the Old Northwest.

Tenskwatawa, like his older brother, was born along the *Hathepnnithiipi* [Mad River, near what is now Clark County, Ohio,] near the village of *Piquea* [*Men Rise From the Ashes*, also called Oldtown, or Old Piqua]. He was born to Pucksinwah [Puckeshinwa, Pukeesheno, *Hard Striker*], a Shawnee *ogima* [war chief] and his Creek-Cherokee wife, Methoataske [*Turtle Laying Eggs in Sand*], prior to the American Revolution [1776-1783]. Tenskwatawa's birth, like his older brother's, was a remarkable one.

Tecumseh was born as a comet passed through the night sky, a sign predicting that he would be a great leader. Tenskwatawa was the third birth in a rare set of triplets. The first-born of the triplets was Sauwaseekau, and the second was Kumskaukau, who most likely died in infancy. Sauwaseekau survived to adulthood, but was killed during the Battle of Fallen Timbers, near modern-day Toledo, Ohio, in 1794. In all, documentation reveals that Tenskwatawa had six brothers and a sister, Tecumpease [*Sky Watcher*, sometimes translated as *Crossing the Water*].

Tenskwatawa started life with the given name Lalawethika. Lalawethika is often translated as "The Rattle," "The Noisemaker," or "He Who Makes A Loud Noise." According to Shawnee historian, Don Greene, the name is more accurately defined when broken into its two segments. The first part of his name comes from *lalawee*, meaning a rattling noise; the second part, *-shika*, Greene explains, is a common clan name, meaning "coming from the ground."

In this light, the name could be defined as "Rattling Bush," or "Rattling Plant." *Alaweeshika,* a Shawnee word that translates as "the snake is rattling," is close in spelling and sound to Lalawethika. Greene also notes that Lalawethika's name identifies him as a member of the *Ka'kineethiileni* [Turtle phratry], which includes reptiles, such as snakes, instead of "a brash, loud-mouth person" as many American historians have characterized him. Greene adds: "It should be recognized that no Shawnee speaker gave the translation as 'Loud Mouth' or 'Noise Maker'," as is often read in American historical accounts of Lalawethika's early life.

Unlike his brother, Tecumseh, who was described as tall, handsome and brave, a great warrior and an articulate and charismatic speaker, Lalawethika is described in most historical accounts as physically small and unattractive and frail with a high, thin voice. Although thought to be present at some of the battles during the Wabash Confederacy War or Little Turtle War of the early 1790s, he did not distinguish himself on the battlefield. As a hunter, he was often forced to rely on others--especially Tecumseh--to provide food for him, his wife and children. Some historic accounts note that Lalawethika was known widely as a braggart despite his lack of early accomplishments and is said to have spent much of his time alone, meditating.

Lalawethika's isolation may be due to the fact that as a child, following the death of his father in 1774 during Lord Dunmore's War, his distraught mother, Methoataske, abandoned her family. She either moved south to live among her former tribe, or moved west of the Mississippi River to live among the Shawnee who had moved as far from American influence as possible. Regardless, her younger children were left in care of the older ones, her oldest son, Chicksika [*Chickasaw Man*], and a married daughter, Tecumpease [*Sky Watcher* or *Crossing the Water*].

According to some writers, Tecumseh became the focus of family attention, while Lalawethika was left to fend for himself. In a childhood accident, Lalawethika blinded himself in one eye while learning to shoot a bow and arrow. This also set him apart from his peers.

Eventually, Lalawethika gravitated toward American settlements and reportedly became a victim of alcoholism. One day in 1805, he is said to have fallen into a coma so deep that he appeared to be dead. He appeared so lifeless that his wife began preparations for his burial. However, Lalawethika awakened as his wife prepared for the ritualistic washing of his corpse, and he awakened a changed man.

During his coma, which he described as a spiritual trance, Lalawethika had a vision. In his vision, he saw himself standing at a junction of two roads. One road led to heaven and the other to hell. First, he chose the road to hell. In this part of the vision, he saw that Indians who had consumed alcohol in life were condemned in the afterlife to drink cups of melted lead. In Lalawethika's vision, all sinners were subject to various forms of torture. Frightened by what he saw, he retraced his steps and traveled the other path to heaven, which he called "the blue road."

At the end of "the blue road," he saw Indians who rejected the white man's ways, especially the use of liquor, were destined for an afterlife of beauty and peace. Upon awakening, he changed his name from Lalawethika to Tenskwatawa, meaning *The Open Door to the Great Mystery*, also translated as *His Mouth Is Open*. Tenskwatawa shared his vision with his older brother, Tecumseh.

Following the signing of the Greenville Treaty at Fort Greenville [Ohio] in 1795, Lalawethika and Tecumseh moved from a village near Greenville and established their new village along Deer Creek in central Ohio Territory, just above the Greenville Treaty Line, which divided Ohio into Indian Territory to the north and United States Territory to the south.

The following year, they moved to the former center of the Shawnee culture, Chillicothe, along the Miami River, where they raised corn and other traditional crops. In 1797, the brothers moved to a site along the Whitewater River, near modern-day Brookville, Indiana, again, outside American territory. Game was more plentiful along the Whitewater River, and they remained there for several years.

While living along the Whitewater, according to some accounts, Lalawethika and Tecumseh were visited by the prominent Delaware war chief Buckongahelas [*Breaker to Pieces*]. Buckongahelas expressed interest in Tecumseh's political message of a proposed tribal coalition of resistance, which once again could stand against American encroachment into Indian Territory. Buckongahelas invited the brothers to live at his village along the West Fork White River, near modern-day Muncie, Indiana. However, other sources make no mention of Buckongahelas' visit. Regardless, the brothers removed to the West Fork White River sometime before 1804; there, Lalawethika became Tenskwatawa.

While living along the White River near the Delaware, Lalawethika convinced Shawnee medicine man, Penagasha [*Changing Feathers*] to accept him as an apprentice. Penagasha gave Lalawethika some instruction in the healing arts, although Lalawethika had not yet had the vision required of a medicine man. When the aged Penagasha died in 1804, Lalawethika attempted to take his place with some limited success. That winter, another epidemic of "white man's illness" hit Lalawethika's village. The novice healer was able to cure some of those stricken, but despite his attentions, many died. During this epidemic, Lalawethika had his transforming vision.

Tenskwatawa, like Tecumseh, held a deep belief that advancing American civilization would doom the traditional Indian lifestyle to extinction. Within his spiritual "awakening" was the message to reject all things affiliated with the *shemanes*. This message, combined with Tecumseh's more political stance that all Indian land was owned in common and could not be sold by individual tribes, became the core beliefs of the new pan-tribal movement.

Tenskwatawa's message was similar to some previous Indian mystics, such as the Seneca Prophet, Handsome Lake, and Neolin, The Delaware Prophet. Neolin's message had inspired the Ottawa, Pontiac, to form an Indian coalition of Great Lakes tribes to resist British encroachment in 1765, a period of armed conflict known as Pontiac's Rebellion. Like Neolin, Tenskwatawa, believed that all American Indians could save their lands and their culture only by returning to "the old ways." Like Pontiac, spiritual admonitions and stern discipline would be important in forming a powerful pan-tribal coalition of resistance.

To Tenskwatawa returning to the "old ways" meant living a virtuous life, avoiding the corruption that came with adopting Euro-American culture and returning to a traditional, pre-contact Indian lifestyle. He preached that guns should be used only for defense; that hunting should be done with bow and arrow; fire should be made with a wooden fire board, and a fire should be kept burning within the home at all times; wearing woven cloth should be avoided and those garments should be replaced with traditional clothing made of dressed animal skins.

Tenskwatawa's disciples were directed not to intermarry with white people and were to be monogamous; they should avoid eating certain foods, such as leavened bread or meat from domestic animals, especially swine; and, above all, they should not consume alcohol. He also encouraged peaceful relations among all Indians, a return to traditional ritualistic observance of religious ceremonies, including regular daily prayer, and a return to traditional farming practices.

Defeat of the once-powerful Wabash Confederacy at the Battle of Fallen Timbers near modern-day Toledo, Ohio, in 1794, led to its dissolution, demoralization of its members and the subsequent loss of Indian lands in the Greenville Treaty of 1795--a treaty Tecumseh refused to sign.

Tenskwatawa's message of spiritual renewal attracted and inspired many disciples. His message of hope convinced many displaced and disillusioned Indians that a pan-tribal force could once again rise and mount a successful resistance to American encroachment. However, Tenskwatawa was not above using tactics of deceit and treachery to convert reluctant Indians to pursue "the old ways."

Tenskwatawa returned to Ohio and re-established a village near Greenville in 1806, but his influence was felt among his Delaware disciples on the White River that winter. [Revered war chief Buckongahelas had died the previous winter, at the age of eighty-four more likely of influenza. However, many were convinced he died of suspicious causes.] During a meeting at Kikthawenund's [*Making a Cracking Noise*] village of Wapeminskink, several Delaware disciples decided to travel to Greenville and inform Tenskwatawa that witchcraft most likely was afflicting their people.

Tenskwatawa maintained that he could look into men's souls and claimed he was able to detect on sight anyone who might be "poisoning the community with evil power." Accused "witches," who confessed their sins openly and ritualistically, could go through a cleansing ceremony. [They could "shake Tenskwatawa's hand," meaning they could pass their hands over a string of beads, said to be made from his own dried flesh.] After confessing their sins and "shaking his hand," Tenskwatawa would accept them as his disciples; however, those who would not admit their trespasses needed to be cleansed through a fiery death. Tenskwatawa, eager to cleanse the Indian community, returned to Wapeminskink with the Delaware disciples.

Many Delaware had adopted Christianity through the work of Moravian missionaries in western Ohio and eastern Indiana Territory. Those accused of witchcraft by Tenskwatawa tended to be individuals who challenged his religious philosophy and spiritual leadership. Tenskwatawa, who was now gaining notoriety as The Shawnee Prophet among Americans, accused the Delaware chief Tetapacksit [*Grand Glaize King*], a former Christian convert, along with a dozen others, of practicing witchcraft and condemned them to death.

Tetapacksit admitted his guilt, but still was tomahawked by The Prophet's disciples and thrown into the fire "half alive." At least one of the other accused, a Moravian convert named Josiah, denied being a witch, but received the same fate as Tetapacksit. During the witchcraft "trials" another of the accused, Chief Hockingpomska, fled his village. And, there are accounts of an elderly woman being slowly roasted over a fire for "four days until she was allowed to die."

Hearing of these events, Indiana Territorial Governor William Henry Harrison sent a message to the Delaware, warning against affiliation with The Shawnee Prophet. Tecumseh, who like Harrison, condemned The Prophet's methods, returned, presumably with his brother, to a village near Greenville.

At Greenville, The Prophet's influence continued to increase, as did Harrison's concerns. As proselytes gathered at Greenville, Harrison sent out a statement designed to discredit The Prophet to all Indians of the region. Harrison challenged The Prophet, "if he is truly a man of God," to perform some type of miracle. A miracle, such as raising the dead or causing the sun to stand still in the sky, would prove that he was truly a representative of Waashaa Monetoo [*The Great Spirit*]. The governor's challenge backfired.

The Prophet had evidently learned – possibly through having lived among Moravian missionaries or through information provided by his brother's British allies - that an eclipse of the sun was soon scheduled to occur on June 16, 1806. Tenskwatawa loudly predicted to his followers that he could make the sun disappear and return on the same day. At the appointed time, Tenskawata emerged from his tent, strode to the middle of the village circle and commanded the skies to darken. As if by "magic," the eclipse followed, the sky darkened as he had predicted; after a few minutes, the sun returned. His accurate prediction of this natural event only served to increase The Prophet's fame and reputation among current and future followers.

Many Indian tribal representatives from throughout the Great Lakes as well as from the southern and western tribes flocked to Greenville to hear The Prophet's teachings. While there, they also heard Tecumseh's plans for an "Indian Nation," politically similar to the "federalism" of the United States. Representatives of the Potawatomi, the Mascouten, the Wyandot, the Kickapoo, the Miami, and possibly tribes from as far as the Mississippi River, the Gulf of Mexico and Canada came to Greenville. Through councils, mutual agreement regarding use of all hunting grounds by all Indians was reached. This was a landmark for the beginnings of Tecumseh's Indian Nation.

Swelling numbers of Indians from varying tribes gathering around the Shawnee brothers frightened American settlers of the area. They took their concerns to the fledgling Ohio State government, which was formed in 1803. Governmental officials – as well as acculturating Shawnee living under the control of chief Catahecassa or Black Hoof - put pressure on the brothers to move out of Ohio.

One of the visitors at Greenville had been the influential Mascouten [Little Prairie People] chief Winibiset [The Crafty One]. He suggested to The Shawnee Prophet that he relocate his village into what was still designated "Indian Country"-- northern Indiana. After a council held near modern-day Terre Haute, the Shawnee brothers received permission from other tribes living and hunting in the region to move to this new location.

In the spring of 1808, the brothers and some sixty followers moved to the suggested site. The new location was called *Kithtippecanunk* [At the Clearing], a former Miami village site near the mouth of the *Ketopkwon* [Tippecanoe River], where it joins the Wabash River, near modern-day Battle Ground, Indiana. The village became known among American officials and settlers as "Prophetstown."

Prophetstown grew quickly as warriors and their families from many tribes came to live. At its peak, American writers estimated Prophetstown's population ranged from as few as six hundred fifty to many as three thousand. Once again, a growing Indian presence caused concern to settlers in the region.

By correspondence in the summer of 1808, The Prophet tried to allay the fears of Governor Harrison and the American settlers in Indiana Territory, which now included what would become the future states of Illinois and Wisconsin. Through a messenger sent to Harrison at the Territorial Capitol of Vincennes, The Prophet maintained that he and all his disciples at Prophetstown intended to live "in peace among the whites." The messenger added his own thoughts, telling Harrison that The Prophet always gave good advice; he promoted religious observance through prayer and he preached abstinence from alcohol.

"He tells us also to work and make corn," the messenger concluded. Harrison's fears were slightly allayed by these words, but he sent a return message that he wanted to meet personally with Tenskwatawa and judge for his self what The Prophet's intentions were.

Increasing discipleship among the tribes of the Great Lakes posed a major problem for The Prophet. At Greenville, and now at Prophetstown, a growing number of followers living near him created a major food shortage. Although admonishing his followers not to eat the white man's food, while living in Ohio, Tenskwatawa had received aid and comfort from the Shakers, a Christian sect living nearby – at least until local settlers and militia threatened the sect with violence if they continued to supply The Prophet. Now at Prophetstown, The Prophet thought he could receive the same sort of aid from Harrison. He did.

The Prophet arrived in Vincennes the following month, August of 1808. As requested, he met with Harrison. During a stay of almost two months, Harrison became convinced that Tenskwatawa was a sincere man of "incredible talents." Harrison wrote that he once believed the Shawnee brothers to be "tool(s) of the British," but now had his doubts. He wrote that creating a positive relationship with The Prophet would prove "advantageous" to the American government and the settlement of Indiana Territory. Meanwhile, Prophetstown continued to grow in population with the arrival of several northern Great Lakes tribesmen, including the Ottawa and Chippewa.

Moved with religious fervor and transfixed with Tenskwatawa's message, little farming was done. Crops at Prophetstown failed, and the winter was one of extreme hardship for the Indian population. To add to The Prophet's woes, sickness hit the village and many died. The following spring, many more deserted The Prophet's cause and Prophetstown.

The Prophet, along with about fifty disciples, made a second trip to Vincennes in July of 1809. Once again he had several personal meetings with Harrison, who described the Indians' condition as "miserable." Tenskwatawa continued to deny any hostile intentions toward settlers or any affiliation with British interests, but this time his assertions had less effect on Harrison. Indian raids on white settlements had continued since their last meeting, especially in the area that would become the State of Illinois. To feed his followers, Tenskwatawa turned to the British for help. The British, although wary of conflict with the United States, responded with much needed supplies.

By 1810, settlers, frightened by continuing Indian raids, pushed Harrison to find a solution to the "Indian problem." The blame was centered on the growing pan-tribal movement at Prophetstown. Harrison sent an emissary, the mixed-blood interpreter Michael Brouillette, bearing annuity gifts requested by The Prophet to feed his people, including one hundred pounds of salt, up the Wabash River to Prophetstown. The Prophet accused Brouillette of being a spy. Not only was Brouillette not allowed to come ashore, he was threatened with death if he attempted to do so. The Indians kept the annuities and the salt, but sent Brouillette unharmed back to Vincennes.

In 1809, a treaty was signed at Fort Wayne between the United States and many "government chiefs." The Treaty of Fort Wayne ceded even more Indian land in Indiana Territory to the United States.

An infuriated Tecumseh began traveling among neighboring tribes, berating the government chiefs and preaching his pan-tribal message of Indian unity.

Harrison again invited Tenskwatawa to visit his headquarters at Vincennes in the summer of 1810. The Prophet did not come. Instead, in August of 1810, it was Tecumseh who arrived. Contrary to Harrison's request that Tenskwatawa bring only a few followers, Tecumseh arrived with several hundred warriors. The citizens of Vincennes were alarmed; Harrison and his aides were annoyed.

After a few days of meetings, Tecumseh returned to Prophetstown. The following summer he arrived at Vincennes again on a surprise visit this time with a slightly smaller entourage. Harrison responded to Tecumseh's arrival by readying the militia and requesting regular soldiers from Fort Knox, three miles to the north. Tecumseh did not stay long at the territorial capitol. Whether he was planning an attack and was thwarted by Harrison's preparations is not known. Regardless, the Shawnee leader continued downriver with an entourage of about twenty warriors; the remaining warriors returned to Prophetstown. For the next several weeks, the Shawnee war chief would be absent, seeking support for his pan-tribal Indian nation among southern tribes.

Before he left, Tecumseh had learned through spies in Vincennes, that Harrison, pressured by Indian raids in southern Illinois, was planning a military "show of force" against Prophetstown. He sent strict orders to The Prophet via his trusted warriors returning to Prophetstown that there was to be no military engagement with Harrison at any cost.

Tecumseh's departure gave Harrison the chance he had been seeking. He assembled an army of Kentucky and Indiana militia, along with some "Yellow Jackets" - American regulars named for the gold and blue uniform frocks they wore – about twelve hundred in all, and marched northward to confront The Prophet in his own village.

After stopping to build Fort Harrison at the site of present-day Terre Haute, Harrison's army reached Prophetstown on November 6, 1811. The commander sent his trusted Indian aide, Winamac, ahead to arrange a meeting with The Prophet. The Shawnee mystic said that he would meet with Harrison the following day.

Some sources suggest that it was The Prophet who convinced Harrison to encamp on a small rise near the village. Other accounts say that it was Harrison alone who picked the campsite because of its easily defensible terrain. Harrison's troops pitched camp on a triangular piece of naturally high ground, above a creek. The campsite was surrounded on three sides by a low, soggy marsh. Harrisons' army camped for the night, several hundred yards from Prophetstown proper.

Although The Prophet may have meant to follow his brother's imperative not to confront the American forces. In the end he disobeyed his brother's orders. Some historic accounts maintain The Prophet bowed to pressure from a small, but militant, group of warriors, mostly Potawatomi. By some accounts, these militant Indians were supported by a small group of British regulars, dressed as Indians. Other accounts stress The Prophet's imagined usurpation of power by his brother, Tecumseh, and instigated the impending fight himself in an attempt to regain sole power.

Regardless, The Prophet was convinced that an early morning surprise attack on Harrison's forces was the best option. Under the philosophy that a decisive victory now would stop the American advancement, Tenskwatawa yielded to the temptation of an all-out surprise attack on Harrison and the American forces the morning of November 7, 1811. It would be his undoing.

The Prophet told his followers of his vision that the bullets of the *shemagana* [soldiers] would fall as "soft as rain;" the Americans would not be able to harm their Indian attackers; victory was certain, the Great Spirit had assured him of that. This would only come true, he added, if Harrison were killed at the outset of the battle.

Safely away from the battle, The Prophet prayed and chanted through the night. Some accounts claim he climbed to the top of a nearby ridge and spent the night on a large, flat rock, known now as "Prophet's Rock." Other accounts report he stayed farther away from battlefield, possible remaining in the village. most accounts agree he urged on some six hundred warriors of differing tribes, who crawled through the tall, damp prairie grasses and silently approached the American camp in the foggy, early morning darkness. The Prophet's prayers did not yield the desired result, nor would his predictions come true.

As the Indians approached in the early morning darkness, a nervous American sentry heard a noise, fired a shot into the deep grass and a wounded warrior cried out. The surprise attack was foiled, and although the Indians at first had the upper hand, the heated battle ended in an American victory.

Most Indians fled Prophetstown. Harrison set the nearly deserted village – along with its now hefty stores of grain – to the torch the following day. Afterwards, he returned to Fort Harrison to care for his wounded, then on to Vincennes. Blame for the defeat fell on The Prophet. Tenskwatawa was taken into custody by some Wyandot warriors and held prisoner at a secluded site along Wildcat Creek, near modern-day Kokomo. There, they awaited Tecumseh's return from his mission to the southern tribes.

Upon his return, Tecumseh, outraged at his brother's disobedience and the blow to the confederation, chastened Tenskwatawa. Tenskwatawa defended himself by saying that his menstruating wife had weakened his powers. Even with the defeat, The Prophet's influence among the Indians was weakened, but not totally gone. Regardless of his animosity toward his brother, Tecumseh kept Tenskwatawa with him.

Tenskwatawa was with Tecumseh during a pan-tribal council near the Mississinewa-Wabash confluence as he tried once again to gain support among the Indians for the British cause in the impending War of 1812, but failed. Tecumseh and Tenskwatawa moved first to Canada, where they lived among the British. While Tecumseh led a combined British-Indian force, Tenskwatawa remained in the rear with British officials who gave him money, shelter and food.

The following spring, 1813, Tenskwatawa appeared at Fort Wayne leading "about ninety" disciples. Tenskwatawa told the fort's commandant that, although the British had tried to lure him into an alliance, he would not join. He professed his lasting friendship with the Americans. The commandant did not believe him and Tenskwatawa left. Presumably, he returned to Canada and his British allies.

Despite his claims of friendship with the Americans, Tenskwatawa joined Tecumseh's forces and was present during several battles against the Americans during the War of 1812. Again, as in the past, he did not distinguish himself as a warrior.

Some accounts maintain that during the Battle of Moraviantown, also known as the Battle of Thames, in which Tecumseh was killed, October 5, 1813, Tenskwatawa was living among the Creek tribe in the south. Other accounts say he was present on the battlefield, but fled to the east with the retreating British troops led by General Henry Proctor, leaving Tecumseh and his forces behind.

After Tecumseh's death, Tenskwatawa did not lost all his influence. He was elected war chief of the remaining pro-British Shawnee and remained in Canada with his followers after the Treaty of Ghent ended the war in 1814. However, his life was changed. No longer a prominent leader among the Indians who followed Tecumseh, he lived among his few remaining followers in birch bark huts near British forts and settlements. The man who once threatened the "government chiefs" with death was now forced to rely on the British government for subsistence. Nor could he return to the United States following an incident in which he thought he had captured a deserting British soldier. He tried to turn the supposed defector over to U.S. officials at Detroit, but was accused instead of kidnapping. He was forced over the next decade to live in poverty, dependent on limited government annuities. Eventually, all his followers deserted him; only his immediate family remained loyal to The Prophet.

After several years in Canada, Michigan Territorial Governor Lewis Cass approached Tenskwatawa with a proposition. A movement was afoot among the United States government to remove the remaining Shawnee from Ohio. Tenskwatawa would make a perfect emissary in assisting with this removal. After spending several months as a pampered guest in Cass' Michigan home, The Shawnee Prophet professed allegiance to the government he once opposed. For his services, he was given money and gifts. One of the most prominent gifts was a well-outfitted, large, white gelding horse, which he reported rode proudly. He returned twice as a paid American agent to the Ohio villages controlled by his former enemy Black Hoof, in 1825 and again in 1827. To Tenskwatawa, this was an opportunity to regain leadership among the tribes of area. There were mixed results.

Tenskwatawa succeeded in convincing some of the remaining Shawnee chiefs still living in Ohio to cede their homelands and move to reservations in the west. During these negotiations, Tenskwatawa, courted by the United States government, claimed to be the "principal chief" of the Shawnee. At first, he was recognized as such, but as the Shawnee journeyed toward Missouri in 1828, a lack of government communication and funding left them stranded near Kaskaskia, Illinois.

Shawnee horses, including Tenskwatawa's prized gift gelding, starved and died. Blame fell to Tenskwatawa.

Other chiefs took control and Tenskwatawa's role was much diminished by the time the Shawnee reached Missouri, where a disgruntled Tenskwatawa was forced to live among the impoverished Shawnee. Later, he was given another horse and selected as a member of a party sent ahead to scout the new Shawnee reservation in Kansas. Again, he attempted to assert himself as a principal chief, but was largely ignored. The following year, the Shawnee, including Tenskwatawa, moved to their reservation in Kansas.

Even in old age and far from the sites of his greatest exploits, Tenskwatawa retained enough fame to sit as a subject for renowned Indian portraitist George Catlin, who had accompanied and illustrated the Lewis and Clark expedition in the early 1800s. Some accounts claim Catlin painted him at his Kansas "village" of four or five houses. Other accounts dispute this claim, saying a sketch was done, and the portrait finished at a later date. Regardless, in his final portrait, Tenskwatawa, The Shawnee Prophet, wore traditional Indian regalia rather than the Euro-American clothing he chose for an earlier portrait by James Otto Lewis.

When Tenskwatawa became ill in his final days, a local doctor visited him and asked to treat The Shawnee Prophet and healer. Tenskwatawa agreed to accept traditional medical care, but not immediately, as he was meditating at the time. He told the doctor to return in three days. By the time the doctor returned, Tenskwatawa's health was so poor that nothing could be done to save his life.

Tenskwatawa, The Shawnee Prophet, died in November of 1837, in present-day Wyandotte County, near Argentine, Kansas; he is buried there.

Most historical sources credit Tecumseh with single-handedly creating the pan-tribal coalition of resistance against American encroachment during the period between 1808 and 1811, sometimes designated as "Tecumseh's War." However, some sources maintain Tenskwatawa's vision and his message of Indian spirituality was the main component in establishment of the final pan-tribal movement of resistance to American settlement of the Indian Territory of the Old Northwest.

Topeah

["Frost on the Bushes," or Francis LaFontaine, or LaFountain]

Miami – French
b. 1810 – d. 1847

Adapted from a portrait oil painting by R.B. Craft, Fort Wayne, circa 1840.

"We feel that we are a poor and feeble remnant of a once influential Tribe of red men. We do trust that our poverty and feebleness will awaken the Sympathy of Our Great Father, the President and open his heart to our prayer that he will grant the petition of his Red Children and cause our wishes to be compiled by the proper department. To the President we make an appeal with great confidence ... Most of the Chiefs who have any weight with the tribe, or capable of aiding them in council have lands, and personal property which the laws of Indiana prohibit the Sale of and we owe debts; [we said in council] that we were willing to remove as soon as we could get permission by a repeal of the prohibitory statute to sell our individual lands, and arrange the debts, and not before ... I trust the President will pardon the freedom with which I write. It is a matter of deep interest to me and to my people. The kindness you manifested toward us in promising to give our affairs a personal examination – when you honored us with a talk at Washington – to cause Justice to be done us emboldens me to request your interposition in our behalf. We do trust that in as much as our people do not like the country assigned them west, our Great Father the President, will cause a change of land to be made with us, and one more suitable to the wants and wishes of the Miami.

– *From a letter written by Chief Topeah to President James K. Polk, dated September 1, 1846, appealing the governmental policy of Miami removal from Indiana.*

Topeah [*Frost on the Bushes*], or Francis LaFontaine, was civil chief of the Miami for six years, from 1841 until 1847, a troubling period for his people. Land held by the Miami for nearly two hundred fifty years was sold to settle mounting debts. These land cessions led to the subsequent removal of all but a few influential Miami in 1846.

As elected chief during this tumultuous transition period, Topeah did all in his power to salvage the best situation possible for the Miami tribe falling into disarray.

Topeah's grandfather, Peter [Pierre Francois] LaFontaine, was a French trader. He came from Canada, via Detroit in 1775 to the main Miami village of *Cecaahkonki* [Kekionga, or Blackberry Patch], located at the site of modern-day Fort Wayne. Peter LaFontaine managed a warehouse at Kekionga for another French trader, Charles Beaubien. He married a Miami woman and around 1780 they had a child, whom they named Francis, the father of Topeah. After Topeah's birth in 1810, his father became commonly known as "the first Francis." He was also possibly known by the Miami name of Wau-no-sa.

Topeah's mother was a relative of the influential Miami leader Wa-pa-se-pah [*White Raccoon*]. Through marriage, the "first Francis" gained some tribal authority, although he was not considered a chief or headman.

Topeah was born near Fort Wayne, Indiana Territory, in 1810, six years before the territory was granted statehood. When Topeah was about eight years old, his father received two sections of land south of Kekionga along the St. Mary's River, as a result of negotiations at the Treaty of St. Mary's in 1818. As his son, Topeah, shared this reserve. However, the LaFontaine family did not move to their new reserve until 1821. A traveler of the period found the first Francis to be "old, hospitable and fluent in the French language."

Two years later, in 1823, Topeah's father petitioned the United States government, requesting to sell one section of his reserve in order to settle his debts. He was given that permission to sell the land, but the government added a provision that Topeah's share of the reserve could not be sold.

With Topeah and his father sharing the same name, there is some confusion as to which Francis signed a number of treaties and annuity payment receipts.

Topeah was only eighteen in 1826 when the Miami negotiated two treaties that year with the United States both known as the "Treaty of the Mississinewa." The signature,"Francis LaFontaine, Wau-no-sa," is found among the list of "chiefs and warriors of the Miami tribe." This signature most likely belonged to Topeah's father.

In order to satisfy mounting debts among tribal leaders and members, the Miami ceded claims to several reserve lands in Indiana, granted through previous treaties. They were rewarded with more than thirty thousand dollars over the following two years, ten thousand dollars in silver and the remainder in goods. Also, the tribe was to receive some fifteen thousand dollars in annuity payments each year thereafter. An annual provision of two thousand dollars was also made for "poor infirm persons of the Miami tribe and for the education of the youth ... as long the Congress ... should think it proper."

Following the Treaty of the Mississinewa, only seventeen Miami retained sizable reserves, including "Francis LaFontaine," who received a section near the mouth of Pipe Creek, where it joins the Wabash River, southeast of Logansport, Indiana. In another section of the documents, Francis LaFontaine, again most likely Topeah's father, is named among several Miami who received a newly built "house, not to exceed six hundred dollars." These cessions indicate that the LaFontaines were among the most prominent Miami.

However, wording in the 1826 Mississinewa documents allowed the United States more liberties among the provisions of the treaty than the Miami were allowed. The government retained the right of eminent domain, reserving rights to an easement through "any of these reservations" for the purpose of building a canal. Also, none of the reserves could be "conveyed without consent of the ... United States."

The "first Francis" died sometime after 1830, possibly 1831 or 1832.

A youthful "second Francis," or Topeah, is described as being "tall, spare and athletic." He was noted for his running ability; he is described in one account as able to "outrun a deer." He wore Miami regalia often and is noted as being fond of ornamentation and "finery."

Sometime between the ages of eighteen and twenty-one, Topeah married Pecongaqua, or Catherine [Cates] Richardville, the daughter of Chief Peshewa [*Wildcat*]. Peshewa, also known as Jean Baptiste Richardville, was, at that time, the wealthy and politically astute civil chief of the Miami.

A life-long member of the Catholic Church, Topeah fathered eight children; four boys and four girls. The first-born boy was Louis, also known by the name of his maternal grandfather, Wapasepah. The others were named Thomas, John and Joseph. Of the four daughters, three: Esther, Francis and Archangel, all reached adulthood, while one daughter died in infancy.

Even while not yet the principal chief he later would become, Topeah was evidently a man of considerable stature among the Miami. His signature can be found on at least three treaties signed at *Paawikami Siipwii* [Forks of the Wabash], one each in 1834 and 1838, on which his signature reads "To-pe-yaw," and a third in 1840.

By signing the third treaty, the Miami ceded a large portion of lands reserved for them in previous treaties. The Miami also agreed to move from Indiana and relocate to a reservation of some half million acres west of the Mississippi. However, Topeah was allowed to retain the sections of land near Fort Wayne, along the St. Mary's river, which had been granted his father in the Treaty of St. Mary's in 1818. And, he and his eldest son, Wapasepah, each received additional, adjoining sections of land at the mouth of Aboite Creek, also near Fort Wayne.

When Topeah's father-in-law, the principal Miami chief, Peshewa, died a year later, in 1841, the task of coordinating the emigration west would fall to Topeah. His election was not without drama.

After Peshewa's death, Miami leaders gathered at the Forks of the Wabash, near present-day Huntington, Indiana, to elect a new leader. None of Richardville's offspring were under consideration. Topeah was one of three men seeking the position of civil chief; Brouillette and Meshingomesia were the other two.

Meshingomesia was on a hunting trip at the time of the election, leaving the contest a two-man race between Topeah and Brouillette. Competition was bitter, and accounts indicate that Brouillette's followers were hatching a plot to kill Topeah. One of Topeah's friends discovered the intrigue and told Topeah. The plot was foiled, and a college-educated member of White Raccoon's band, Michael Chappeen, stood before the assembly, his hand on his knife, and nominated Topeah, a relative of White Raccoon. With knife still in hand, Chappeen asked if anyone wanted to challenge the nomination. None did, and Topeah was chosen chief. He was thirty-one years old.

Although Chappeen's threats may have played a part in Topeah's election, Francis LaFontaine, although not as politically adept as his father-in-law, Richardville, is said to have been a charismatic leader. Governmental leaders and American traders outside the tribe were very aware of his considerable influence among the Miami. Not only was he was able to control his own village, subchiefs and family as a politician; as a businessman, he also was very astute.

After being chosen chief, Topeah moved from his house on the prairie between Huntington and Fort Wayne and made the Forks of the Wabash his home. Near his new residence, he opened a store. The store also became headquarters for a once powerful Miami Nation now in decline.

Although Topeah did not directly receive great tracts of land through treaty grants, through his marriage to Catherine Richardville, he controlled considerable amounts of property and wealth, which had been accumulated by the Richardville family. By the time of his death, Topeah had amassed a personal fortune amounting to some two hundred thousand dollars, according to estimates.

Topeah's term as civil chief was brief, but it was an important time for his people. The majority of his days were involved with overseeing land transfers and financial matters for the Miami. Land had increased in value from just over a dollar an acre to three dollars; and some land was being sold for as much as five dollars an acre.

During this period, the threat of Miami removal from Indiana loomed ever closer. One of LaFontaine's tasks was finding a way to save a deteriorating Miami nation from economic disaster. Federal law, noted in the Mississinewa Treaties of 1826, forbade Indians from individual sales of property gained through treaty grants. Not only did this confront the tribe with severe economic hardship, but also with the possibility of violent and abrupt removal.

News of the forced removal of "The Potawatomi Preacher," Menominee [*Rice Eater*] and his band from their reservation in 1838 and the subsequent Trail of Death – a forced march of some six hundred sixty miles from northern Indiana to Kansas - was still fresh in the minds of Topeah's Miami people.

In an attempt to prevent such a forced eviction of the Miami to the west, Topeah followed political policies established by Chief Peshewa, but he and the Miami no longer had enough influence or power to halt the machine of U. S. governmental removal set in motion by the Indian Removal Act of 1830. Although many Miami were forced to relocate, Topeah was successful in keeping nearly half of the Miami Nation, mostly those of mixed ancestry, in Indiana.

In 1844, Thomas Dowling of Terre Haute received fifty-five thousand dollars through a governmental contract to remove the Miami from Indiana. In 1845, Topeah sent his oldest son, Wapasepah, and several sub-chiefs to view their proposed Kansas reservation. Wapasepah and his colleagues returned with satisfactory reports and preparations began for emigration.

Although still a young man at the time of Miami emigration, Topeah's health was beginning to fail. He had grown to a huge weight of nearly three hundred fifty pounds and was feeling ill by the time he left his home to accompany his people to their new lands in Kansas Territory.

Under military supervision the removal of a "once influential Tribe of red men" from Indiana started at Peru on October 6, 1846. Three canal packet boats traveled up the Wabash River to Fort Wayne, stopping along the way to pick up more displaced Miami passengers. Two days later, the loaded boats arrived at Fort Wayne, where they joined two other boatloads of Miami emigrants.

A combined party of five boats left Fort Wayne, traveling east on Indiana's Wabash and Erie Canal. At its confluence with the Miami and Erie Canal in Ohio, the boats turned southward toward the Ohio River. Traveling down the Ohio, the packet boats stopped at Louisville, the emigrants boarded a steamboat, "The Colorado II," and continued the long journey west. The Miami arrived at their Kansas reservation November 9, 1846.

Although the forced Miami migration was difficult, it was not as disastrous as that of the Trail of Death, where fifty Potawatomi died. Six of nearly four hundred Miami died on the month-long exodus and two births were recorded.

Some accounts record that Topeah also was planning to move his family west of the Mississippi. But on his return home to the Forks of the Wabash from Indian Territory, while in St. Louis, Topeah was taken ill. He continued his journey up the Wabash River by steamboat as far as Lafayette, Indiana. Once there, his condition worsened. He disembarked and was taken to an abandoned building to rest. He died, April 13, 1847, in Lafayette at the age of thirty-seven.

A rumor surfaced that Topeah's death was the result of a plot to poison him, but that rumor was discounted. His body was embalmed and transported by wagon from Lafayette to his home at the Forks.

Topeah was buried first near his home at the Forks of the Wabash; later his remains were disinterred and reburied near Huntington in Mount Calvary Cemetery on land that he had donated.

Topenebee

[Topinbee, Tuthinipee, Thu-pe-ne-bu, Topeeneebee,
Topanepee; "He Who Sits Quietly," or
"A Quiet Sitting Bear"]

Potawatomi
b. 1770? – d. 1826?

Adapted from a portrait painting by Van Sanden, undated, circa 1820's.

"Father, we do not care for the land or the money, or the goods offered us. What we want is whiskey! Give us whiskey!"
— Topenebee's sarcastic reply to Michigan Territorial Governor Lewis Cass' comments concerning his indifference toward his people brought about by his intemperance, spoken at the signing of the first Treaty of Chicago, 1821.

Topenebee [*He Who Sits Quietly*] was principal *wkama* [leader] of the St. Joseph Band of Potawatomi more than forty years.

An avowed enemy of American expansionism early in his life, he fought against American aggression with the alliance of Great Lakes Indian tribes during President Washington's Little Turtle War of the early to mid-1790s. He also was empathetic with the pan-tribal movement of the Shawnee brothers, Tecumseh [*Panther Passing Across*] and Tenskwatawa [*The Open Door*] and was a British sympathizer during the War of 1812 between the United States and England.

Topenebee was a member of *Mko dodem* [the Bear clan] of the St. Joseph River of Lake Michigan band. No documentation surrounding his birthdate seems available, but an estimated timeline appears to place the date sometime following the French and Indian War, which ended in 1764. Topenebee's role as influential leader among the Potawatomi came not only through birth, but also through the marriages of his children and relatives.

Topenebee was the son of Anaquiba, an *okema* [chieftain] of the *Neshnabe*, or *Bode'wadmiyuk* [True People, or Potawatomi]. His mother, also a Potawatomi, was named Katabwe. Anaquiba's *otan* [village] was on the *Sohq-wah-se-be* [St. Joseph River of Lake Michigan] near present-day Niles, Michigan, down river of modern-day South Bend, Indiana.

Topenebee was related by marriage to several notable historic figures of the period. His sister, Kaukeama, married a metis [French and Indian] trader named Burnett. Through this marriage, Burnett became an adopted member of the Potawatomi. Their son, William Burnett, later became civil chief of the Potawatomi. In the early 1800s, William allied himself and his followers with the pan-tribal movement of Tecumseh and The Shawnee Prophet, which advocated spiritual, political and armed resistance to American expansionism. William, according to historic sources, fought on the side of the Indians at the Battle of Tippecanoe, November 9, 1811.

Topenebee's niece - other sources suggest his daughter - married Leopold Pokagon [*Rib*]. Pokagon, who ascended to the role of chief after Topenebee's death, played a pivotal role at the 1823 Treaty of Chicago. Through Pokagon's influence during treaty negotiations and later favorable judicial interpretation, his Potawatomi band was allowed to remain on reserves in the Territory of Michigan. Unfortunately, Potawatomi from what are now the states of Indiana, Michigan, Wisconsin and Illinois were forced by the United States government from their homelands onto reservations west of the Mississippi River in 1838.

One of Topenebee's daughters, Madeline, married wealthy and influential French trader, Joseph Bertrand. Bertrand operated a trading post along the St. Joseph River, near modern-day Niles. The Madeline Bertrand (Berrien County, Michigan) County Park is located at the former trading post site.

Another of Topenebee's daughters married Wesau, a Potawatomi war chief.

Topenebee also fathered a son, named Topenebee the Younger. In early adulthood, the younger Topenebee was accused of murdering a relative. Following his father's death, he escaped retribution through adoption into Chief Pokagon's family.

Although not especially noted for his prowess in battle, Topenebee twice played a significant role in the failed defense of the Wea and Kickapoo village of Ouiatenon against American military attacks in the spring and summer of 1790.

Two forces of mounted Kentucky militia, one under the command of Charles Scott, the other under James Wilkerson, were ordered to attack Indian villages along the Wabash in retaliation for Indian raids in Kentucky. The *nodwe* [American enemies] under Scott attacked Ouiatenon in May. Scott routed the Indians and destroyed more than four hundred acres of cultivated corn. Wilkerson led the second raid in July and destroyed the replanted crops and routed the Indians living there.

Topenebee also participated in the Battle of Fallen Timbers, fought near modern-day Toledo, Ohio, in August of 1794. This was the climatic battle of the *megatkiwin* [war] between the United States and the Miami Alliance, or Wabash Confederacy, which ended four years of hostilities known as Little Turtle's War. Topenebee's signature appears on the treaty of peace, signed at Greenville, Ohio, in 1795.

On the Greenville Treaty, his name is translated as "Thupenebu." In the wording of the treaty, he is designated as the first on the list of "Putawatames of the River St. Joseph." He was one of the few Potawatomi chiefs to sign this significant treaty. Although he professed continued *eitokmite'k* [peace] with the United States during the council, his later actions called his allegiance to the United States into question.

In 1800, Topenebee joined *Miowmik* [Miami] war chief, Me-she-kin-no-quah [*Little Turtle*], in advocating peaceful relations with the United States. Together, they requested governmental assistance in promoting agricultural pursuits among their people. The following year, he, along with Little Turtle, advocated a temperance movement in an attempt to keep to liquor out of the hands of their tribal members.

In 1802, Topenebee represented the Potawatomi during a tribal council with Indiana Territorial Governor William Henry Harrison. The council was held at Harrison's estate, Grouseland, located near the capitol in Vincennes. At this meeting, discussions were held regarding additional cessions of Indian land. These cessions would be finalized three years later in 1805 at the Treaty of Grouseland, on which his signature is listed as "Topanepee."

Although a resident of southern Michigan, and with no Potawatomi villages located south of where the *Ke-top-e-kon* [Tippecanoe River] empties into the Wabash River in northern Indiana, his name appears on a treaty signed at Vincennes in 1804. This treaty ceded Indian rights to historic saline [salt] springs located in southern Illinois near the Ohio River west of Shawneetown.

During the same period of time, Topenebee and other leaders of Indians located in northern Indiana, and Mascouten leader Winibiset [*The Crafty One*], who lived in the Illinois Country, gave Tecumseh and The Prophet permission to locate the center of their pan-tribal movement at *Kithtippekanunk* [At the Clearing] amidst their mutual hunting grounds. This new village, located at the confluence of the Tippecanoe and Wabash rivers, near modern-day Lafayette, Indiana, became known among the American settlers as Prophetstown. The

Shawnee brothers arrived there in the spring of 1809 with some sixty followers. Within a year population estimates jumped into a population range of anywhere between six hundred-fifty and three thousand warriors from various tribes.

During the period of unrest on the Indiana frontier between 1807 and 1811, designated by American historians as "Tecumseh's War," Topenebee, along with Potawatomi chiefs Five Medals and Winamac, continued to petition the U.S. government for assistance in creating an agricultural society. Although many farm implements, other equipment and personnel were provided, including a blacksmith, the Potawatomi, as a people, generally refused to abandon traditional hunting and gathering practices to build fences, grow corn and raise livestock.

Despite these outward gestures of friendship and peace toward the American government, documentation reveals that Topenebee was one of several chiefs, who if not overtly active in the pan-tribal resistance of Tecumseh and The Prophet, kept in close communication with the Shawnee brothers at Prophetstown. He may or may not have been present at the Battle of Tippecanoe, but many of his tribal members, including his son-in-law, William Burnett, were there.

Despite his early pleas for abstinence from spirituous liquors among his people, following the Indian defeat at Tippecanoe, Topenebee eventually developed a taste for *ish-kot-e-waw-be* [whiskey]. Lured by British money and gifts, especially liquor, he became a staunch British sympathizer during the War of 1812.

Although the evidence is speculative, he may have been one of the major organizers of the August, 1812, attack on the evacuees of Fort Dearborn, the American military and trading outpost along the southern shore of *Mitch-asa-gai-gau* [Lake Michigan] at modern-day *She-gog-ong* [Chicago]; however, documentation also reveals that Topenebee sent a message of warning to local trader John Kinzie, revealing that the occupants of the *wa-ka-i-gan* [fort] should be wary of the impending Indian attack, now known as the Fort Dearborn Massacre.

After the War of 1812, he remained a principal Potawatomi leader. His name appears as "Topeeneebee," on the Treaty of Spring Wells, signed near Detroit, Michigan, in 1815. His signature, spelled "Tuthinepee," is also on the 1818 Treaty of St. Mary's. After the 1818 treaty, he led his people to Chicago to receive their annuities. The last treaty he signed was the Treaty of Chicago in 1821.

The Treaty of Chicago ceded to the United States, with the exception of a few reserves, all Potawatomi lands in lower southwestern Michigan and additional lands in northern Indiana. In all, Topenebee signed at least six treaties that sold or ceded Potawatomi *aukee* [land] to the United States.

Later, Topenebee became a Baptist church supporter and was friendly with the Reverend Issac McCoy, who moved his mission to the St. Joseph River, three miles southwest of the village of Niles, Michigan near Bertrand's trading post.

In his final years, Topenebee's consumption of alcohol worsened as he watched the Potawatomi nation decline. His *gi-nib-own* [death] may have come in 1826 when, supposedly intoxicated according to Rev. McCoy, he fell from his horse.

However, at least two other later dates for his death are given: 1833 and 1840. However, these dates may reflect the death of his son, Topenebee, the Younger.

Wach-e-kee
[Watch-e-kee, *Beautiful (or Fine-looking) Womam;* also, Watasakwe, *Warrior Woman*]

Miami – Illiniwek? – Potawatomi
b. 1810? – d. 1878?

Adapted from a portrait painting by Laura Hunt, dated 1916, taken from an earlier undated lithograph.

Wach-e-kee was the last young female among the Indians of eastern Illinois to be honored with the personal name of Watasakwe, meaning "*Warrior Woman.*"

Watasakwe's legendary courage and leadership in the face of a marauding enemy established a traditional ceremonial ritual, which was conducted once each generation. During this ritual, one young woman was selected by the tribe to become the embodiment of Watasakwe's heroic, courageous spirit. The young maiden, who was to possess beauty, intelligence, courage and modesty, was designated as "Warrior Woman," in honor of the original, spiritual heroine who led the defeated remnants of her tribe to victory over a band of maurading *Irinakhoiw,* or Iroquois [*Real Adders or Snakes*], invaders from the Northeast.

Beginning in the mid-1600s, parties of fierce warriors of Iroquois, a confederacy of Five Nations living in today's upstate New York, carried out annual summer raids against western tribes, traveling on foot as far as modern-day St. Louis, Missouri. The well-armed Iroquois were one of the first Indian tribes to use firearms in warfare.

Dutch settlers, the first Europeans to claim what is now New York State, had provided the Iroquois with guns and enlisted them as allies against the encroaching British. Better armed than any of the other tribes, the Iroquois cut an annual swath of terror through what would become the States of Ohio, Indiana and Illinois, traveling on foot and by canoes. The feared Iroquois killed, ransacked and plundered spoils of war, including captives. They displaced many western tribes who sought safety in other locations

By the late 1600s, annual Iroquois raids had driven several tribes from their traditional homelands. In an attempt to avoid further invasive contact with the Iroquois, many tribes living in what is now Indiana, including the Potawatomi and Miami, had relocated and were living among the Kickapoo and Illiniwek in what is now central and southern Illinois. About this time Watasakwe's legend began.

According to legendary accounts, while Watasakwe's tribe was living in eastern Illinois, along the *Can-o-waga,* or *Pick-a-mink,* known on modern maps as the Iroquois River, when the Iroquois conducted another successful raid against her people. Many warriors of Watasakwe's tribe were killed and the remaining survivors fled.

As the now-homeless survivors of Watasakwe's village huddled in fear and darkness, the young maiden devised a plan to retaliate against the hated Iroquois, and inspired her people with unwavering courage.

Watasakwe's strategy was to lead a surprise attack under the cover of darkness, catching the Iroquois while they were distracted with the celebration of victory. Watasakwe believed her people could exact revenge on the Iroquois before they could respond. Aware of the potential danger an attack on the Iroquois posed, and fearful of another devastating defeat, the few remaining warriors of the tribe refused to embark on the dangerous mission. Undaunted by the men's refusal, the women of the tribe responded to Watasakwe's urgings and eagerly volunteered to follow the brave Warrior Woman.

With Warrior Woman as their leader, the women began preparations to fight the Iroquois. Humiliated by the courage of their women, the men soon relented and joined the expedition. Through Watasakwe's inspiration and leadership, the Iroquois were surprised and defeated.

According to legend, in times of trouble Watasakwe's spirit still "guards over the tribe." Watasakwe's spirit, which can be embodied by the most fair among women, reminds her people of this legendary victory against overwhelming odds. It was believed that selecting a young maiden and ritualistically confirming the name of "Warrior Woman" upon her, Watasakwe's courageous spirit would be revived.

From that time on, every generation of Watasakwe's people selected one young woman, determined to be the most "accomplished" one; the one having Watasakwe's attributes of beauty, modesty, intelligence and courage was selected to bear her name. During the ritual, one beautiful, modest girl gave up her own personal name and became Watasakwe, the "Warrior Woman"- in honor of their great heroine. The last recipient of this honor was the adopted daughter of Chief Tamin – Wach-e-kee.

Wach-e-kee is believed to been born around 1810. She may have been of *Miowmik* [Miami] descent or of mixed Miami-Potawatomi or Illiniwek heritage. According to her great great grandson and Wach-e kee family historian, George Godfrey, a Potawatomi, she may have been kidnapped in her youth and/or adopted by Potawatomi chief Tamin. Tamin's village was along the *The-a-ki-ki* [Kankakee River] in what is now eastern Illinois.

Around 1824, Wach-e-kee became "wife" to successful American fur trader Colonel Gurdon Saltonall Hubbard. Among the Indians of the area, Hubbard was known as *Pa-pa-ma-ta-be* [Fast Walker] because he was said to have once traveled seventy-five miles on foot in one day.

Hubbard operated an American Fur Company trading post at Bunkum, modern-day Iroquois, Iroquois County, Illinois, along the Iroquois River. A well-traveled path, known historically as Hubbard's Trace, linked Hubbard's trading post with the growing settlement of *She-gog-ong* [Chicago], located on the southwestern shore of *Mitchasagaigau* [Lake Michigan].

Hubbard's business dealings had made him rich; but, instead of including Wach-e-kee in his success, Hubbard thought his association with a *kwe* [Indian woman] lowered his status among his white Americans. After two years of "marriage", he "gave" Wach-e-kee to his best friend and partner, Noel LaVasseur, a common practice of Euro-American traders living briefly among the Indians. Hubbard subsequently moved away from the Kankakee and built a large house in Danville, Illinois. Once established in Danville, he married a white woman.

According to one historical account, LaVasseur and Wach-e-kee claimed the other to be their true love. Together, they had two sons and a daughter. But LaVasseur, too, abandoned his new bride within a few years. Around 1835, he moved from the trading post he established in 1820 to live in the village of Bourbonnais, Illinois. Meanwhile, Wach-e-kee, a victim of the United States' Indian Removal Policy of the 1830s, was banished to a reservation near Council Bluffs, Iowa, where supposedly, she lived among a mixed group of Kickapoo and Potawatomi.

Wach-e-kee reportedly returned to her former Illinois home, traveling on foot from the western Iowa reservation on three separate occasions: once to visit her former husband LaVasseur; once for a family reunion; and once to visit her sons who had become storekeepers in Galena, Illinois.

Wach-e-kee visited her sons in Galena during the mid-1850s, yet by the time she arrived, one of her sons was dead; the other died during her visit. Ten years later, she and her daughter traveled from Kansas--

again on foot--for a family reunion. However, her first visit to her former homeland was to visit LaVasseur in 1842.

When Wach-e-kee arrived at LaVasseur's newly built, expansive and expensive Bourbonnais home, she was not welcomed. Her former husband's new wife, Ruth Bull, was reportedly put into a panic by Wach-e-kee's arrival, and LaVasseur sent her away. Wach-e-kee dutifully returned to the reservation at Council Bluffs, but LaVasseur did, evidently, have a soft spot in his heart for her.

Iroquois County, Illinois, was platted in 1836, and LaVasseur was elected as one of its first commissioners. In 1837 LaVasseur, in his capacity as commissioner, suggested the county's governmental seat be named Watseka, a corruption of the term for "Warrior Woman" - Watasakwe.

Wach-e-kee's later life is surrounded by vague information. Documentation shows that she married a third time, this time to a white man named Francis Bergeron, who was adopted by the Potawatomi through this marriage.

LaVassuer claimed in his later years that Wach-e-kee had died at Council Bluffs about 1878 and was buried at the former Potawatomi reservation.

Another account claims the Bergerons moved to Kansas, and Wach-e-kee died there. Supposedly, the once-young maiden and the traditional source of tribal pride had been buried along the banks of a Kansas stream. The stream later flooded and washed away her remains.

Some Bergeron descendents claim Wach-e-kee and her husband were forced from Kansas onto the Potawatomi Reservation in Oklahoma, where they both passed away.

Weyapiersenwah
[Wehyahpiehehrsehnwah, Whirlpool; or, Blue Jacket]

Shawnee
b. 1745? – d. 1810?

Adapted from a work by Lorence Bjorklund, dated 1969.
No known authentic image exists.

"From all quarters we receive speeches from the Americans,
and not one is alike. We suppose they intend to deceive us."
          – Blue Jacket, April 1789.

"We as a people have made no war, but as a people we
are determined to meet the approaches of an enemy,
who came not to check the insolence of individuals, but
with a premeditated design to root us out of our land…"
          – Blue Jacket, at Detroit, November 2, 1790.

"Remember, brothers, you have all buried your
war hatchet. Your brothers, the Shawnoes, now
do the same. We must think of war no more."
          – Blue Jacket, Treaty of Greenville, Ohio, 1795.

"We have deluged the country with blood to satiate our
revenge, and all to no purpose. We have been the sufferers.
The Great Spirit has shown us the vanity of these things.
We have laid down the tomahawk, never to take it up again.
If it is offered to us by the French, English, Spaniards,
or by you, our white brethren, we will not take it."
          – Blue Jacket, quoted in The Chillicothe Fredonian, 1807.

Weyapiersenwah [*Whirlpool*] was an *okema* [leader] of the
shaawanooki [Those of the South], or Shawnee, during a period of
Indian resistance in the late eighteenth century known as the Wabash
Confederacy War or Little Turtle War. He is most noted for his role
in the formation and leadership of the Wabash Confederation, which
consisted of seven Algonquin-speaking Indian tribes of the Old
Northwest. Those tribes included the Miami, Potawatomi, Delaware,
Seneca, Chippewa, Ottawa and the Shawnee.

During the late 1700's, the Wabash Confederacy maintained
that American expansionism should be limited to areas south of the
Pelewathiipi [Ohio River]. Despite his prominence as a war chief
and *psaiwinenothtu* [great warrior] among the Shawnee and the
Wabash Confederacy, many modern historians have down played
Weyapiersenwah's accomplishments.

There is a popular, although erroneous, belief that Weyapiersenwah's true identity was that of Marmaduke Van Swearingen, an American captured by the Shawnee.

According to a legend that has been perpetuated by novelists and is portrayed in "historic" pageants, the Shawnee captured "Duke" Van Swearingen when he was a young man. After passing various physical tests, he was adopted into the tribe and rose through the ranks to become the famous war chief, Blue Jacket, a name that supposedly referred to the color of the coat he was wearing at the time of his Shawnee capture. However, several reliable scholars who have studied Weyapiersenwah's life in depth have refuted this story.

These scholars note that a Van Swearingen family lived in Fayette County, Pennsylvania, during the mid to late 1700's. Yet, birth dates in the Van Swearingen family Bible are not compatible with the older Shawnee warrior, Weyapiersenwah. The age difference between the two men is about fifteen years, according to Shawnee historian Don Greene. Greene also notes that Van Swearington was a Shawnee captive named "Blue Pocket," not Blue Jacket.

Also, according to accounts of those who knew him, the Shawnee known as Blue Jacket spoke only a few words of English. If Van Swearington were captured at the age of seventeen years old, as accounts claim, he would certainly have been fluent in English by that age. The most solid evidence that Van Swearingen was not Blue Jacket comes from the results of DNA testing carried out in the year 2000. DNA samples taken from descendents of both men reveal Blue Jacket was a full-blooded *Shawanoe* [*Southerners*, or Shawnee].

Blue Jacket was born sometime during the 1740s, possibly as early as 1730, in what is now the State of Pennsylvania. Greene, in his "Historic Shawnee Names of the 1700s," dates Blue Jacket's birth as "about 1735." At birth, his personal Shawnee name was *Sepettekenathe*, or Big Rabbit. Sometime before 1778, in keeping with Shawnee tradition, he adopted the warrior name of *Weyapiersenwah*, meaning Whirlpool.

Blue Jacket had at least three wives, the first being noted only as a "Shawnee woman." Two others are recorded by name: Margaret Moore, an adopted American captive from Virginia, and Eau Claire Bebe, or Clearwater Baby, the metis daughter of French trader, Jacques Duperon Bebe and a Shawnee woman.

With Margaret Moore, Blue Jacket had two children who survived to adulthood, Joseph and Nancy. With Clearwater Baby, he had at least three children: George Blue-Jacket, Mary Bluejacket and Jim Bluejacket. Jim Bluejacket was an associate of Tecumseh [*Panther Passing Across*] and was killed fighting with Tecumseh and the British during the War of 1812.

Weyapiersenwah was an honored war chief among the Shawnee for many years. According to some accounts, he became war chief around 1775; in others, he "succeeded Black Snake as War Chief in 1785." Following the murder of Cornstalk, a peace-advocating chief of the Shawnee, and prior to the rise of Tecumseh, Weyapiersenwah became war leader of the Shawnee. Beginning in the late 1780s, he was one of the main architects and commanders of the Wabash Confederacy.

Also known as the Miami Alliance, the Wabash Confederacy was a militant coalition of Algonquin-speaking tribes, including the Shawnee, which formed to meet armed resistance to continuing American encroachment into Indian Territory.

Some noted historians claim that Blue Jacket's role in the leadership of the confederacy was diminished through accounts told by Miami adoptee William Wells [*Apekonit*]. Wells became Indian Agent at Fort Wayne [Indiana] following the defeat of the Confederacy by the Americans at the Battle of Fallen Timbers near modern-day Toledo, Ohio, in 1794.

According to some accounts, Wells intentionally magnified the role of his Miami father-in-law, Meshekinnoquah [Little Turtle] as founder and leader of the confederation. Little Turtle no doubt played a large role in the formation and leadership of the confederacy.

But the Miami war chief correctly predicted the coalition could not defeat the American forces under General Anthony Wayne and abdicated his leadership to Weyapiersenwah prior to the Battle of Fallen Timbers.

Weyapiersenwah accepted and continued as leader of the resistance until Wayne and the American army defeated the Indian confederacy at Fallen Timbers. After the defeat, the confederacy dissipated.

Weyapiersenwah lived most of his life in what would become western Ohio. By 1772, he was living along what is now called Blue Jacket Creek, located at the headwaters of the *Msimiyamithiipi*, or Great

Miami River, the site of modern-day Bellefontaine. Not yet a Shawnee war chief, his principal activity at this time was farming.

In 1774, Blue Jacket joined the Shawnee Chief Hokolesqua [*Cornstalk*] in the fight against Pennsylvania and Virginia militia during the dispute over rights to Indian land in eastern Ohio. The Ohio land was claimed by the British colony of Virginia as spoils won in the French and Indian War [1754-1762]. An armed conflict, known as Lord Dunmore's War, led to seizure of Indian lands west of the *Pelewathiipi*, or Ohio River.

Blue Jacket participated in that war's major battle, October 6, 1774. The site was Point Pleasant, where the Kanawaha River flows into the Ohio River, in what is now the State of West Virginia. At the time, the area was claimed by the British colony of Virginia, as was the Ohio Territory, also known as "The Middle Border." Defeated in that battle, the Shawnees lost the one-year war that followed and ceded all claims to lands in Virginia.

Primarily because of continuing American encroachment into Indian Territory, Blue Jacket sided with the British during the American Revolution [1775-1783]. During the Revolution, Blue Jacket settled along the *Hotaawathiipi*, or Maumee River. There he became a close associate of the Miami war chief Little Turtle. Along with his relative, Blackfish, another Shawnee chief, Blue Jacket attended the 1785 Council of Western Nations at Detroit.

During this council, the tribes vowed to halt the American aggressors at the Ohio River, a boundary set by British at the Treaty of Fort Stanwix in 1768. In the Fort Stanwix treaty, all land north and west of the Ohio had been designated by the British as Indian Territory.

In 1784, following the victory of the rebellious American colonies over Great Britain, all claims to lands once held by England, including the vast expanse of Indian Territory, was claimed by the newly formed United States. Three years later, in 1787, Congress ratified the Northwest Ordinance. The land once designated as Indian Territory was annexed by the United States and named the Northwest Territory. Wording in the ordinance "granted" specific rights to Indians living in the area that would become the states of Ohio, Indiana, Michigan, Illinois, Wisconsin and Minnesota; however, those words soon would ring hollow.

Land in the Northwest Territory was surveyed awarded to veterans of the American Revolution, or sold to land speculators and businessmen. Indians of the area vowed to resist the intrusion of squatters and land grabbers. A coalition of tribes formed into the Wabash Confederacy. Raids on American settlements and armed conflicts between American and Indian forces were about to commence.

By the year 1788, Blue Jacket established a farm along the Maumee River and is known to have maintained a herd of cattle. That same year, during a raid into Kentucky, Blue Jacket, Blackfish and their warriors captured the legendary American frontiersman Daniel Boone. Boone was adopted into the Shawnee tribe and given the name Big Turtle. Boone later escaped and returned to Kentucky.

By 1790, Blue Jacket was the major leader of the Shawnee faction of the Wabash Confederacy. The confederacy soundly defeated American generals Josiah Harmar [1790] and Arthur St. Clair [1791]. After Little Turtle resigned his position as head war chief of the Confederacy in June of 1794, Blue Jacket assumed the role of principal commander. However, his coalition forces were defeated at Fallen Timbers, along the Maumee River near the Maumee Rapids, west of present-day Toledo, Ohio, August 20, 1794. After that defeat, the Confederacy dissipated; and, with great reluctance, Blue Jacket accepted the terms of peace.

Following Fallen Timbers, Blue Jacket signed the Treaty of Greenville [Ohio] in 1795. The treaty ceded Indian claims to most of the land in eastern and southern Ohio Territory and a portion of what is now the State of Indiana. The Greenville Line, stretching at an angle through central Ohio, from Lake Erie to the Ohio River, became the new western boundary of the United States.

After signing the treaty, Blue Jacket visited Tecumseh at his village along Deer Creek [Ohio] to advise Tecumseh, the new leader of continuing Indian resistance, about the treaty's terms. Blue Jacket opted not to join in Tecumseh's plans of creating a pan-tribal alliance and Indian Nation.

Blue Jacket moved to Detroit the following year and was still living there in 1801. Two years after Ohio became a state in 1803, he signed the Treaty of Fort Industry [1805], ceding additional Shawnee lands in Ohio and setting the western boundary of the United States at the *Potakihiipi* [Sandusky River].

Although he had become an apostle of Indian neutrality, in 1807 he returned to Ohio and lived for a period of time with fervent pan-tribal leaders Tecumseh and his brother, Tenskwatawa [The Open Door], who was now known by Americans as The Shawnee Prophet. Although empathetic, there is no documentation of his joining or advocating the brothers' pan-tribal movement.

There are several accounts of Blue Jacket's death.

Some accounts say he died at Bellefontaine, January 26, 1810. Others maintain that he died in Michigan Territory, along the Detroit River, sometime between 1808 and 1810. Still other historic accounts report that he participated in the Battle of Frenchtown, January 23, 1813, during the War of 1812. Still other historians say he died on an undetermined date following the War of 1812.

Where Weyapiersenwah or Blue Jacket is buried remains a mystery.

Winamac
[Winnemack, Winnemac, Wynemac, Ouinemeg, Ouenemek, Winemac, Wenameac, Wenamech, Winnimak, Wenaumeg, *Mudfish,* or *Catfish*]

Potawatomi
b. 1767? – d. 1812

Adapted from a "special cachet…with a drawing of chief Winamac on it," produced locally in Winamac, Indiana, commemorating National Air Mail Week, May 15-21, 1938. No known authentic images exist.

Winamac [*Catfish*] remains a prominent *kiwe'nke' dodem* [clan name] among *Neshnabe*, or *Bode'wadmiyuk* [the True People], or Potawatomi, even today. In the Old Northwest during the late eighteenth and early nineteenth centuries, the name has led to historical confusion concerning two Potawatomi leaders, both known as Winamac. To add to the confusion, there are other Potawatomi of prominence also named Winamac.

According to noted Potawatomi historian R. David Edmunds, Winamac, "a chief from the *Sohq-wah-se-be* [the St. Joseph River of Lake Michigan], which flows through northern Indiana and lower Michigan," is identified as a member of a Potawatomi delegation that visited Montreal, Canada, circa 1700, on a mission to exchange prisoners with the *Irinakhoiw*, or the Iroquois, [*Real Adders* or *Snakes*]. However, this Winamac lived a century before two contemporaries with the same name gained notice – or notoriety - during the chain of events leading up to and taking place during the War of 1812 between Great Britain and their former colonies, now known as the United States.

History reflects that, following the American-Indian conflicts in the Old Northwest Territory during the early 1790s, two Winamacs emerged as political opposites. One Winamac allied himself with the *Nadowe* [Americans], the other with the *Saganash* [British]. With both bearing the same name and both being from the tribal segment known as Wabash Potawatomi, a great deal of conjecture arises concerning these two Winamacs and the conflicting roles they played in the Indian history of the Indiana Territory.

Spelled in a variety of ways on a number of early treaties and in other frontier documentation, there is little information to indicate clearly which Winamac signed which treaty, and to which Winamac writers of this period and subsequent historians refer.

Some historians speculate that one of these Winamacs may have been the son of a Potawatomi father and a *Miowmik*, or Miami [*All Beavers, All Friends*] mother. This speculation may be due to documented information regarding his close ties with the Miami. Many Miami joined the Wabash Confederacy, an alliance of Algonquin-speaking tribes formed in the late 1780s to militarily resist American encroachment into Indian lands.

Following General Anthony Wayne's victory over the Wabash Confederacy at the Battle of Fallen Timbers [near Toledo, Ohio] in 1794, many Miami leaders, including the noted war chief Meshekinnoquah [*Little Turtle*], expressed their desire for peaceful relations with the powerful Americans. During this period, a Potawatomi named Winamac also is noted as a consistently active supporter of American policy.

"Wenameac" appears among the signatures of the "Pattawatimas of Huron" on the 1795 Treaty of Greenville [Ohio], which ceded most of the southern portion of the present-day State of Ohio and a small, but significant, area of southeastern Indiana Territory to the United States.

Although having little, if any, claim to Indian land in the southern part of the Indiana territory, "Wenamech" was one of three Potawatomi to sign the 1805 Treaty of Grouseland. This document ceded Indian claims to lands along the Ohio River as well as portions of what is now southern Illinois. Since this treaty was negotiated with Indiana Territorial Governor William Henry Harrison, this Winamac is most likely the one who is documented as Harrison's "trusted aide."

During the late 1790s and early 1800s, a Winamac is documented as a messenger, scout and spy for Harrison. This work endeared him to Americans, and his service to the United States led to several visits to Washington, D.C. Yet, as an advocate of treaty negotiations with the Americans, especially at the 1809 Treaty of Fort Wayne and its subsequent large cessions of Indian land, he was a *neshab* [traitor] in the eyes of pan-tribal Shawnee leaders Tecumseh [*Panther Passing Across*] and Tenskwatawa [*The Open Door*], The Shawnee Prophet and their allies.

On one occasion, Tecumseh is recorded as insulting this Winamac and threatening his death.

During a meeting between Harrison and Tecumseh at the Indiana Territorial capitol in Vincennes in the early fall of 1811, a confrontation between Tecumseh and Harrison's aide, Winamac, erupted. In a heated exchange between the two political leaders, Tecumseh rose to his feet and called Winamac a "black dog." The frightened Potawatomi, seated nearby, "recharged his pistol" and drew it on Tecumseh, who had drawn a tomahawk. Peace between the two political rivals finally was restored, but the confrontation ended the council.

Meanwhile, a Winamac reportedly was living in friendship with Tecumseh and The Prophet at *Kithtippecanunk* [at the Clearing], a village known to the Americans as Prophetstown.

According to several historical accounts, this Winamac was an avowed disciple of the Shawnee brothers' anti-American, "Indian Nation" movement. This Winamac has been documented as a *pasigwin* [minor chief] and a skillful warrior. This Winamac is believed to be a "full-blood" Potawatomi.

Historians describe this Winamac as a consistently, outspoken enemy of American advancement. He appears to be a devoted disciple of pan-tribal resistance, although he, along with the equally the militant, anti-American Mascouten [*People of the Little Prairie*] war chief, Winibiset [*The Crafty One*], defied the Shawnee brothers' teachings of Indian brotherhood by conducting raids against other Indians in addition to American settlers. According to many historical account, these ill-advised raids against American settlers in the Indiana Territory precipitated Harrison's military advance against Prophetstown. Winamac is noted as one of the most militant warriors living at Prophetstown. He is listed, along with Miami chiefs White Loon and Stone Eater, among the leaders of the group that convinced The Prophet to defy Tecumseh's orders forbidding military confrontation with the Americans.

According to some accounts, it was Winamac and his allies who convinced The Prophet to attack Harrison's encamped troops at the Battle of Tippecanoe, near modern- day Battle Ground, Indiana, on November 7, 1811. Harrison's victory at this bloody battle led to the destruction of Prophetstown and momentarily crippled Tecumseh's pan-tribal movement.

However, even this definitive black and white division between pro- and anti-American Indian leaders is clouded with shades of historical gray. Continuing confusion between these two Winamacs has some historians melding them into one.

Some accounts contend that only one Winamac existed. These accounts have a devious Winamac acting as a double agent, using his trusted position among the Americans to ultimately benefit the Indian resistance of the Old Northwest.

One such narrative contends that, during the march against Prophetstown, Harrison directed his trusted interpreter, spy and scout,

Winamac, to seek out The Prophet and establish a time, date and place to hold a council of peace.

Historian and Kentucky militiaman, Robert Breckinridge McAfee, who served with Harrison as a lieutenant during this period, writes that Winamac came to Harrison, "professing friendship and loyalty," and then traveled ahead to Prophetstown. His account says that Winamac not only warned The Prophet of the Americans' advance, but joined White Loon and Stone Eater in advocating an ambush on Harrison's troops before they could get to The Prophet's *otan* [village].

Most historians agree that a Winamac was a major spokesman of a militant faction at Prophetstown and most agree it was a Winamac and his warriors who pressured The Prophet into disregarding Tecumseh's strict orders of non-confrontation. But a few writers contend no one named Winamac was present during the Battle of Tippecanoe.

These accounts claim that, after issuing his warning to the Indians, Winamac left Prophetstown and deliberately avoided rendezvousing with Harrison's army. Instead he traveled south along the opposite bank of the Wabash River on a mission to bring Indian reinforcements back to Prophetstown. Still, most accounts identify a Winamac as one of the principal Indian leaders during the foggy, early morning attack which ended in defeat for Tecumseh's coalition. The confusion continues.

Although Harrison, himself, notes in his diary that Winamac did not return to his camp after being sent on his mission to Prophetstown, the governor never seemed to waiver in his trust of the Indian.

After the Battle of Tippecanoe, a warlike Winamac led an unsuccessful siege of Fort Wayne [Indiana]. During the siege, this Winamac tried, but failed to conduct, a devious assassination of the commandant of the *wa-ka-i-gan* [fort], an inept, drunken Captain Rhea. After British reinforcements from Fort Detroit were diverted by now-General William Henry Harrison's American troops to Fort Wayne, this Winamac and his Indian allies withdrew.

After failing at Fort Wayne, a Winamac is said to have conspired with Main Poc's sons-in-law, Black Partridge and Mad Sturgeon, in organizing an attack on Fort Dearborn. Fort Dearborn, located on the lower, western shore of *Mitchsagaigau* [Lake Michigan], in the area of *She-gog-ong* [present-day Chicago, Illinois] was the United States' most isolated outpost of America's western frontier.

Yet, other writings put a friendly Winamac at the side of American captain and Miami adoptee William Wells [*Apekonit,* Carrot] as Wells led a relief column to the besieged fort. Some writers maintain that American commanders sent Winamac ahead alone, carrying the message that the fort should be abandoned.

Other accounts say that Winamac delivered his message to Fort Dearborn as instructed, but then informed his Indian allies of the route Dearborn evacuees would take on their way to refuge at Fort Detroit – as well as their time of departure.

Still, some historians claim that, after Winamac guided Wells and a cadre of Miami comrades to Fort Dearborn, Winamac turned on Wells and actually lead the massacre of the fort's escaping inhabitants.

In the final analysis, the conclusion that only one guileful, scheming Winamac acted alone has trouble withstanding the historical test. Documented history proves at least two notable Winamacs served on opposite sides of the British and American conflict during the War of 1812.

After the war ended in 1815, documented accounts place a peaceful Winamac at home in his village along the Wabash River at the mouth of Crooked Creek, some ten miles west of Logansport, Indiana. The name of "Wynemac" – or at least his "X" – appears on The Treaty of Maumee Rapids in 1817, four years after the documented death of his more warlike contemporary. Most sources place this "peaceful" Winamac's death in the year 1821.

Stiffening the proof that Winamac was not a single, dual-natured character, undisputed documentation shows a second Winamac, one in service with the British, died during an 1812 gun battle against American envoy Spemica Lawba, or James Logan, in an Ohio swamp near modern-day Defiance.

Present-day Winamac, Indiana, founded in 1839, the county seat of Pulaski County, is located exactly where an historical Indiana map places "Winamac's Village." However, local historians still try to arrive at a conclusion as to the correct origin of this community's place name.

To further add to the mystery, some writers believe the place name may have come via a fourth Winamac, one who lived in a village there around 1818, existing peacefully and without historical note on a sandy west bluff overlooking the Tippecanoe River.

Winibiset

[Wenebeset, Wapakee, *The Crafty One*; also, Main Poc, Main Poche, Marpock, Maipock; *Withered Hand, Lame Hand, Left Hand, Crippled Hand*]

Mascouten
b. 1765? – d. 1816

Illustration based on description and artistic imagination.
No authentic image is known to exist.

"You have caught me; like a wild horse is caught with a lick of salt, you have hobbled me. I can no longer range the woods as I please. You must now get a bell and put it on my neck [so] I shall always be in your hearing ... this will enable you to know at all times where the warriors of the west are and what they are about."
— Winibiset's profession of loyalty to Indian agent William Wells [Apekonit] at Fort Wayne, 1808.

Winibiset [*The Crafty One*] was noted in 1808 by Fort Wayne Indian agent William Wells [*Apekonit*, Carrot] as being one of the "most influential warriors of the west."

Winibiset possessed in one person many of the attributes shared by two of his contemporaries, the renowned Shawnee brothers, Tecumseh [*Panther Passing Across*] and Tenskwatawa [*The Open Door*], The Shawnee Prophet.

Like Tecumseh, Winibiset was a skilled orator, an active organizer and a fierce warrior; like The Prophet, he also claimed to be a holy man or *wabeno.* Serving as both a shaman and a war chief, Winibiset garnered respect, not only among his own people, but that of other tribes of the Old Northwest.

Winibiset was born in a Mascouten, or *Maskuta,* village in what is now lower southwest Michigan sometime in the mid-1760s. The Mascouten were closely allied with the Kickapoo, with whom they merged after 1800. Born with no thumb or fingers on his left hand, Winibiset became convinced that this deformity was a "mark of the *Kshe'mnito* [Great Spirit]." *Wekimtagosh* [French traders] identified him through this physical defect, referring to him as Main Poc, or Withered Hand. The *Sagnanash* [British], and later the *Nagowe,* or *Gotakin* [Americans], altered the French pronunciation. The British referred to him as "Marpock," while some American references use "Maipock."

Physically, Winibiset is described as a large, burly man, who wore his hair long. To add to his physical intimidation, he often wore an ornamental belt, which he decorated with human scalps. On occasions, he wore strings of bear teeth and claws and strings of hawk and owl beaks around his neck and ankles.

He rarely had fewer than three wives at any one time and is known to have fathered at least two sons and three daughters.

As a warrior, historical accounts credit him with extraordinary courage in battle; as a holy man, he spent long periods in isolation and meditative silence. He is also noted for fits of rage.

As a *wabeno*, Winibiset claimed to possess many mystical powers. He claimed he could change form and become various animals; he could see the future; and was, according to him, immune to any injury, especially in battle. He also claimed the ability to cast evil spells, but could also use his power to heal and prepare protective charms to benefit others. According to Winibiset, he could even make rain.

Sometime after 1795 when many tribes of the Old Northwest ceded millions of acres in what would become the State of Ohio and a small portion of southeastern Indiana to the United States through the Treaty of Greenville [Ohio], Winibiset, who did not sign the treaty, moved west, deeper into what remained Indian Territory. He settled on the *The-a-ki-ki* [Kankakee River], at its junction with the Des Plaines River, where the confluence forms the Illinois River. This *wabeno*-warrior attracted many followers to his new village.

From his new location, the warrior Winibiset led raids against the Piankashaw villages along the lower Wabash River. He was said to have personally killed many Piankashaw during these raids. During this time, with the help of allied tribes, he also waged an ongoing war against the Potawatomi's traditional enemy, the Osage, who lived west of the Mississippi River in what is now the State of Missouri. On his many raids against the Osage, he and his followers also attacked American settlements found along the way.

Winibiset's father was a war chief who professed hate for the Americans and instructed his son in the same beliefs. Winibiset clung to this philosophy most of his life. This hatred was the catalyst that would draw him to the pan-tribal coalition being formed by Tecumseh and The Prophet.

Winibiset was a strong leader who did not take kindly to rivals, such as the newly spiritually awakened Shawnee Prophet. But after hearing from Shawnee messengers about the "magic" of Tenskwatawa, Winibiset became interested in The Prophet's message of a return to

Indian spirituality, rejection of all things European, and resistance to American incursion in Indian Territory.

In 1807, Winibiset accepted an invitation from the Shawnee brothers to visit their village near Greenville in what was now the State of Ohio. Winibiset arrived at Greenville around November and spent nearly two months at the Shawnees' village. After many conversations with Tecumseh and The Prophet, Winibiset agreed with them in some ways, but not in all.

Winibiset rejected the Shawnee brothers' policy of abstinence from alcohol. Winibiset believed his powers came directly from The Great Spirit through his use of alcohol. Neither would he espouse Tecumseh's teachings of Indian brotherhood; he vowed to continue his raids against the Osage. Common ground was discovered, however, when it came to American incursion.

Winibiset, Tecumseh and The Prophet all agreed that Americans were "children of The Great Serpent" and "troublers of the Earth." Like Tecumseh, Winibiset also agreed that a combined Indian force, with help in the form of arms, ammunition and food from the British, could defeat the Americans; a feat the Wabash Confederacy had failed to accomplish in the early to mid-1790s. After his visit to Greenville, Winibiset became a major political and military ally of the Shawnee brothers.

Winibiset departed Greenville in December for his home along the Kankakee River in today's Illinois. On his way, he passed through Fort Wayne in northeastern Indiana Territory.

Encouraged by Indian agent William Wells to winter at the fort, by spring "The Crafty One" and several of his tribesmen had cost the American government some eight hundred dollars in food and other supplies. During his winter stay, the wily chief convinced Wells that he was considering peace with the Americans, and he welcomed westward American expansion.

Based on this misguided information, Wells picked Winibiset as a member of the Indian delegation he was scheduled to escort to Washington in the spring of 1808. The purpose of the delegation was to impress "Marpock" [as Wells refers to him], and the other invited chiefs with the size of America's population, with its political power and its military might. Marpock agreed to the journey. In November of 1808, he arrived back at Fort Wayne accompanied by two warriors and two *ikwe* [wives].

On the journey to Washington, somewhere around modern-day Wheeling, West Virginia, Wells writes that Marpock came into an ample supply of *ish-kot-e-waw-be* [whiskey]. From that point on, the trip became unsettling for Wells.

Wells writes that Marpock was under the influence of liquor most of the time. For the rest of the journey to Washington, Marpock stayed mostly in his hotel room. He was belligerent to hotel staff and his traveling companions, and he professed reluctance to participate in any political meetings or talks with American leaders. Marpock did, however, on one occasion, meet personally with President Thomas Jefferson.

Dressed in his buckskins, Marpock told the President Jefferson in no uncertain terms that, if Indians were to remain neutral in American affairs, America should likewise stay out of Indian affairs - such as his ancestral battles with the Osage. He also flatly rejected any overtures from the President that Indians should take up agricultural pursuits. This meeting finished, while other Indian members of Wells' party toured the city, Marpock retired to his room for the remainder of the Washington visit.

On the return trip, Marpock rejected meetings with Maryland Quaker missionaries. Wells reports that Marpock stayed to himself most of the time, walking in the woods and gathering fruits and nuts. At one point on the journey, Marpock became ill and was bedridden for several weeks. Upon his recovery, he demanded that Wells take him back to Fort Wayne immediately. During the remainder of the trip, the erasable chief often threatened violence on members of the party. Wells described Marpock's behavior throughout the excursion as "insufferable."

Upon his return, as he had promised, Winibiset continued his war against the Osage. But in 1810, things began to go wrong for Winibiset. Despite his *wabeno* status, in a battle with the Osage near modern-day St. Louis, Missouri, he suffered a serious gunshot wound. To save face regarding his claims he could not be injured, a wounded Winibiset told his warriors that he had seen the bullet coming and intentionally jumped in front of it to protect his wife. Regardless, his warriors began to lose confidence in his powers. Unable to walk as the result of his wound, he was transported back to his village by canoe.

By spring Winibiset had recovered. He moved his village to a location north of present-day Peoria, along the Illinois River. From there, he traveled among neighboring tribes, rallying support for Tecumseh's pan-tribal coalition, which was now centered at the village of *Kithtippecanunk [at the Clearing]*, located in northern Indiana at the confluence of the Wabash and Tippecanoe rivers. The Americans knew the village as Prophetstown.

By June, he left Illinois and settled south of Detroit, near the British Indian Agency at Amherstburg, Ontario, Canada. That winter, he stayed in Michigan and was not present during the 1811 Battle of Tippecanoe. The American victory and subsequent burning of Prophetstown dealt a crippling blow to Tecumseh's pan-tribal movement. However, with the upcoming War of 1812 looming, Winibiset remained active in recruiting other tribes to join Tecumseh and ally themselves with the British to halt American encroachment into Indian Territory.

By the summer of 1812, war between Britain and the United States had been declared. Marpock and some twelve hundred of his warriors joined forces with Tecumseh and the British under the command of Major General Isaac Brock. Together, Marpock and Tecumseh participated in several battles, but during a battle at the bridges over the Canard River in July 1812, the aging Mascouten received the second gunshot wound of his life.

This time, Marpock was wounded in the neck by a musket ball. Although the wound was not physically serious, it dealt another serious blow to his invincible *wabeno* reputation. In an effort to regain his legend of invulnerability, he vowed to kill and scalp any retreating Americans he could find.

When no American soldiers could be found, Winibiset took the scalp of a dead British soldier and returned in brief triumph. However, his deception backfired. When the dead soldier's companions recognized the flaming red hair of the scalp Winibiset had taken, he was ridiculed by the British soldiers.

His humiliation resulted in a second attempt to regain his former status. Marpock went on a rampage against the Americans and was at the forefront of several skirmishes.

Then in the summer of 1812, he sent riders to the Illinois Potawatomi war chiefs, Saugenash [*Englishman*, or Billy Caldwell] and Nuscotemeg [*Mad Sturgeon*], urging Caldwell and Mad Sturgeon to attack the American garrison at the western outpost of Fort Dearborn near *She-gog-ong* [*Place of Wild Onion*], or modern-day Chicago. The resulting attack on the escaping American garrison – known as the Fort Dearborn Massacre - led to the death of Wells and many American soldiers and civilians.

In August of 1812, Marpock assisted General Brock and Tecumseh's company of Indians in capturing American-held Fort Detroit. He remained to hold the fort in the face of twenty-two hundred advancing American reinforcements led by General William Henry Harrison. Finally that winter he left the fort on a recruiting mission to rally support for Tecumseh among the Kickapoo, Sauk, Fox and Potawatomi.

In the following spring of 1813, Marpock returned to the fighting around Detroit. By this time American forces had retaken Fort Detroit. The British retreated into Canada, but Winibiset did not follow them. Instead he retired with his warriors into the Michigan woods and awaited the outcome of the war.

Winibiset settled for a while along the St. Joseph River, near present day South Bend, Indiana. All the while, he continued to rally support for Tecumseh. But, upon news of Tecumseh's death, Winibiset moved farther south to a new camp on the Yellow River in northern Indiana. From there, he and his warriors continued to raid settlements on the Indiana and Illinois territorial frontiers.

Winibiset was in disbelief when he heard that the British had surrendered to the Americans at the 1815 Treaty of Ghent. He traveled to the British fort at Mackinac in northern Michigan Territory to learn if these rumors were true. Finding they were, he became disheartened. By some accounts, he settled on the isolated eastern shore of Lake Michigan, near modern day Manistee. By other accounts, he returned to his village on the Yellow River.

Now in old age, Winibiset lost much of his influence among the Indians. He was deaf and in poor health. According to some sources, he died during a hunting trip near Manistee, in Michigan Territory in 1816. He never made peace with the Americans, and he never signed a land cession treaty.

His place of burial is unknown.

Recommended Reading

Allison, Harold. *The Tragic Saga of the Indiana Indians*. Paducah, KY: Turner Publishing Company, 1986.

Anson, Bert. *The Miami Indians*. Norman, OK: University of Oklahoma Press, 1970.

Barce, Elmore. *The Land of the Miamis*. Fowler, IN: Benton Review Shop, 1922.

Barnhart, John D. and Dorothy L. Riker. *Indiana to 1816: The Colonial Period (History of Indiana, Vol. I)*. Indianapolis, IN: Indiana Historical Bureau and Indiana Historical Society, 1971.

Baxter, Nancy Niblack. *The Miamis*. Indianapolis, IN: Guild Press, 1987.

Beckwith, H. R. *The Illinois and Indiana Indians*. New York, NY: Arno Press, 1975.

Berthrong, Donald J. *An Historical Report on Indian Use and Occupancy of Northern Indiana and Southwestern Michigan*. New York, NY: Garland Publishing, 1974.

Borneman, Walter R. *The War That Forged a Nation*. New York, NY: Harper Collins, 2004.

Carter, Harvey Lewis. *The Life and Times of Little Turtle: First Sagamore of the Wabash*. Urbana: IL: University of Illinois Press, 1987.

Cave, Alfred A. *The French and Indian War*. Westport, CT: Greenwood Press, 2004.

Cayton, Andrew R. I. *Frontier Indiana: A History of the Trans-Appalachian Frontier.* Bloomington, IN: Indiana University Press, 1996.

Churchill, Ward. *Indians 'R' Us: Culture and Genocide.* Toronto, Ontario, Canada: University of Toronto Press, 1993.

Clark, Jerry E. **The Shawnee.** Lexington, KY: University of Kentucky Press, 1993.

Dodge, Jacob Richards. *Red Men of the Ohio Valley, 1650-1795.* Springfield, OH: Ruralist Publishing Company, 1860.

Dunn, Jacob P. *True Indian Stories with Glossary of Indiana Indian Names.* Indianapolis, IN: Sentinel Printing Company, 1909.

Eckert, Allan W. *Johnny Logan: Shawnee Spy.* New York, NY: Little, Brown & Company, 1982.

Edmunds, David R. *Tecumseh and the Quest for Indian Leadership.* Boston, MA: Little, Brown & Company, 1984.

Edmunds, David R. *The Potawatomis: Keepers of the Fire.* Norman, OK: University of Oklahoma Press, 1978.

Edmunds, David R. *The Shawnee Prophet.* Lincoln, NE: University of Nebraska Press, 1983.

Edmunds, David R., and Francis A. Levier. *Kinsmen Through Time: An Annotated Bibliography of Potawatomi History.* Metuchen, NJ: Scarecrow Press, 1987.

Feest, Christian F. *Indians and a Changing Frontier: The Art of George Winter.* Indianapolis, IN: Indiana Historical Society and Tippecanoe County Historical Association, 1993.

Fowler, William M. *Empires at War: The French and Indian War and the Struggle for North America (1754-1763)*. New York, NY: Walker and Company, 2005.

Frost, John. *Border Wars of the West: Frontier Wars of Pennsylvania, Virginia, Kentucky, Ohio, Indiana, Illinois, Tennessee, Wisconsin*. Auburn, NY: Derby and Miller, 1853.

Giorgiady, Nicholas P., Louis G. Romano and Richard P. Klahn. *Indiana's First Settlers-The Indians*: Milwaukee, WI: Franklin Publishers, 1968.

Godfroy, Chief Clarence (Ka-pah-pwah). *Miami Indian Stories*. Winona Lake, IN: Light & Life Press, 1961.

Grumet, Robert Steven. *The Lenapes*. New York, NY: Chelsea House, 1989.

Guernsey, E. Y. *Indiana; the Influence of the Indian Upon its History with Indian and French Names for Natural and Cultural Locations* (map). Indiana Conservation Department, Publication no. (22), 1933.

Hamlin-Wilson, Gail, ed. *Biographical Dictionary of the Americas*, 2nd ed. Newport Beach, CA: American Indian Publishers, 1991.

Hamlin-Wilson, Gail, ed. *Encyclopedia of Indiana Indians*. St. Clair, MI: Somerset Publishers, 1998.

Harrison, Wm. Henry. *The Papers of William Henry Harrison, 1800-1815*. Indianapolis, IN: Indiana Historical Society, 1994.

Horan, James D. *The McKenney-Hall Portrait Gallery of the American Indian*. New York, NY: Crown Publishers, 1972.

Horsman, Reginald. *Expansion and American Indian Policy, 1783-1812*. Norman, OK: University of Oklahoma Press, 1992.

Hoxie, Frederick E., ed. *Encyclopedia of North American Indians*. New York, NY: Houghton, Mifflin Company, 1996.

Hurt, R. Douglas. *The Ohio Frontier: Crucible of the Old Northwest, 1720-1830*. Bloomington, IN: Indiana University Press, 1996.

Hutton, Paul A. **"William Wells: Frontier Scout and Indian Agent."** Indiana Magazine of History, Vol. 74 (1978): Pgs. 183-222.

Jablow, Joseph. *Illinois, Kickapoo and Potawatomi Indians*. New York, NY: Garland Publishing, 1974.

Kinietz, Vernon. *Delaware Culture Chronology*. Indianapolis, IN: Indiana Historical Society, 1946.

Kinietz, Vernon. *The Indians of the Western Great Lakes, 1615-1760*. Ann Arbor, MI: University of Michigan Press, 1965.

Kinietz, Vernon and Ermine W. Voegelin, eds. *Shawnee Traditions: C. W. Trowbridge's Account*. Ann Arbor, MI: University of Michigan Press, 1939.

Lamb, E. Wendell and Lawrence W. Shultz. *Indian Lore*. Winona Lake, IN: Light and Life Press, 1964.

Lamb, E. Wendell and Lawrence W. Shultz. *More Indian Lore*. Winona Lake, IN: Light and Life Press, 1968.

Lilly, Eli, et al. *Walum Olum; or Red Score: The Migration Legend of The Lenni Lenape or Delaware Indians*. Indianapolis, IN: Indiana Historical Society, 1954.

Malinowski, Sharon and George Abrams, eds. *Notable Native Americans*, 2nd ed. Farmington Hills, MI: Gale Publishing Group, 1994.

McAfee, Robert Breckinridge. *History of the Late War in the Western Country*. Lexington, KY: Worsley and Smith, 1816.

McNamara, William. *The Catholic Church on the Northern Indiana Frontier, 1789-1844*. Washington, D.C.: Catholic University of America, 1931.

McPherson, Alan. *Indian Names in Indiana*. Monticello, IN: privately printed, 1994.

Meginness, John F. *Biography of Frances Slocum, the Lost Sister of Wyoming: A Complete Narrative of Her Captivity and Wandering Among the Indians*. Manchester, NH: Ayer Co. Publishers, 1977.

Nester, William R. *Haughty Conquerors: Amherst and the Great Indian Uprising of 1763*. Westport, CT: Praeger Publishers, 2000.

Parkman, Francis. *The Conspiracy of Pontiac*, Vols I-II. Lincoln, NE: University of Nebraska Press, 1994.

Pokagon, Simon. *O-gi-maw-kwe Mit-i-gwa-ki or Queen of the Woods*. Hartford, MI: C. H. Engle, 1899.

Prucha, Francis Paul. *American Indian Treaties: History of a Political Anomaly*. Berkley, CA: University of California Press, 1997.

Rafert, Stewart. *The Miami Indians of Indiana: A Persistent People, 1654-1994*. Indianapolis, IN: Indiana Historical Society, 1996.

Richards, Clifford H. *Little Turtle: The Man and His Land*. Fort Wayne, IN: Allen County-Fort Wayne Historical Society, 1974.

Sleeper-Smith, Susan. *Indian Women and French Men: Rethinking Cultural Encounter in the Western Great Lakes*. Amherst, MA: University of Massachusetts, 2003.

Sokolow, Jayne A. *The Great Encounter: Native Peoples and European Settlers in the Americas, 1492-1800*. Armonk, NY: M. E. Sharpe Publications, 2002.

Stuntz, Ervin. *The Incredible Wheel of Time*. Plymouth, IN: self - published, 1983.

Sugden, John. *Blue Jacket: Warrior of the Shawnees*. Lincoln, NE: University of Nebraska Press, 2000.

Sugden, John. *Tecumseh's Last Stand*. Norman, OK: University of Oklahoma Press, 1985.

Sword, Wiley. *President Washington's Indian War: The Struggle for the Old Northwest, 1790-1795*. Norman, OK: University of Oklahoma Press, 1993.

Tanner, Helen Hornbeck. *Atlas of the Great Lakes Indian History*. Norman, OK: University of Oklahoma Press, 1987.

Tanner, Helen Hornbeck. *Indians of Ohio and Indiana Prior to 1795*. New York, NY: Garland Publishing, 1974.

Thom, Dark Rain. *Kohkumthena's Grandchildren: The Shawnee*. Indianapolis, IN: Guild Press, 1994.

Thom, James Alexander. *Panther in the Sky*. New York, NY: Ballentine Press, 1990.

Thom, James Alexander. *The Red Heart*. New York, NY: Ballentine Press, 1998.

Tregillis, Helen C. *The Native Tribes of Old Ohio*. Bowie, MD: Heritage Books, 1993.

Unrau, William E. *The Emigrant Indians of Kansas: A Critical Bibliography*. Bloomington, IN: Indiana University Press, 1979.

Unrau, William E. *White Man's Wicked Water: The Alcohol Trade & Prohibition in Indian Country, 1802-1892*. Lawrence, KS: University Press of Kansas, 1999.

Van Hoose, Willam H. *Tecumseh: An Indian Moses*. Canton, OH: Daring Books, 1984.

Voegelin, Carl F. *Shawnee Stems*. Indianapolis, IN: Indiana Historical Society, 1940.

Weslager, Clinton A. *The Delaware: A Critical Bibliography*. Bloomington, IN: Indiana University Press, 1978.

Weslager, Clinton A. *The Delaware Indians, a History*. New Brunswick, NJ: Rutgers University Press, 1972.

Weslager, Clinton A. *The Delaware Indian Westward Migration*. Wallingford, PA: Middle Atlantic Press, 1989.

Wiggins, Felicia S., ed. *Mother Earth, Father Sky: Native American Wisdom*. Kansas City, MO: Andrews and McNeel, 1999.

Williams, Joyce G. and Jill E. Farrelly. *Diplomacy on the Indiana-Ohio Frontier, 1783-1791*. Bloomington, IN: Indiana University Press and Bicentennial Committee, 1976.

Willard, Shirley, *Trail of Death Commemorative Caravan, 1998*. Shawnee, OK: Citizen Potawatomi Nation, 2000.

Winger, Otho. *Last of the Miamis: Me-shin-go-me-sia, The Last Tribal Chief of the Miamis*. North Manchester, IN: L. W. Shultz Publishing Company, 1968.

Winger, Otho. *Lost Sister of the Miamis.* North Manchester, IN: L. W. Shultz Publishing Company, 1968.

Winger, Otho. *The Frances Slocum Trail.* North Manchester, IN: The News-Journal, 1943.

Winger, Otho. *The Potawatomi Indians.* North Manchester, IN: L. W. Shultz Publishing Company, 1968.

Winter, George. *The Journals and Indian Paintings of George Winter, 1837-1839.* Indianapolis, IN: Indiana Historical Society, 1948.

Index

L

M

Printed in the United States
87931LV00011B/7-18/A